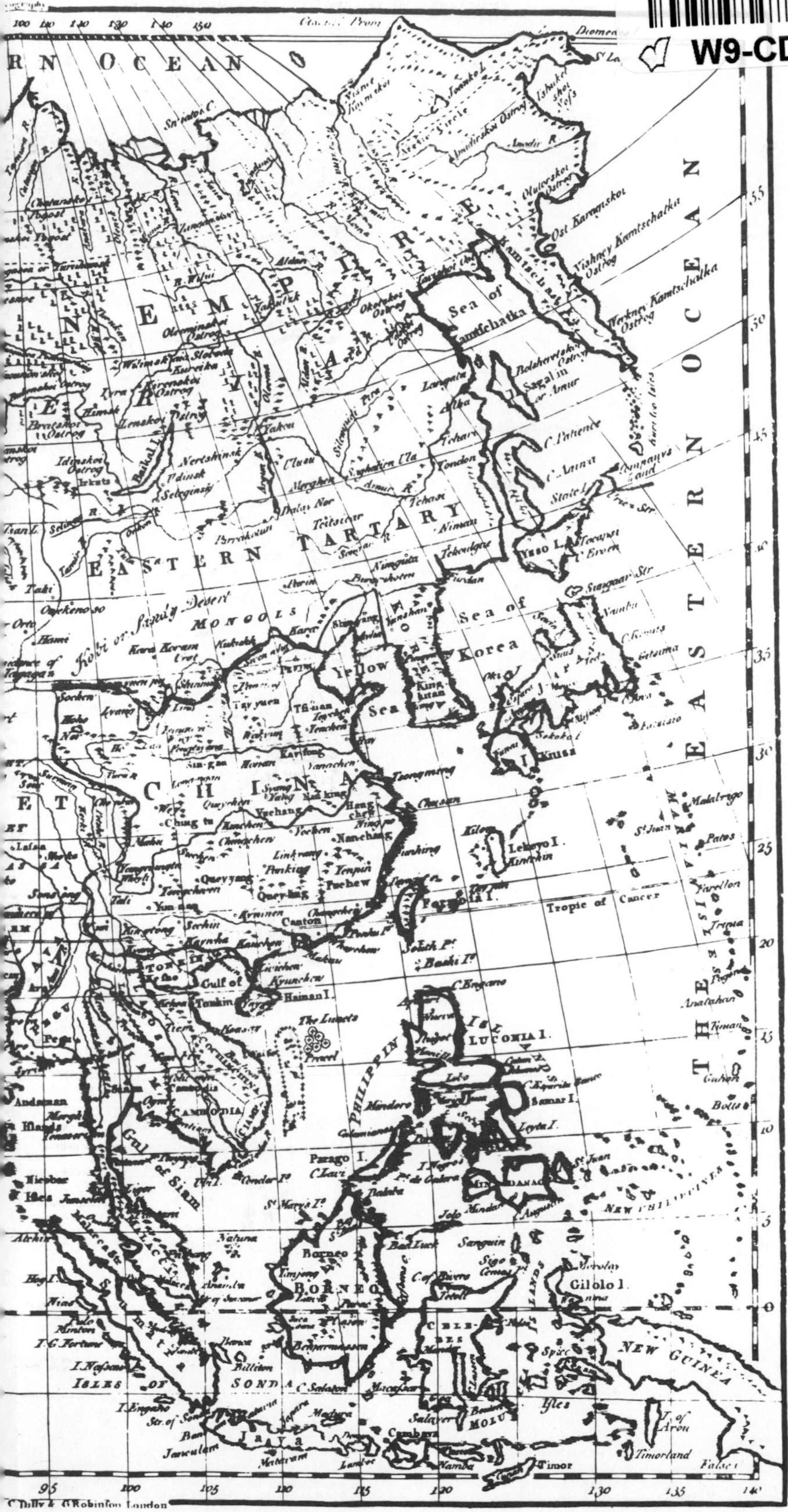

SENTIMENTAL IMPERIALISTS

SENTIMENTAL IMPERIALISTS

The American Experience in East Asia

JAMES C. THOMSON, JR.

PETER W. STANLEY

JOHN CURTIS PERRY

Foreword by John King Fairbank

1817

HARPER & ROW, PUBLISHERS, New York

Cambridge, Hagerstown, Philadelphia, San Francisco,
London, Mexico City, São Paulo, Sydney

094429

FIRST EDITION

Designer: Sidney Feinberg

Library of Congress Cataloging in Publication Data

Thomson, James Claude, 1931–
  Sentimental imperialists.
  Includes index.
  1. East Asia—Foreign relations—United States.
2. United States—Foreign relations—East Asia.
I. Stanley, Peter W. II. Perry, John Curtis.
III. Title.

DS518.8.T486 1981	327.7305	79–1689
ISBN 0–06–014282–0		AACR2

81 82 83 84 85 10 9 8 7 6 5 4 3 2 1

For Diana, Mary-Jane, and Sarah Hollis

Contents

Acknowledgments

This book is the result of a subject in search of three authors.

Each of us has been worrying for a long time about the absence of any readable, reliable, and up-to-date book that can tell the general reader about the extraordinary multicultural complexity called "American–East Asian Relations." We have all three spent extended periods of time in Asia; two of us have served in the United States government, both in Washington and abroad, on civil or military assignments; and most important, we have long tried to teach American students—and, more informally, virtually anyone willing to listen—about this subject.

But we have never found a book that put it all together: those often forgotten patterns of the past that define the shape of the present and future. So, forced by circumstances, we have written one.

Inevitably, this book borrows from the thinking and writing of countless others—generations of teachers, authors, and participants in the American–East Asian experience. We are especially indebted to friends and colleagues at Harvard University, Carleton College, and Yale University. And in this circle of indebtedness, two figures inevitably loom most large: John King Fairbank and Edwin O. Reischauer, who have done more than any other two Americans to explain East Asia to their fellow citizens.

It is customary to say in ritual acknowledgments that the authors—despite their great gratitude—bear all responsibilities for the shortcomings of their book. In our case, however, since our intellectual debt is so large and multiple, we insist on sharing everything, both praise and blame, with our friends, mentors, colleagues, and those who came before.

Foreword

This book is dedicated to the idea that our troubles in East Asia have come from both sides—from the non-fit between American ways and East Asian ways. If we want peaceful relations, it is not enough to understand the East Asian peoples. We have to understand ourselves too. In fact, since we have generally been more active, expansive, or aggressive than the East Asian peoples, our conduct needs the closer scrutiny.

Sentimental Imperialists offers a perspective which all of us ought to get in school but seldom do. The book traces our contact with the third of humanity who live in East Asia but hardly figure in our class-rooms, peoples who today form a major center of the world economy and soon will outproduce Western Europe.

Our ignorance has been costly. We can no longer afford to know so little. Take for example our performance during the recent Cold War when we fought in Korea (1950–53) and then in Vietnam (1965–73). Our chief mistake, that led up to our Vietnam disaster, was to see only "international communism" at work. We underestimated the power of Vietnam's "national communism," and it defeated us. Yet it is now at sword's points with the "national communism" we had also failed to see in China. Our ignorance led us to defeat both in China and in Vietnam. Righteous cold war zeal could not substitute for realistic knowledge.

Vietnam had never even been on our maps. Those few Americans who knew that it existed called it Annam because the French, after they began to seize the area as a colony in 1858, used the medieval

Chinese name *an-nan,* "the pacified south." After the Vietnamese drove the French out in 1954, we got involved because of global security concerns, to stop the spread of "monolithic international communism" which we believed was directed from Moscow. A national communist revolution was more than we could comprehend. A similar failure of comprehension had accompanied our expulsion from China. The American public leadership, both in and out of government, had backed Chiang Kai-shek (Jiang Jieshi) and Nationalist China as our allies in World War II. After such a long public relations build-up, Americans could not accept the facts of Nationalist weakness and defeat in the late 1940s. Many of us preferred to attribute that weakness to a communist conspiracy in the State Department like the one Joe McCarthy wildly alleged, but could never prove.

Another problem has been our failure to put East Asia into our image of world history. Only a few hundred years ago, the world's big centers of culture and population were in Asia. India, China, and even Japan were bigger than any countries in Europe. The Europeans were have-nots; they voyaged overseas to seek the riches of the Indies.

And as long as the countries of East Asia were merely bigger than the countries of Western Europe in population, Westerners could live with the fact and still keep "The Far East" at a geographic and ideological distance, as masses of "backward" or "colonial" peoples with quaint cultures.

Other examples of American ignorance, misunderstanding, and wishful thinking in our East Asian relations could be cited. But overall, our failings have been due to our difficulty in understanding far-distant East Asian societies and cultures that come from a separate historical tradition.

Trade and migration, investment and industrialization, as they spread out from Europe after 1500, had fostered the growth of America on the west and Russia on the east. Thus Europe's expansion eventually spawned the superpowers of today, for both the Americans and the Russians in their wide-open spaces sedulously imported West European technology and culture until they could go ahead on their own.

And since the world is, after all, round, Russians and Americans eventually met, both in Alaska and northern California as well as in China, Japan, and Korea, on both sides of the Pacific. The American continent, however, proved more productive than Siberia. Even though Russian explorers reached the Pacific by 1637 during the founding of New England, Americans in time inherited the British tradition of maritime trade and naval power and made the Pacific an American lake.

As industrialism and modern mass nationalism continued to spread around the globe, East Asian peoples eventually found two styles of development confronting them, one Anglo-American, one Soviet Russian. The Anglo-American style, first on the scene, stimulated Japan to develop her own overseas trade and naval power. The Soviet style, coming later, inspired in China a bureaucratic mobilization of peasant muscle power under the Chinese Communist Party that now rules China. Korea remains unhappily divided between the two styles.

This bit of world history has been the context of the American experience in East Asia. We crossed the largest ocean, went the farthest away from home (literally halfway round the world), and penetrated the greatest non-Western civilizations. Why we expanded so, for good and ill, is a fascinating question. Why we have fought five wars in East Asia since 1898 (but none before then) is a very disturbing question.

To deal with American–East Asian relations requires a triple focus, a focus on each of the cultures in itself and then on their effects on each other. Living and studying abroad, using the necessary Asian languages, are a necessary preparation. So also is an intimate grasp of American history and of how American policy is made. Thus far only a handful of scholars—including the authors of this book—have qualified for this exacting task.

James C. Thomson, Jr., grew up in China, studied its language and history, and then for five years (1961–66) worked on China policy in the State Department and the White House. This was an invaluable first-hand experience of the policy making process. In 1969 he published *While China Faced West: American Reformers in Nationalist China, 1928–37.*

Peter W. Stanley's book, *A Nation in the Making: The Philippines and the United States, 1899–1921* (1974), has made him a leading specialist on Philippine-American relations. He is particularly conversant with the ethos of our expansion into the Far East.

John Curtis Perry has spent years in Japan and taught at Connecticut College, Carleton, and is now at Tufts' Fletcher School of Law and Diplomacy. His book, *Beneath the Eagle's Wings: Americans in Occupied Japan* (1981), analyzes the experience of American reformers in Japan just as Thomson does in China and Stanley does in the Philippines.

In addition to their own experiences in each country, two of these authors have lectured together in the Harvard course on American–East Asian Relations. The careers of all three have criss-crossed. Thomson and Perry got the best of two worlds by securing their B.A.s at Yale and their Ph.D.s at Harvard. Thomson and Stanley both studied at Cambridge University in England. Stanley is and Perry was at Carleton College. All this has benefited their smooth collaboration in this judicious and fast-moving volume.

No other book shows so neatly the comparability of American efforts in the various lands of East Asia, nor poses so clearly the issue—can't we do better in the times to come? This book can help us do so.

—JOHN KING FAIRBANK
December 1980

A Note on the Spelling of Chinese Words

There are now two predominant but not entirely satisfactory ways of representing Chinese words in roman letters: the traditional English Wade-Giles system, and the much newer but widely accepted pinyin system. Since virtually all of the books, monographs, and articles on which this book is based used the Wade-Giles transliteration, but most future writings will use pinyin, we have decided upon the following compromise:

1. All Chinese words, including the names of people and places, will be printed in the Wade-Giles form.
2. On first mention, however, all such words will be followed, in parentheses, by the pinyin version of their spelling (unless the two spellings are identical).
3. The index will list *both* versions, and the indexing will be cross-referenced.

A
General Map
OF
NORTH AMERICA
DRAWN FROM THE BEST SURVEYS
1795

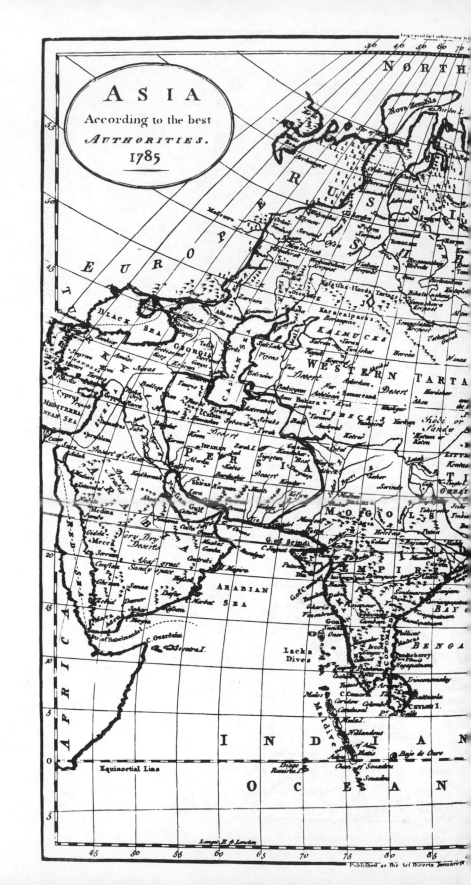

A S I A
According to the best
AUTHORITIES.
1785

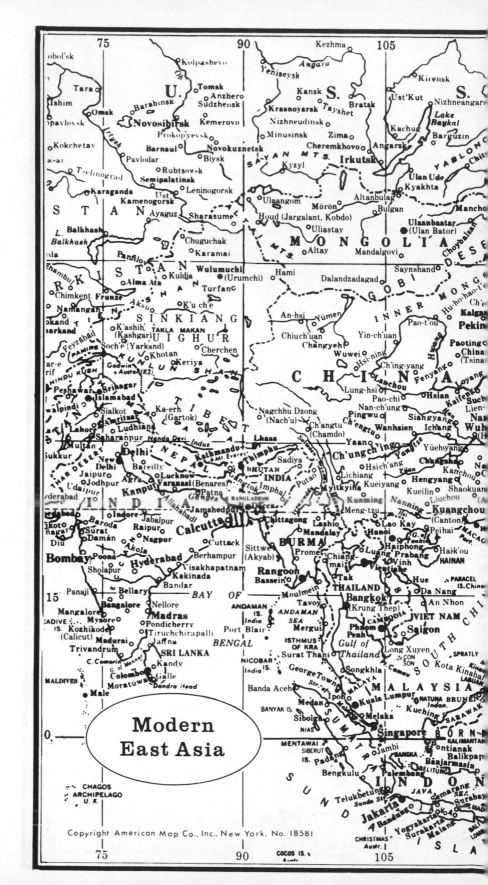

Modern
East Asia

SENTIMENTAL IMPERIALISTS

Prologue

THERE IS SOMETHING both odd and persistent about America's two centuries of relations with the countries of East Asia. What seems odd is that Americans, so far removed from Asians in space, time, language, and culture, should nonetheless thrust repeatedly toward that "Far West." Yet to Asia they persisted in journeying, from the end of the War of Independence right up to the present—as traders and missionaries, adventurers and consuls, soldiers, sailors, and marines, and later, tourists, airmen, experts, and investors.

This westward push, though small in numbers at the outset, produced important cumulative results. One was the rise of national hopes and myths about East Asia and its peoples—especially the Chinese and Japanese, but eventually also others. Another was the development of a small but growing constituency of Americans who shared strong desires about Asia and its future—to exploit it, "civilize" it, "Christianize" it, win its "hearts and minds," or perhaps all four. A further result was American entanglement from the beginning in a larger process: the efforts by the European powers to force open Asian doors for Western trade and the alien institutions that went along with trade. This meant American complicity in the use of superior weaponry against resistant Asians. Finally, the U.S. push into East Asia made Americans both catalysts and participants in an unforeseen and sometimes slow-developing process of great potency: the revolutionary transformation of increasingly nationalistic societies. In that process, another power, part Asian, would eventually play a significant role: that vast Eurasian state, Russia; and Americans and Russians, coming from opposite direc-

1

tions, would meet and sometimes collide at the center of Asian revolutions.

By the end of these first two centuries—the 1980s—America's Asian involvement would seem not merely persistent but also violent and costly. The record would show not only spasmodic American use of force in East Asia in the nineteenth century but, beginning in 1898, some wars that left very deep scars: against the Spanish Philippines, and then—more prolonged and brutal, 1899–1902—against Filipinos who rejected annexation by the new American overlords; against the expanded Japanese empire, 1941–1945, culminating in America's nuclear bombing of Hiroshima and Nagasaki; against the People's Republic of China (and North Korea), 1950–1953; and, most interminably and perhaps most destructively, against North Vietnam and its allies, 1965–75.

For a nation which had early renounced "foreign entanglements" in keeping with General Washington's farewell address, that is a record which demands a fuller exploration in search of explanations.

Why, for instance, was it American naval vessels that shoved open that sealed-off archipelago Japan—and thereby helped launch both the militarized Japan that bombed Pearl Harbor and the economic superpower of the 1980s?

Why did America agree—by a President's decision and one Senator's vote—to annex the Philippines and thereby make the United States a colonial power in Asia with a territorial stake in the region?

What gave rise to America's grand and recurrent dreams about the reshaping of China—dreams, and actions, that brought the United States into a long, poisonous conflict with Japan?

What produced such intense American fears of the Communist wing of the Chinese revolution—and such alarm and recriminations after Mao Tse-tung's (Mao Zedong's) victory in 1949?

What caused six American presidents to believe that the American national interest was at stake in former French Indochina between 1950 and 1975?

Why, as the Vietnamese were winning and the Americans were losing, did the Chinese and Americans end their twenty-two years of hostilities and renew an old but turbulence-ridden habit of friendly mutual exploration?

Why has the United States so often been obsessed and preoccupied with China when Japan has been, since 1890, America's chief trading partner in Asia, and became, after World War II, the most important American ally outside the European community?

Why is Russia's (and the U.S.S.R.'s) role in East Asia so universally ignored by historians and policymakers, despite the fact that the Russians reached the Pacific in the seventeenth century, have pressed upon China and Japan intermittently since the nineteenth century, have encouraged Asian revolutionaries since 1919, and have long been America's nearest Asian neighbor and rival, across the Bering Strait?

And why has it been so difficult to achieve that rarity of the late 1970s and early 1980s: a situation in which China, Japan, and the United States (though not the U.S.S.R.) are all on a plateau of peaceful and protective relations with one another?

Finally, one faces at least one recurrent and more cosmic question: Were Americans—and American policy—generally "imperialist"? If so, which of them, in what sense, when, and regarding which nations and issues in East Asia?

Many conflicting answers to some of these questions have been suggested over the decades. Some make much sense; some no sense at all. It is easy to simplify, polemicize, and cast blame. It is also easy to complicate, obfuscate, and cast no blame.

But the questions remain significant for those who want to understand America's Asian past. And for those who need to understand America's Asian future, they are urgent.

The story of the American involvement is too important to be lost, in times of relative East Asian quietude, lest one of those other times, of violent and unfathomable American entanglements, suddenly takes hold. Americans and Asians both have too often been taken by total surprise, knowing nothing of what has come before.

So, let us begin at the beginning.

(1)

East Asia in the American Mind

EAST ASIA IS A GEOGRAPHIC and political reality, a *place* with certain identifiable economic, cultural, and geological attributes. It is also a conceptual abstraction. East Asia is a name, a shorthand symbol, for the cluster of ideas and images that people have about that part of the world. Perhaps if information were perfect and minds objective, our images would correspond exactly with reality. Then there would be little significant distinction between the place and the ideas people have about it. But clearly this is not the case. Asia is vast and complex, and even today our information about it is relatively meager. Such images as we have are no more than selective responses to some part of the whole that has caught our eye.

In our own time, East Asia has meant many different things to Americans. To some, the dominant image has been the human degradation of famine, poverty, disease, and overpopulation; to others, despotic and corrupt government. Some Americans still associate the region primarily with its great cultural traditions; more, probably, view it as a complement or rival to the industrial economy of the West—its docks loaded with Toyotas and Hondas awaiting export. Even in the case of individual countries, there is little agreement. What some admire as the economic miracle of Japanese recovery from the second World War others denounce as a nightmare of pollution, or deplore as cultural debasement. The People's Republic of China has been called both the model of a just society and the epitome of repressive dictatorship.

Ideas and images such as these are not faithful representations of the place they purport to describe. Nor should we expect them to

4

be; that is not their function. They are attempts to organize thought in such a way as to make a remote place mean something specific in terms of the thinker's experience and concerns. As such, these particular ideas tell us a good deal more about ourselves than they do about Asia. That is one reason they are important to the historian. Understanding our reaction to other societies is a useful way to come to a better knowledge of our own.

Moreover, the way people think about a place is subtly but vitally related to the way they act toward that place and the sense they make of the way it deals with them. It is customary, for example, to say that American-East Asian relations began in 1784 with the pioneering voyage of a merchant vessel named the *Empress of China*. That is accurate as far as it goes, but it really tells us very little. Ships sailed to many places in those days—the Middle East, for example—made profits, and returned home without kindling interests and myths as extravagant and lasting as those that quickly enveloped American thought about the Far East. Why was such a ship sent at that time? Why did its success matter enough to attract great attention? What did people expect of China and the Far East? Why did this commercial beginning lead so quickly to the mythologizing of China as part of the meaning of America and the justification of American civilization? As these questions suggest, the deepest roots of the American–East Asian encounter are to be found in the ideas underlying visible acts and formal milestones.

In the beginning, East Asia was at best an idea on the periphery of the American mind. Most Americans of the late eighteenth and early nineteenth centuries probably had no idea about, or attitude toward, East Asia at all. This is hardly surprising.

Prior to the middle of the nineteenth century, the number of Americans who had ever been to any part of East Asia themselves was extremely small—almost certainly less than a thousand people alive at any one time. Of these, only a tiny minority had recorded their impressions in a form that could reach the general public. Missionaries are an example. Ordinarily in that period, missionaries were one of the principal sources of information about distant non-Christian cultures. Prior to 1840, however, there were only twenty American Protestant missionaries in all of China, and none in Japan or the Philippines. The flow of information such a small band of people could generate was inevitably very limited. Symptomatically, Americans wrote almost no books about East Asia. The shelf list of the Widener Library at Harvard University records only sixteen items about China, Japan, or Korea published in the United States prior to 1840. What this means is that for a long time, at the outset, East Asia was an esoteric subject. Absorbed in domestic political, social, and economic issues of the first importance, very few Americans knew, and almost none cared, about East Asia.

In colonial and revolutionary America there was practically no informed opinion about East Asia. People knew that the region was there, of course, and that it was a source of luxury products such as tea, silk, spices, and porcelain. There were advertisements for imports like these in colonial newspapers, and occasionally they identified the geographic sources of the goods in general terms. Beyond this, there was a sense that Asia was a place of antiquity, splendor, and riches. One finds occasional references in those years to the Manila Galleon, for example, and the great flood of wealth that had historically drained out of China and India, by way of the Philippines, to the Spanish viceroyalty in Mexico. In 1771, Philip Freneau and Hugh Henry Brackenridge wrote a poem for the commencement exercises at Princeton entitled "The Rising Glory of America," in which they foresaw poetically a day when America would expand to continental dimensions and tap this commerce for itself. Grandiose and anachronistic, their vision completely missed the actual course of future commerce between Asia and America. Omitting China altogether, they prophesied a future in which

> fleets shall then convey rich Persia's silks,
> Arabia's perfumes, and spices rare
> Of Philippine, Coelebe and Marian isles,
> Or from the Acapulco coast our India then,
> Laden with pearl and burning gems of gold.

Apart from this sort of thing and the third- or fourthhand information that a few merchants might gain through their European connections, there was simply a huge vacuum. By and large, Americans did not even read what was written and published elsewhere about Asia. Studies of the best libraries of the colonial era reveal that they contained almost nothing dealing with the other side of the Pacific. Accordingly, not only sophisticated questions concerning the nature of government and society but even the simplest questions of geography and ethnicity in East Asia were clouded in mystery.

Benjamin Rush, a Philadelphia physician, was one of the most learned men in America, an intellectual confidant of John Adams and Thomas Jefferson. During the debates over the Articles of Confederation in 1776, Rush shared with Adams a new piece of information he had acquired. Adams was sufficiently impressed to write it down with his notes on the debate: "China is not larger than one of our Colonies. How populous." At about the same time, Jefferson and Benjamin Franklin apparently discovered the subject of China in books that they saw in Europe during their diplomatic service there. As late as 1785, a year after Americans had entered the China trade, George Washington expressed surprise when informed that the Chinese were not white. He hastened to add, however, that he had long known them to be "droll in shape and appearance."

This ignorance on the part of the most knowledgeable men in America is important, because it suggests that in the mid-1780s, when direct commerce was inaugurated between the newly independent United States and Canton,* Americans discovered China intellectually and culturally for themselves. The initial American response was formed in at least relative isolation from the great contemporary debate in Europe over the quality and worth of Chinese civilization.

During the sixteenth and seventeenth centuries, Europeans had developed a highly idealized image of China on the strength of reports from Jesuit missionaries. The Jesuits admired the high ethical character of Confucianism and the virtuous results it seemed to produce in the political society of China. Their views were picked up and carried into the eighteenth century by natural-law philosophers and Enlightenment writers, ranging from Leibnitz to Voltaire, who saw in China a model for much that they wished to achieve in Europe. Idealizing China's scholar-bureaucrats and the examination system through which they were chosen, the Europeans imagined that China's administrative institutions epitomized the rule of reason. Misapprehending the Chinese concept that the emperor ruled under the "mandate of heaven,"

---

* Here is a nice first example of the complexity of Chinese names, especially place-names: "Canton" is the traditional European rendition of the name in local dialect; Wade-Giles would romanize it "Kwangchow;" in pinyin, it becomes "Guangzhou." We choose to stay with "Canton."

embodying the principles of social and ethical harmony, they concluded that China's sovereign, unlike their own, must be a philosopher-king.

By the second half of the eighteenth century, however, this conception of China had come under serious attack in Europe. For one thing, critics of the Enlightenment—tories and radicals, romantics and conventional Christians—set out to discredit the Chinese model as part of their attack on the rationalists who had adduced it. The image of China became, to this extent, a casualty of cultural and intellectual conflicts inside Europe. Moreover, discrediting the Chinese model proved quite easy, because it had been inflated out of all proportion by the intellectual needs and the internal dynamic of Enlightenment thought. Once the number of traders and missionaries in China increased, it was only a matter of time before reports of infanticide, poor treatment of women, and political despotism began to filter back to Europe. At this point, the model collapsed under its own weight. Samuel Johnson expressed the change most trenchantly. At one point in his life, Johnson had given thought to writing stories with Chinese themes; later he growled to Boswell that the Chinese were a "barbarous" people, lacking an alphabet and devoid of all arts except pottery.

Aspects of this European debate did eventually cross the Atlantic. But Americans' initial images of China, in particular, and East Asia, more generally, were their own, not reflections of a conflict within European culture. American ideas about East Asia derived in the beginning from the experience of commerce there and the application to that commerce of a body of general principles about the relationship of commerce to foreign relations.

As the poem by Freneau and Brackenridge suggests, direct commerce between America and Asia had been desired for many years before it finally began. During the colonial period, Americans had been forbidden by the mother country either to trade on their own account east of the Cape of Good Hope or to import Asian and East Indian products from any place other than Britain. Since there was a strong market in the colonies for teas, spices, and Asian luxury goods, merchants understandably chafed under these restrictions. Even before the revolution had ended, some of them started planning to take advantage of independence to open a direct trade of their own with the Orient. The return of a traveler during the revolution with dazzling tales that sixpenny fur pelts sold at Canton for a hundred dollars apiece spurred them on. Finally, in 1784, Robert Morris and his associates sent the *Empress of China* from New York to Canton and back by way of the Cape of Good Hope. Her voyage returned a profit of better than 25 percent.

Profits of this magnitude were especially welcome at just that moment, because, in retaliation for the revolution, American traders had been shut out of the British mercantile system in the Western Hemisphere. A widely read pamphlet by Lord Sheffield smugly predicted that independence would reduce Americans to relative poverty. For this reason, Americans felt a special need for new markets and new sources of supply to balance their international payments; and China, with its attendant imagery of magnificence, seemed the perfect answer. By 1790, every port of consequence between Salem, Massachusetts, and Norfolk, Virginia, had sent at least one vessel to Canton. A decade and a half later, on the eve of Jefferson's embargo in 1807, about fifty voyages a year were being made between the United States and China or, on a lesser scale, the Philippines.

This trade reinforced the existing imagery of Asia as a place of munificence and splendor. The products were luxuries, not necessities—tea, spices, silks, porcelain. The profits, for at least some of the traders some of the time, were spectacular. Moreover, they were preeminently young men's profits—profits that required daring, innovative, unconventional behavior in a remote and almost totally alien place.

For these reasons, and also because of the practical impossibility of maintaining active control of Canton activities from the United States, most of the great Boston families that came to dominate the trade chose to send their own young sons to head operations at the Chinese end. John P. Cushing, the richest of the New England China merchants, went to China at the age of sixteen, became a partner in Perkins and Company at nineteen, returned home within a few years to live off his investments, and cleared a cool $983,000 at the age of forty-two, when the firm was liquidated. John Murray Forbes, to take one other example, went out to China at seventeen, became a partner in Russell and Company at age twenty, and left China for good at twenty-five with a fortune that contributed to the building of several major American railways. The *American Quarterly Review* wrote admiringly in 1835: "This trade has upon the whole been the most profitable in proportion to its extent of any branch of our foreign commerce, and has been the principal source of some of the largest fortunes to our merchants."

It seemed to follow that the challenge and potential of China were peculiarly appropriate to America. If it was a young man's trade, doubtless it was also a young nation's trade. Everybody knew, of course, that in actual fact Britain dominated the Canton trade—and did so to such an extent that American merchants there had to transact their business in bills of credit and exchange drawn on London banking houses. But the British position in China at the turn of the century seemed to Americans very much a historical anachronism, vulnerable to the inroads of Yankee ingenuity. It was a product of mercantilism, depending upon artificial state-imposed monopolies that gave control of British trade at Canton to the same organization—the East India Company—that controlled the supply of Indian opium that was used to purchase Chinese exports.

By and large, Americans built better ships, sailed them more efficiently, and realized better profits from them than Britons did. So, once independence freed them from the binding power of the East India Company's monopoly at Canton, it seemed that the only important obstacle remaining was to find a substitute for Indian opium as an item of trade with the Chinese. A number of products were found that met this need at least partially and temporarily. (We shall have more to say about them in a following chapter.) And when the Napoleonic wars interrupted European commerce with China, it began to appear that Americans might indeed come someday to rival or even surpass the British. For the first time, but not the last, Americans expressed an earnest faith that in a fair competition based upon price and quality, Chinese would *choose* to trade with them.

To prophesy a specifically commercial relationship of major dimensions between the United States and China in this way was not simply to reiterate the mid-eighteenth-century faith that Asia was a place of great riches that Americans might someday tap. For one thing, the image had become much more precise. People no longer lumped together everything from Persia to Acapulco. They spoke, instead, of specific ports, like Canton and Manila, and specific products traded there. But more important than this, commerce suggested to Americans of that period dynamic and progressive consequences that went beyond the static image of riches and wealth.

The men who conducted American foreign relations at the time of the revolution and in the first decades of independence had given a great deal of thought to the role of commerce in relations between sovereign states. They were heirs, in this respect, to a whole generation of European officials and philosophers; and they drew selectively and knowingly upon European models.

It was widely recognized in late-eighteenth-century America, for example, that the premises of British foreign policy had changed dramatically during the age of Walpole. The traditional foreign policy of the English Whigs had been to intervene politically and militarily on the continent of Europe to maintain a balance of power there. Walpole, by contrast, tried to disengage Britain from the rivalries of the continental powers, in order to free British resources for the development of maritime commerce. While Hapsburgs and Bourbons exhausted each other in struggles to control one or another corner of Europe, he argued, British merchantmen and warships could freely course the oceans to establish in other continents a commercial empire of far greater value.

Plainly, there were lessons to be drawn from this line of thought for the American relationship with Asia. One was that, if Americans wished to maximize their maritime commerce without risk of entanglement in European rivalries, they should give special attention to Asia, the richest part of the non-European world. Another was that, in their relations with Asia, Americans should avoid political, diplomatic, and naval involvement, so as to preserve their flexibility, reduce their risks, and free their energies for commerce. Conceivably, success in the competition for Asian commerce might do for young America what similar successes had previously done for Britain: namely, make it a great, powerful, and wealthy country. This was an attractive prospect for a new nation lacking military and naval power deployable in distant waters, but greatly in need of a commercial bonanza to balance its foreign trade.

Walpole's Britain was by no means the only model of a commercially oriented foreign policy known to eighteenth-century Americans. Diplomats assigned to the continent of Europe during the American Revolution learned of the different but complementary approach of the bourgeoisie and the Physiocrats of the French Enlightenment.

In one respect, the French model was dramatically at odds with the British. Walpole conceived of commercial empire as an aspect of national power. The French Physiocrats, on the other hand, saw commerce as a *supra*national bond between peoples. They perceived in the growing eighteenth-century trade between Europe and the Asian, African, and American continents a sign of the economic interdependence of the various peoples of the world. This conception was highly elitist, based as it was upon Europe's importation of such luxury products as West Indian sugar, African chocolate and coffee, and Asian teas and spices. Nevertheless, true believers theorized that, without the distortions caused by political interference or national rivalries, the free exchange of goods at market price ought to be mutually beneficial to all parties. If people everywhere in the world traded a little of what they had (but others lacked) for things they lacked (but others had), the world would be a better, richer, more comfortable place. In such a world, one theorist observed, people would be united like "threads of silk."

To realize the benefits of economic interdependence, the Physiocrats argued, a new conception of foreign relations was necessary. The proper goal of foreign policy henceforth, they concluded, ought to be the promotion of international harmony and the easing of economic exchange. Here was a moral sanction for placing commerce at the center of a nation's foreign policy.

Americans of the revolutionary era identified themselves with the values of this new, virtuous economic diplomacy. And from it, as from the Walpole model, they drew profound implications for the relationship between the United States and East Asia. In the nature of the thing, the American presence in East Asia had to be commercial and cultural only; it was beyond the capacity of the country to maintain effective naval power in so distant a place and therefore pointless to try to force diplomatic relations upon the Chinese, even if Americans had wished to do so. The economic emphasis of American-East Asian relations was a result of America's strategic and diplomatic weakness, not of its virtuous principles. In fact, the American position in China and the Philippines, such as it was in those early years, depended upon naval and diplomatic power just as much as that of any other nation. But the power in question was not American. Had not British warships and diplomats opened the way to foreign traders, Americans would probably have had no commerce with China at all.

But weakness of this sort had compensatory advantages. By leaving the dirty work to other nations, Americans were free to conceive their own role more constructively. To those familiar with Enlightenment views concerning foreign relations, the nearly complete absence of the American government from the scene improved the environment for an economic relationship based upon the mutually beneficial exchange of goods. It was credible, in this light, that commercial relations between the United States and China might contribute to the improvement and elevation of peoples on both sides of the Pacific and might ultimately forge a new harmony of races and interests. This gave high ethical sanction to what might otherwise have seemed merely a matter of balancing payments and scrounging profits.

There was, however, at least one serious obstacle to this happy union of national interest, commercial aspirations, and *supra*national morality. The notion that mutually beneficial commerce could be an engine of social improvement and international harmony supposed that the participants in the commerce respected each other and had something genuinely constructive and of real value to offer each other. This necessarily made relations between Asia and the United States anomalous, since neither party really respected the other as a cultural peer, and the Americans, for their part, had a great deal of trouble finding anything more constructive to trade than opium or Mexican silver.

It is now clear that most Americans who traveled to China in the first decades of contact between the two countries were, at best, ambivalent and, more typically, hostile toward the culture, polity, and people they found there. It is true that there were American champions of the Chinese, men who admired and defended the Chinese people and their civilization. It is also true that personal friendships of genuine commitment sprang up between some Americans and Chinese in the early years, especially between certain American merchants and their Chinese counterparts. Yet by and large, China and its people struck their early American visitors as both strange and unattractive.

The least critical of the early Americans appear to have been the merchants. Even they found much to dislike, however. At superficial levels, they noted what they called "peculiarities," like eating dogs, binding women's feet, and listening to unpleasant, squeaky music. They commented unfavorably upon idolatry, polygamy, and vices such as gambling and prostitution. Most of them were frustrated, and many angered, by Chinese xenophobia, including the abusive nicknames given to Westerners. Yet, though all these things registered negatively, the traders as a group plainly did not find them important or truly offensive. Foreigners were a bit more put out over what some called the universal dishonesty of the Chinese in business dealings. (Stuart C. Miller recounts in his book *The Unwelcome Immigrant* the story of an American in China who unwittingly purchased a wooden ham, which a Chinese had cleverly painted and covered with real fat to give the appearance of authenticity. The truth finally appeared when the ham began to smolder in his oven! Americans could appreciate the humor of this variation on one Connecticut peddler's wooden nutmegs.) Even in this case, most of the Yankee traders were ambivalent rather than thoroughly critical. One reason for this was that some of the hong merchants—including Houqua, who was considered the greatest of them all—were celebrated for their integrity and reliability. Another was that the Yankees themselves had a reputation for hard trading and shrewd dealing, and many of them clearly relished the challenge provided by the Chinese.

What did offend and outrage the traders, however, was an apparent lack of dynamism in the Chinese civilization. To an outsider, Chinese society looked static; the heroic, striving, progressive virtues so highly valued by Western man seemed to be lacking. The military were inept. The soldiery and the people appeared alternately vicious and cowardly. Science and technology, whatever their great past, seemed backward. Worst of all, the Chinese seemed not to care. "If the world were like the Chinese," one merchant said in disgust, "we should yet have worn fig leaves."

In this criticism of the Chinese for stagnancy, one sees something more than simply ethnocentrism and provincialism. Both of these qualities, to be sure, were present on both sides of the encounter; but it would be a mistake to dismiss Americans' negative reactions on those grounds alone. The Americans who first directly encountered the Chinese—and indeed the Filipinos also, whom they held in even lower regard, as simply tribal natives—conceived of themselves as the cutting edge of Western civilization in one of its most dynamic and dramatic phases. In their own minds, they were the exemplars of mechanical and scientific ingenuity, industrial progress, ethical nationalism, and constructive revolutionary republicanism. The Frenchman St. Jean Crèvecoeur captured the spirit of this exhilaration in his famous volume *Letters from an American Farmer*, published in 1782, only two years before the *Empress of China* sailed for Canton. America, he wrote, was "a modern society."

We have no princes, for whom we toil, starve, and bleed. We are the
most perfect society now existing in the world. Here man is free as
he ought to be. . . .

He is an American, who, leaving behind him all his ancient prejudices
and manners, receives new ones from the new mode of life he has
embraced, the new government he obeys, and the new rank he holds.
. . . Here individuals of all nations are melted into a new race of men,
whose labors and posterity will one day cause great changes in the
world. Americans are the western pilgrims, who are carrying along with
them that great mass of arts, sciences, vigor, and industry, which began
long since in the east. They will finish the great circle.

What, then, was an American? asked Crèvecoeur. He was a man who
was venturesome by choice, and who carried with him in his great
adventure the hope and future of human society. For people with
such a faith—such a mission—stagnation in others was more than just
a challenge to cultural relativism. It was an anti-historical force, an
obstacle to the realization of the American character in its profoundest
dimension.

Missionaries, the only other sizable and articulate group of Americans in China during the early decades, were more outspoken. What
seemed merely peculiarities and irritations to merchants were signs
of serious moral failure when seen from the missionary perspective.
Gambling, drunkenness, infanticide, and the calculated debasement
of women attracted particular attention. But frequently the missionary
indictment broadened out from such particulars to encompass the
whole of Chinese life. S. Wells Williams, who came in time to a relatively favorable and pluralistic appreciation of China, also called it "a
defective civilization." A Baptist missionary at Ningpo (Ningbo) wrote
in 1850 that the Chinese were a people "whose character is in many
respects the least lovely and the most hopeless of all on earth." At
times, the horror of it all seems practically to have defied intelligible
description. In one account the Chinese people are said to be "rapidly
sinking" into a "foul relentless malady . . . indescribable, unutterable,
and inconceivable."

The terrible thing, of course, was not the "foul malady" itself, but
that the people were sinking into it "relentlessly"—that they responded
so little and so poorly to the means of salvation offered by the missionaries. This was extremely frustrating; and in time some missionaries,
attempting to account for the recalcitrance of the Chinese people,

concluded that China and its cultural paraphernalia were literally the work of the devil—that the Chinese language, for example, had been created by Satan as an instrument to seal these people in their wretched perversion, proof against evangelization. (Even secular-minded Americans have sometimes had similar ideas about the language!) And yet, such was the nature of the missionaries' task that the worse things were, the greater and more glorious was the challenge of meeting them in the service of God. "We should be glad if it were possible to lay hold upon one lofty principle in this demoralized people," one lamented, ". . . but we can only hope that this gross darkness is an indication of the dawn of a brighter day."

In a variety of ways, then, Americans both secular and religious found China not simply a market but a profound cultural challenge against which to test their assumptions and their faith about themselves. In numerous contexts, they portrayed China as the very antithesis of the United States: despotic rather than libertarian; stagnant rather than developing; pagan rather than Christian; cowardly rather than heroic; cruel rather than cherishing toward its women and children. The list could easily be several times as long. In thus portraying the Chinese, however, Americans regarded China and America not as separate, rival species of civilization but as the two extreme ends of a single historical continuum.

Crèvecoeur, in the passage quoted earlier, said, "Americans are the western pilgrims, who are carrying along with them that great mass of arts, sciences, vigor, and industry, which began long since in the east." Then he added, "They will finish the great circle." It was a commonplace of early Romantic thought that civilization had followed what was termed the "westward course of empire." Having begun in the East, in China and India, it was said, civilization had moved steadily westward in its successive stages of development— from the Far East, through Persia and Egypt, to Greece, Rome, the Italian city states, France and Spain, Britain, and finally America. The dynamic elements in this movement had been the growth of progress and enlightenment. From the Catholicism and monarchism of the Mediterranean world, for example, civilization had developed toward the liberal Protestant and parliamentary regime of Britain, and eventually matured in the republicanism of the United States.

Hence the cultural significance for the people of the time of bridging the Pacific Ocean. Although much of the early China trade really went via the Cape of Good Hope and the Indian Ocean rather than the Pacific, the latter route captured Americans' imagination. Across the Pacific's almost unpopulated expanse, the world's newest, most enlightened civilization (or empire, as they might have said) confronted its oldest, most decadent one. Americans crossing that great sea and living among the Chinese brought into direct contact the two extreme ends of the continuum of civilized life. This made America's role in China a matter of world-historical significance, its arrival a moment of fulfillment for the whole human race.

As Caleb Cushing said shortly before leaving on the country's first official diplomatic mission to China, "For though of old, it was from the East that civilization and learning dawned upon the civilized world, yet now, by the refluent tide of letters, knowledge is being rolled back from the West to the East, and we have become the teachers of our teachers. I go to China . . . if I may so express myself, in behalf of civilization." The *Democratic Review,* in a vivid physical metaphor, hailed "the transition of our fresh blood into the collapsing veins of stagnant nations, renewing and reinvigorating the life of Time."

Moreover, fulfilling the civilization's destiny led directly to realizing America's own unique potential. To tap the trade of Asia and plant there the seeds of enlightened civilization, Americans needed an effective means of access, what people of the time romantically termed a passage to India. The long and perilous voyages around the Cape of Good Hope (the preferred route) or through the Straits of Magellan were too precarious a basis upon which to build a relationship of such great presumed importance. The real challenge was to link China to the centers of American population and production. In the first decades after independence, these were still on the Atlantic seaboard and in the trans-Appalachian river valleys. Between them and the direct route across the Pacific stretched a vast region still considered inhospitable, ill suited to agriculture, and uninhabitable in large part even by Indians, a region then known as the Great American Desert.

For more than two generations, linking the public careers of Thomas Jefferson on the one hand and John Quincy Adams and Thomas Hart Benton on the other, the search for a passage to India was perhaps the greatest attractive force that propelled Americans beyond the farming frontier into the vast continental void. Gradually, the narrow idea of the American continent as a barrier to be crossed—an enlarged version of the Isthmus of Panama—gave way to a developmental calculus. By the 1840s, when Asa Whitney directed attention to the possibility of a transcontinental railroad, Asia was being depicted as potentially a major stimulus to the economic growth of the American interior: "The road which transports mineral wealth and Asiatic merchandise from the borders of the Pacific to the bosom of the Great Lakes, will return in almost limitless quantities the swelling produce of the Mississippi valley to minister to . . . the necessities and growing demands of the overpopulated countries of Asia."

Populating and developing the interior of the American continent, it was argued, would pave the way for a new cultural nationalism. The most prominent advocate of this view was undoubtedly Thomas Hart Benton, Senator from Missouri, a leader of the Democratic party, and one of the most celebrated orators of the age. In speech after speech, all over the country, he decried the civilization of the Atlantic seaboard as an Anglo-American hybrid, inappropriate as a cultural expression of American nationality. In the freedom of the trans-Mississippi West, by contrast, American man, responding to the American natural environment, was creating a new, definitively American civilization. This "free, original life," as Walt Whitman was later to call it—free from the stratification and the dead hand of the European past—was, to many, the true American culmination of the westward course of empire. In this way, the American relationship to Asia became an indispensable part of the central myth of this country: that the United States is both the fulfillment of history and the dawn of the future.

From that day to this, Americans have repeatedly felt a need to prove themselves and test their civilization in Asia. As if by witnessing there what we wish to believe of ourselves we might discover conclusively the meaning and justification of our national life. Capturing this mood with poignancy, Walt Whitman wrote,

> Inquiring, tireless, seeking that yet unfound,
> I, a child, very old, over waves, toward the house
>   of maternity, the land of migrations, look afar,
> Look off over the shores of my Western sea—having
>   arrived at last where I am—the circle almost
>   circled;
> For coming westward from Hindustan, from the vales
>   of Kashmere,

From Asia—from the north—from the God, the sage,
    and the hero;
From the south—from the flowery peninsulas, and
    the spice islands,
Now I face the old home again—looking over to it,
    joyous, as after long travel, growth, and sleep;
But where is what I started for, so long ago?
And why is it yet unfound?

(2)

East Asia As It Really Was

FROM EARLIEST TIMES, American myths were to collide with Asian realities. Not that Asians would be lacking in myths about Westerners, those big-nosed, pink-faced people whose habits were so absurd. But it was the Western myth bearers who journeyed to Asia first, not Asians to the West. And what did they find? What was this East Asia, newly discovered by young America—by the seamen who had sailed to Canton in 1784, and by those of the *Lady Washington* and the *Grace* who entered the closed waters of Japan in 1791 in vain pursuit of trade?

In the first place, American mariners of those years had wandered into a distinctive, separate, and isolated zone of the planet: namely, the zone of East Asian civilization, whose center was the Chinese imperial state. The distinctiveness, separateness, and relative isolation of this civilization must be underscored. From time to time, of course, Chinese civilization had had cultural and commercial contacts with the Mediterranean and with Europe—usually through the changing series of middlemen who dominated the trade routes of central Asia, southern Asia, and the Middle East. But these waves of contact had far greater impact—first on the silk-hungry elite of the Roman empire, then on the backward medieval Europeans of Marco Polo's day, and last on the philosophers of the European Enlightenment—than they ever had on the Chinese. Europe was infinitely far away. To the Chinese, its existence was uninteresting, if true. And the middlemen blunted the sharpness of cultural exchange. The imperial government in Peking listed European travelers vaguely and inaccurately, from time to time, among the Southeast Asians who regularly came to present tribute and gain trade—a matter to which we shall return. China was untouched and entirely devoid of curiosity.

A further feature of Chinese civilization, as Americans found it, was its longevity and relative stability. The China to which American ships sailed had been in business as a cultural and political entity for over nineteen hundred years—this despite intervals of collapse, disunity, and turmoil, and despite long periods of conquest and rule by foreigners. China was first unified in 221 B.C. The last Chinese Emperor, successor to this original empire, abdicated in 1912 as a very small boy. After a term as puppet "Emperor" of Manchuria under the Japanese in the 1930s, he eventually became a gardener in Peking under Chinese Communist rule, was very happy, it was said, and was sorry about his past sins.

To account for this unique phenomenon of stability, we must focus on yet another major feature of Chinese civilization: the Confucian state. What was this resilient institution? The answer requires some subdivisions. For the institution's chief elements were, first, an all-encompassing ideology, namely Confucianism; second, a universal Emperor; and third, a large bureaucracy of scholar-officials.

Confucianism was China's social and political cement for nearly two thousand years. It was an ideology based on the general principle of proper behavior according to one's status in a hierarchical society. It prescribed the right conduct for all human relationships—from parent and child and husband and wife, all the way to ruler and subject. The central principle of Confucian government was, in theory, government by goodness—government by the moral prestige of the ruler.

At the apex of the state and ideology was the universal Emperor. It was his duty to maintain the moral nature of government, and thereby to retain the Mandate of Heaven. If he didn't, things would go badly, and he would probably lose his throne unless he somehow restored order, justice, and tranquillity. The Emperor's benevolence was available to Chinese and non-Chinese alike, as long as they behaved with right conduct; hence his rule was universal, emanating from the center of what the Chinese viewed as the civilized world.

But the real key to imperial control of China's vast territory was an elaborately developed administrative bureaucracy of scholar-officials. These were men who achieved imperial appointment through immersion and success in the Confucian ideology—that is, the study of the classics—men who were tested through the famous "examination system," a Chinese invention, and who rose up through the nine ranks of the civil service. The bureaucracy was the essential instrument of government—in the collection of revenues, the supervision of vital public works and flood control, the administration of justice, and the preservation of law and order. Confucian scholar-officialdom was the non-hereditary aristocracy of China, the product and perpetuator of orthodoxy. It was an aristocracy that nonetheless permitted mobility, since the bright peasant boy theoretically could—and sometimes did— enter the ranks of this class through, in effect, cramming for the exams. This took time and money, but clans and villages would sometimes pool their resources with success to back the local genius.

These chief elements of the Confucian state were reinforced by the language of the ideology: the common written language of classical Chinese, and a common body of literature. Literacy, together with study of the classics and proper behavior according to one's status— all this constituted the route to political power. The Emperor was absolute, although he constrained himself by concepts of moral rule. Emperors and even dynasties might come and go; but the bureaucracy remained as the key to running the empire, and so did its ideology. Therefore, new emperors and dynasties tended to adjust. And hence the extraordinary degree of political and cultural continuity.

To those features of Chinese civilization so far described, one should add that the stability, continuity, and isolation combined with the ideology to produce two things: intellectual complacency and a sense of cultural superiority.

There were good grounds for both attitudes. China was indeed the oldest and most advanced culture in the world known to China. On its inner Asian frontiers were the horsemen and nomads of the steppe. They were a periodic military threat of considerable magnitude but were obviously culturally inferior. To the south and southwest were either similarly backward tribal peoples or petty princedoms under China's influence. Korea was firmly in the Chinese cultural zone, and Japan had borrowed heavily and regularly from China's language, thought, and institutions. To borrow a Western psychiatric joke, China didn't have a superiority complex—China *was* superior.

This brings us to a critical problem for nineteenth-century Sino-American relations: imperial China's view of foreigners. Because of the backwardness of most of the foreigners China had known—Jesuit missionaries excepted—the Chinese assumed all foreigners to be backward and, in the Chinese sense of the word, "barbarian." China was therefore profoundly ill prepared for the advent of a breed of barbarians whose high level of weaponry was matched by a high level of civilization. Traditional China had no precedent and no mechanism for coping with such a development. Worse still, traditional China had developed a complacency that blinded it to such a new kind of threat. Unpreparedness compounded by complacency were the major causes of China's nineteenth-century trauma.

To be sure, traditional China had learned from earliest days how to coexist with certain types of barbarians, including those who actually conquered China. After all, during almost half of the past thousand years, China had been under alien dynasties. One should note as well a fact of considerable significance for later developments: the dynasty that ruled China when America "discovered" China was itself a foreign dynasty.

In 1644, powerful tribes from the northeast (now Manchuria) had overthrown the decaying Ming dynasty, occupied Peking (Beijing), and established the Ch'ing (Qing) or Manchu dynasty. They spread their garrisions through China, but, much more important for their success, they came to terms with the old Confucian bureaucracy and adopted the style and trappings of the Chinese imperial tradition. At the same time, the Manchu rulers and their retainers kept their separateness from the Chinese in order to preserve their rule. They forbade intermarriage and forced the Chinese to wear the queue or pigtail as a sign of submission.

The significance of the ruling foreign dynasty for the later years can now be glimpsed. It tended to blunt and delay the rise of Chinese nationalism in response to the West, since genuine Chinese nationalism was subversive to the foreign dynasty, and the dynasty's paramount interests were dynastic, not national.

There is another aspect to Sino-barbarian relations that deeply affects the story of the nineteenth century—one which concerns the traditional mechanism of coexistence, not with barbarians who ruled China, but with those who visited or touched on China.

In the development of the Chinese state, even the barbarian peoples could have access to China's benevolence if they performed the proper rituals to acknowledge China's self-evident superiority. Hence the rise from the earliest times of tributary relationships between the

Chinese ruler and lesser rulers from far places. In part this was originally a form of control over difficult neighbors who had been quelled (the purer sense of a tributary relationship). But it tended to outgrow the narrow confines of victor and vanquished. Barbarians were expected to draw near the throne in Peking from time to time bearing ritualistic gifts, and in exchange would be rewarded with imperial benevolence. Imperial benevolence meant not only lavish gifts from the palace but, inevitably, access to Chinese merchants and markets.

Increasingly, then, the tributary relationship became a cover for a trading relationship. Since the merchant class ranked low in the Confucian order, international trade itself was not officially encouraged; yet by the back door of tributary missions, it tended to thrive. In due course, various points of entry for tributary missions were established, both in inner Asia for the overland traders, and along the southeastern China coast for those who came by ship. Representatives of foreign rulers—or sometimes men pretending to be such—would come with an entourage of merchants, leave them at these points of entry to do excellent business with their Chinese counterparts, and proceed to Peking to perform the formalities—among them the famous athletic feat of the kowtow (kou tou), or the three kneelings and nine prostrations, in the Emperor's presence.

So the tribute was mutually beneficial. It reassured the Chinese of their superiority and benevolence and of the barbarians' proper submissiveness; it lined the palaces of barbarian rulers with Chinese luxuries; and it lined the pockets of barbarian and Chinese merchants with cash.

Lest this system seem exotic, recall that Americans after World War II developed their own international rituals of mutual benefit. There has been in recent decades the ceremonial journey to Washington by the Asian, African, or Latin American head of state; the offer of tribute in the form of renewed verbal pledges to the "Free World" cause and perhaps the offer of military base rights; and finally the full benevolence of the American ruler, manifested in the form of a private helicopter or set of monogrammed golf clubs for the visitor, a moon rock for his wife (in the 1960s, a silver model of the Alamo)—and, of course, that welcome increased flow of military and economic aid.

But back to Canton, and to the arrival of the *Empress of China*. Those American sailors aboard that vessel were very late and not alto-

gether witting participants in a "Canton system" of foreign trade that
had grown up within the old evolving institution of tribute as a cover
for trade. It is the Canton system that formed the increasingly incon-
venient mechanism by which Ch'ing China kept the trade and other
activities of the seagoing barbarians—including Englishmen, continental Europeans, and Americans—under careful control. Once that system became intolerable to the barbarians, something had to give; and
that something, in due course, was the Ch'ing empire, not the barbarians.

There were, beyond the rigid Canton system, further puzzlements,
frustrations, cultural shocks, and even outrages, that American seamen
and their compatriots—for instance, traders, missionaries, and consuls—faced in the reality of late Ch'ing China. Chinese, on close inspec-
tion, seemed very strange, even barbaric. The men wore gowns, the
women trousers, and the men's pigtails (or queues) seemed grotesque.
They wrote and read from top to bottom, from right to left; they
used chopsticks instead of knives and forks; and their language was
outlandish.

There were some heavier truths, not just curiosities, for the Westerner: They *did*, in South China at least, eat "puppy dogs"; they practiced infanticide with female babies or sold them later into servitude;
they widely practiced polygamy through concubinage; their legal system seemed bizarre, capricious, and violent (beheadings, for instance);
they worshiped strange and multifarious gods, those of Buddhism,
Taoism, and animism; and the condition of the poor and the sick
seemed appalling even in terms of America in that era. So, positive
American myths about China had to contend with some repugnant
realities; and negative views found gradual reinforcement.

China, though the matrix of East Asian civilization and America's
first point of contact, was not, however, the only place American traders
sought to pry open. There was also that other focal point of nineteenth-
century transformation: the islands of Japan.

The most extraordinary phenomenon of the nineteenth-century
history of East Asia was the radical contrast between China's response
to the West and Japan's response. What were the features that might
help to explain such a contrast?

First, Japan was a state whose most striking quality was that of
isolation. Its isolation from the rest of the world exceeded that of China;
it was even isolated from China. This was an isolation that derived

both from geography and historical experience. For it was Japan's fate to be geographically insular—which made it reasonably defensible, in fact historically invulnerable to invasion and conquest (though in the thirteenth century it faced a nearly disastrous threat from the Mongol rulers of China, whose ships were destroyed in a storm). Japan had also seen enough of the incursions of Western powers in the Pacific region in the sixteenth century to sense a foreign danger and to impose on itself a policy of self-isolation and seclusion.

Yet despite its isolation, Japan fell well within the orbit of Chinese civilization. And proximity to such a vast neighbor produced a second identifiable quality, that of self-consciousness—consciousness of Japan's separateness from the dominating force of East Asia, and therefore national self-consciousness from the earliest days, and a patriotic mythology to support that national self-consciousness. Such elements could form a promising foundation for the development of later nationalism in a distinctly Western sense of the term.

Japan's proximity to ancient and highly civilized China encouraged a sense of inferiority. The Japanese were made aware of the youth of their culture. Japan not only lay at the fringe of China; it periodically imitated that culture and borrowed heavily from it—initially through the vehicle of Buddhism (arriving via Korea), and most notably in the sixth through ninth centuries when a wholesale attempt was made to create in Japan a replica of T'ang (Tang) Dynasty China by importing the Chinese written language and Chinese legal and political institutions. Korea played a vastly important, although generally unacknowledged, role as a cultural filter between China and Japan, particularly in the early centuries of the encounter.

Even while adding to a sense of inferiority to the mother culture, such imports created a tradition of conscious cultural borrowing—and a tradition of willingness to learn from others—that was to serve Japan well in the nineteenth century.

Despite the early adoption of the Chinese model of imperial government, political power in Japan had soon reverted to a patchwork of fiefdoms, a network of competing clans led by a hereditary aristocracy of warrior lords. The Emperor and court became in due course only one of a series of rival power centers; and eventually imperial rule, though never formally abolished, was eclipsed by a series of strongmen who controlled the court, took the title of shogun, or barbarian-quelling generalissimo, and sought to perpetuate their family rule. Thus developed a tradition of strongmen standing behind showpiece front men.

After a long interval of civil warfare, in 1600 the leader of the Tokugawa family succeeded in defeating his rivals, and he soon completed a unification of the country. In order to preserve their victory, the Tokugawa shoguns imposed a freeze on the feudal structure of the country as it had existed at the time of their victory—with those clans that fought on the Tokugawa side given special status in perpetuity. Because the Japanese were wary of the political implications of European Christian missionary endeavors, the shogunal government banned Christianity and imposed a policy of seclusion on the nation, forbidding Japanese to leave or most foreigners to enter. Between the mid-sixteenth century and the mid-seventeenth century, Portuguese and then Spaniards had traded freely with Japan, and their missionaries had created a community of Japanese Christian converts that eventually totaled about 300,000, including some feudal lords. Such a foreign incursion, and such successes, bore ominous overtones for the Tokugawa, who knew of the colonial expansion of Spain into the Philippines and feared the consequences for Japan. Western religion appeared to demand a loyalty to Western prelates that was subversive to Tokugawa rule.

The Tokugawa shoguns took up residence in Edo (now Tokyo), away from the imperial court at Kyoto; and by a series of checks and balances, including an elaborate hostage system, rival feudal lords were kept in a state of general submissiveness. The result was more than two centuries of relative stability and remarkably effective isolation up until the arrival of Commodore Matthew Perry, U.S.N., in 1853.

A further characteristic of Japan as Americans found it was an outgrowth of Tokugawa feudalism: the men, the spirit, and the traditions of a military elite. During the Tokugawa era, aspects of Chinese Neo-Confucianism, or later philosophical and political refinements of Confucian doctrine, seeped into Japan and were grafted onto old feudal military values. The result was the creation of a strict hierarchy of four social classes, in which the top class was that of warrior-administrator, or samurai. It was this class of feudal retainers, well lettered in the Confucian tradition and imbued with the spirit of Bushido—or "the way of the warrior"—that was to provide much of the energy and initiative for Japan's transformation when the country's doors were finally opened.

On the Asian mainland by the 1790s, the Chinese empire appeared at the zenith of its power, wealth, territorial extent, and cultural achievement. The Ch'ien Lung (Qianlong) Emperor, patron of the arts, was completing nearly sixty years on the throne—a golden age. Tribute missions still came to Peking from far and wide, and seafaring traders were largely restricted to the port of Canton. Stability and serenity must have seemed assured to the empire and its clients. And off the coast, in the Japanese archipelago, the Tokugawa shogunate was drawing to the end of its second century of enforcing a frozen feudal structure at home and a policy of strict isolation from virtually all foreign contact. Despite internal tensions, feudalism and isolation promised a continuation of security and stability to the nation as well as power to the shogun.

Yet, a brief hundred years later, by 1895, East Asia was destined to become a world turned upside down. By that year, imperial China lay prostrate, tied up like some giant Gulliver in a network of Western-imposed unequal treaties—treaties that gave foreign merchants and officials rule over China's ports and commerce, gave foreign mission-aries unlimited access to the Chinese hinterland, and gave foreign governments and entrepreneurs control over China's economic exploi-tation and potential industrial development. By then, too, the dynasty in Peking owed its continued survival largely to foreign indulgence. Even so, the breakup of China—"the carving up of the Chinese melon" by foreign powers—appeared imminent to the Chinese and foreigners. China's humiliation was nearly total.

Meanwhile, Japan in 1895 was also to be a nation transformed through the shock of Western intrusion, but transformed in a radically different direction. By that date, the shogunate had been abolished, the entire feudal structure dismantled, the Emperor "restored," and a revolutionary thrust toward Westernization and national strength was under way at breakneck speed. By then Japan was grudgingly being judged a grown-up by the West—to such an extent that *its* un-equal treaties with the West were terminated. (The move toward sym-bolic adulthood was to reach one of its more bizarre successes forty-five years later when the Japanese were decreed to be honorary Aryans by Dr. Goebbels, the propaganda chief of Nazi Germany.)

But most striking of all, in 1895 small Japan had just inflicted a disastrous military defeat on proud, huge China in a war over Korea. Though temporarily obstructed by the West, Japan now stood eager for its own rightful helping of the Chinese melon.

Yes, indeed, a world turned upside down.

But can one now make the tempting leap and assume that the West's impact—the actions of Americans and their European colleagues—brought on *in toto* that massive transformation? That without the West's arrival, Ch'ing China and Tokugawa Japan would have remained substantially unchanged?

Such questions fall in the realm of hazardous speculation. But some further Asian realities must be noted in attempting a reply.

The fact of the matter is that serious tensions seem to have been building up in both the societies under scrutiny. They are most vivid in the case of China. For there were already signs at the very end of the eighteenth century that the Manchu dynasty was moving into one of the classic phases of decline that are recurrent through Chinese history. In 1796, the White Lotus Rebellion erupted in the west and northwest; it began as a minor revolt against tax collectors, but soon spread with such force—and with anti-dynastic overtones—that it took eight years of imperial effort (and cost five years of revenue) to crush it. By the mid-nineteenth century the most devastating war in Chinese history, the fifteen-year Taiping Rebellion, had broken out, and the dynasty was barely saved by a rallying of Chinese scholar-generals and the provision of Western arms. And in the first years of the nineteenth century, floods and drought and famine began to take a terrible toll.

These were traditional signs of a dynasty that had grown fat and corrupt; signs, too, of a bureaucracy that had bled the people through taxes (for even the Confucian bureaucracy fell prey to most of the evils of bureaucracy), and that had let public works and flood control fall into disrepair. Such signs were compounded, we now know, by a fantastic population rise—a doubling of the Chinese population in the century from 1750 to 1850. Western incursion or not, that puzzling demographic revolution would have shaken the rulers of the nation.

So, with or without the Western impact, the Manchu dynasty appears to have been in trouble. The question is when it would have collapsed, and what would have replaced it, in the absence of the Western incursion.

Meanwhile in Japan, a different type of change seemed to be taking place beneath the rigid surface. The growth of urban culture was fostered by the shogunate's development of the capital city at Edo, a city full of retainers and hostages serviced by an increasingly strong merchant class. Osaka also rose and flourished, prospering from its location at the head of the Inland Sea. Along with urban culture came the rise of a money economy, together with increasing indebtedness on the part of the feudal lords. Simultaneously, there were visible signs of restiveness below the frozen order: a new surge of nationalism under the slogan of restoring the Emperor in order to strengthen the state and achieve Japan's destiny. How long Tokugawa society could have survived the mounting pressures is an open question. Again, the course that change would have run in the absence of the Western stimulus is impossible to predict.

But the stimulus came, and in very strong doses, to both traditional organisms, China and Japan. Japan responded with urgency and immediacy, China with sluggishness and complacency. And it is out of those responses—and America's reactions—that the hopes, fears, conflicts, and tragedy of American–East Asian relations in the twentieth century inexorably flow.

(3)

Commerce and Investment:
The China Market

IN THE BEGINNING, commerce with China was the heart of American–
East Asian relations. Without it, there would have been almost no
Americans living on the Asian continent and little in the way of incentive or accommodations to draw Asians to the eastern side of the Pacific.
So exclusively commercial were American interests that for the first
six decades of contact, during which Japan was altogether closed to
the Western world, the United States did not even have a formal diplomatic representative in China. As late as the 1850s, American consuls
in China's ports were being elected informally within the local merchant community.

The Chinese preferred no diplomatic representation; it made the
foreigners appear dependent and inferior. Since in orthodox Chinese
thought the Middle Kingdom was economically self-sufficient and culturally the center of civilization, it needed nothing from the outside
world. As the Ch'ien Lung Emperor told a British emissary in the
eighteenth century, China already possessed all things "in prolific abun-
dance." Even within the empire, commerce was an occupation of very
low status.

On the other hand, it was understandable from the Chinese perspective that foreign barbarians should seek exposure to Chinese culture and access to Chinese wealth. To make this possible, seaports
were opened to those barbarians submitting to the rules of the tributary
system. Korea, for example, paid tribute and carried on trade through
Shanhaikuan (Shanhaiguan). The tribute port for Siam was Canton.
Overland trade from Russia entered through Kyakhta. When the

31

"Western Ocean barbarians" from Europe arrived, they were assigned to Canton.

In 1760, well before the first Americans arrived, the trade at Canton was systematized. The Ch'ing dynasty was still strong enough at that time to set the terms. Like any other barbarians who wished to trade, the Europeans had to accommodate themselves to the Chinese world view. China's interest, in this case, was to control the degree of Western penetration and segregate the foreigners from direct contact with the Chinese government and people. Since the imperial government refused to deal with other governments as its equals, and Westerners were becoming testy about performing the kowtow, the simplest thing was to arrange a purely commercial relationship.

A guild (the Co-hong) of about a dozen Chinese merchant firms (or hongs) was given the exclusive right to trade with Westerners at Canton and, in return, made responsible for the Westerners' conduct. For the purpose of trading with this monopoly, foreign merchants could establish "factories"—places of business, or trade depots, for foreign "factors" or trade representatives, and their staffs, outside the walls of the Chinese city. There they were to remain, with even their own Chinese employees chosen for them and guaranteed by the hong merchants. The absence of American diplomats in later years suited this system perfectly, because ordinarily the Chinese viceroy at Canton chose to deal with the foreigners indirectly through the hong merchants. In the Chinese view, foreign consuls were merely spokesmen for the merchants of their nationality; and in the American case, this was literally true.

The success of the early American trade with Canton was a minor miracle. Confined to their factories and dependent upon the same hong monopolists for both the sale of their imports and the purchase of their exports, American merchants at the China end of the trade lived a commercially precarious existence. On early voyages, a supercargo was sent aboard each ship as business manager; but this quickly gave way to the establishment of permanent commission houses at Canton, which acted as agents for various American clients. The commission houses, since they were on the spot, were presumed to know more than a supercargo and could judge market trends and product quality with a seasoned eye. Certainly they tried; and a few, such as Russell and Company, Olyphant and Company, and Augustine Heard and Company, became fixtures on the China coast, extending their activities to Shanghai and other treaty ports after the Opium War and eventually investing in the operation of steamships on Chinese waterways.

During the Canton period, however, these houses operated very largely in the dark. Three or four months distant from their principals in the United States, and deprived of any direct access to or firsthand information about the condition of Chinese markets and crops, they were pretty much at the mercy of the hong merchants with whom they dealt. It suited the purposes of the hong merchants that the better American houses should survive and continue the trade; but for every Forbes or Cushing who made a fortune, there were many more who failed.

The critical problem was to find something the Chinese wanted to buy. This was a difficulty faced by all foreign merchants, but it was particularly acute for Americans. Part of the difference was conceptual, and part was a reflection of the undeveloped state of the American economy. Britain, for example, had an established industrial sector, especially active in the production of textiles. Accordingly, British traders in the eighteenth century approached China not only as a source of luxury products, but also as a market. Americans, on the other hand, produced almost nothing for export but foodstuffs and raw materials. They went to China to buy tea, porcelain, nankeens, crepes, and silks, not to sell the products of American factories. Later, of course, this would change. In the 1820s, the United States began to export large amounts of cotton textiles and some raw cotton to China. By the end of the century, sewing machines and kerosene were also important. But in the beginning, Americans conceived of the China market simply as a mechanism for generating funds with which to purchase Chinese goods.

One thing the Chinese would always accept in trade was silver. There was a strong demand in China for the Mexican silver dollars that were still widely used as currency in the United States. So if all else failed, ships could be sent to Canton with a quantity of silver specie to be used for the purchase of tea. Plainly, however, it was a poor bargain to drain the country of hard currency in order to buy a beverage.

An alternative was to sell something—usually Southern cotton—in England and obtain a credit thereby on one of the London banks. This credit, in the form of a note or draft or bill of exchange, could then be sold in China to finance the purchase of Chinese goods. Drafts on London were in great demand in China as a means of transferring home to the British Isles wealth that Englishmen and Scots had won in India. Ironically, the balance of trade between Britain and India was so lopsided that one of the only reliable ways for Britons in that part of the empire to send money home was to convert it into Indian opium and sell that in China for drafts on London or for silver with which to purchase such drafts.

Thus Americans had an opportunity to convert cotton into a medium of exchange that would buy tea and silk in Canton. But the process was cumbersome, costly, and dependent upon the good offices of a British banking house. About 6 percent of the original value at the American end was lost in commissions and banking charges beyond the normal costs of transacting business at Canton. American merchants calculated that if they had a commodity to export and sell directly in China, they could take a loss of 5 percent on it and still come out more profitably than they would using drafts on London.

This made the search for a salable cargo particularly important. Many expedients were tried, including such unlikely staples as sea slugs (bêche-de-mer) and the famous ginseng, a phallic-shaped root supposed to reinvigorate declining males. Until the War of 1812 interrupted it, the most promising of these expedients was the trade in sea otter and seal pelts from Oregon and sandalwood from the Hawaiian Islands. Sooner or later, most portions of the China trade gravitated to the port of New York; and John Jacob Astor, a New Yorker, established a trading post at Astoria, in the Oregon Territory, hoping to dominate the fur trade as well. But the route around Cape Horn to Oregon and across the Pacific to Canton was dominated by merchants from Boston and Salem.

It was a trade requiring extraordinary courage and ingenuity. The ships, designed to navigate the coastal waters of the Pacific Northwest, had to be small. Typically, they were only sixty-five to ninety feet long and about a hundred to two hundred and fifty tons. In these little craft, a crew composed mostly of young men in their late teens or very early twenties spent as much as three years away from home, engaged in strange and dangerous activities. At the outset of the voyage, they beat around South America, through the roughest waters in the world. Then, having sailed up the western edge of two continents, they traded back and forth along the coast and up the rivers of what are now Oregon, Washington, and British Columbia, sometimes fighting for their very lives against Indian raiding parties. It took between a year and a half and two full years to make a cargo for Canton in this way. Then, after leaving Oregon, they sailed across the world's largest ocean and put in to trade within sight, sound, and smell of a civilization dramatically different from their own. Finally, a return cargo made, the little vessels would sail from Canton with their competitors on the favorable winds of early January and race home through the Strait of Sunda and around the Cape of Good Hope, past pirates and uncharted reefs, hoping to beat their rivals to the markets of Boston.

The most salable and lasting of all the expedients, however, was opium. Here, again, Americans followed a British lead. The East India Company had begun to export opium from India to China during the second half of the eighteenth century. Although the importation of opium was illegal and the West was still too weak to force its will upon China, the trade survived and grew. It did so because it suited the purposes of local Chinese officials, who used its illegality as a pretext for collecting bribes from would-be importers.

Americans broke into the opium trade early in the new century by developing an independent source of supply in what is now Turkey. The first American-owned opium cargo arrived in Canton in 1805 from Smyrna. A little over a century and a half later, the United States government would spend millions of dollars to stifle the growth of opium poppies as a commercial crop in Turkey. But in the early nineteenth century, Boston firms such as Perkins and Company encouraged the Turks, in order to circumvent the British monopoly on Indian opium. Eventually, every major American China trade firm except Olyphant and Company involved itself either directly in Middle Eastern opium or in the carrying trade in opium between India and China. Olyphant abstained because of the strong religious convictions of its senior partner. These principles and his use of the firm to support missionary work made him such an oddity in the Canton environment that old-timers there called the Olyphant headquarters "Zion's Corner."

The American opium traffic was, in fact, an early and primitive example of multinational enterprise. The traders, tactics, and responsibility were American; the opium was largely Turkish, although Americans began to break into the Indian market by the 1820s; the capital was largely British, secured from the great international banking house of Baring Brothers; and the marketing in China was carried out with the connivance of Chinese officials and Perkins's, business partner, Houqua, the greatest of the hong merchants. At times during the years just after the Napoleonic wars, the Perkins syndicate brought in as much as one-quarter of all the opium that entered China through Canton. The total American share of the market may have been as high as one-third.

There were problems for the Americans even with opium, however. The Turkish product was inferior to its Indian competition, and the only way in which Americans could hope to cut into the British position was by dealing in high volume. This led to several difficulties. For one thing, high volume in a basically illegal operation carried on across great distances with primitive business techniques produced repeated gluts in the market. This drove down prices and reduced or eliminated profits. Then, too, the scale of the American challenge provoked British countermeasures. The East India Company, which initially responded by increasing its own production, lost monopoly control of Britain's China trade in 1834. Whereupon, former "country" firms (i.e., independent shipping and mercantile firms that had operated in the shadow of the East India Company) such as Jardine, Matheson and Company, rose to prominence with the backing of British industrial interests and introduced a new level of dynamic, sophisticated, highly capitalized competition for all aspects of American trade at Canton.

Finally, of course, opium became a source of contention with the Chinese government. Periodic crackdowns on the trade led to incidents that embittered relations and occasionally cost lives. After 1821, opium had to be unloaded outside of Chinese jurisdiction and kept on storeships anchored downriver from Canton. But this in no way reduced the trade. Chinese who had paid silver in advance came to the ships at their own risk and ferried the drug to shore. By all accounts, many of those who did so were in the employ of Chinese officials. This tense, ambiguous, fundamentally dishonest situation could not last.

By the late 1830s, the ravages caused by opium led the government to undertake a major effort to suppress the trade altogether. At the order of an imperial commissioner, Lin Tse-hsu (Lin Zexu) British and American merchants surrendered the opium on their storeships in 1839. But China was by then no longer able to dictate the terms of the trading relationships. In retaliation, the British government, through the Opium War of 1840–1842, overthrew the whole Canton system.

Lacking naval power in the Pacific, the United States remained neutral during the war. Americans accepted the benefits of the British victory, however, among them the continuation of the opium trade. American firms at Canton were actively trading opium again as early as 1842. Russell and Company, successors to Perkins and Company, dominated the American part of the trade in these years. Two decades later, *Hunt's*, a leading American commercial journal, actually proposed that the United States cultivate opium in California to improve its position in the China market. All told, opium is one of the most discreditable aspects of American–East Asian relations, as both Nationalists and Communists in China have repeatedly emphasized in this century. The opium trade finally dried up in the years between 1880 and 1913, when China began to grow increasing quantities of its own opium within the country. After the turn of the century, the use of the drug declined.

The Opium War ended in 1842 with the Treaty of Nanking (Nanjing), which, along with a supplementary document the following year, introduced the treaty system. Since it suited the principles of Chinese statecraft to lump all barbarians together—the better to play them off against each other—the privileges won by Great Britain were voluntarily extended to the United States as well. To nail this down, however, an American commissioner, Caleb Cushing, traveled to Macao and there, in July 1844, signed the Treaty of Wang-hsia (Wangxia). This assured the United States not only certain specified rights, but also what diplomats call "most-favored-nation" status, the guarantee that this country would receive whatever benefits China accorded to any other nation. Britain already had such a provision, and other powers obtained it in due course. In this way, a Chinese tactic became a Western snare. As treaties multiplied over the years, China found itself caught in an intricate and ever-growing web.

The trinity at the center of the treaty system was treaty ports, the treaty tariff, and extraterritoriality. The original round of treaties, in the 1840s, opened five Chinese ports to Western trade and settlement; eventually the number would rise to more than eighty. To encourage trade through these ports, the Chinese tariff was fixed by treaty at a mere 5 percent and collected for China by the Imperial Maritime Customs Service, nominally an agency of the Chinese government, but actually staffed and directed by foreign inspectors. The Maritime Customs, which was largely a British operation, served a useful purpose, freeing the customs from diplomatic and political pressures and assuring the Chinese central government a reliable and efficient source of revenue. On the other hand, it was clearly an infringement of China's sovereignty. Extraterritoriality placed Westerners in China under the laws and courts of their own countries, exempting them from the rules by which Chinese had to live. This not only protected persons against such vagaries of the Chinese legal system as torture and collective responsibility, but also brought their business under the shelter of Western laws of contract.

In each of these nineteenth-century treaty ports, a foreign section or international settlement was built alongside the existing Chinese city, usually on the banks of a navigable waterway. Governed by foreign consuls (of whom the British was almost always *primus inter pares*) and protected by gunboats anchored offshore, the foreign section was a small, self-conscious outpost in the midst of a vast and alien civilization.

The threat implicit in the overwhelming cultural and numerical presence of Chinese on all sides turned the community in upon itself. At the same time, however, the absence of Western women and children—there were 250 men and thirteen women at the Shanghai Christmas dance in 1861!—turned life within the community away from the privacy of the home toward public activities. To an unusual degree, institutions such as the club, the church, and the racecourse structured society. This made for a certain masculine camaraderie and deflected sensuality into a great deal of heavy eating and hard drinking. But it also emphasized the importance of rank, ritual, and bearing. For many, it was a lonely, rootless life in a stifling and precarious society. Albert Heard, a partner in Augustine Heard and Company, said that one endured China in order to make enough money to leave.

This was hard, even on the more favorable terms of the treaty port era. Information was probably the single most important requirement for success in this commerce; and for this the merchants in treaty ports were dependent upon second- or thirdhand reports. Since American merchants did not go upcountry themselves, they had little or no sure sense of Chinese crops and markets, political developments, climatic patterns, and transportation or distribution systems. Nor could they speak with authority about financial conditions or prices even in other treaty ports. This was not entirely their fault: two different kinds of currency problems complicated the task. Between China and the United States, the problem was the exchange rate for gold and silver. Since the United States was on the gold standard and China was on silver, everything traded between the two countries was bought in one currency and sold in another. And because the value of silver in terms of gold fluctuated by as much as 10 to 20 percent—often for reasons that could not have been foreseen from the vantage point of a Chinese treaty port—potentially profitable ventures could easily fail for this reason alone. Within China, the problem was regional variations in the standard unit of currency, the tael. In the late 1860s, for example, if the haikwan (haiguan) tael used by the Maritime Customs in its accounts had been assigned an index value of 100, the Hankow (Hankou) tael would have been valued at 104, the Tientsin (Tianjin) tael at 106, and the Shanghai tael at 111.4. This made a chaos of accounts.

Moreover, there continued to be problems finding a market for American exports to China. During most of the century, opium kept the balance of trade favorable to the West. But as the United States industrialized, the commission houses came under growing pressure to dispose of the products of American factories—this time "factories" back home. Cotton textiles were a particular embarrassment. Beginning in the 1820s, volumes of them were exported to China, where they accumulated in the warehouses of firms like Augustine Heard, draining capital and eroding clients' confidence in the effectiveness of the firm. Only at the end of the century was a sizable market found in faraway North China and Manchuria. For all the rhetoric about a China market of vast dimensions, the principal American role in China during the nineteenth century was in shipping.

In all questions of information, currency, and markets, the commission houses relied upon a Chinese go-between called the "comprador." Compradors were an adaptation to Western commerce of an established Chinese institution, the *ya-hang*, or licensed broker. Unlike a broker, however, the comprador was an employee of the house whose business he handled. The immediate antecedents of treaty port compradors were the purchasing agents and stewards who had worked for foreign houses at Canton under the supervision of the Co-hong. There, "ship compradors" had arranged for the provisioning and repair of vessels, and "house compradors" had handled relations with the

Chinese staff and kept accounts in Chinese currency. Both were part of the control apparatus of the Canton system, one of their principal tasks being to report on foreigners' conduct.

After the Treaty of Nanking ended the Canton system, most of the established hong merchants left the trade. To replace them, the role of the comprador grew. Now hired directly by the firm, he was separated from the mechanism of control. In fact, compradors now profited by detaching themselves from Chinese jurisdiction. Living in the treaty ports under the protection of Western law, they were immune to the "squeeze" by which Chinese officials profiteered at the expense of merchants and businessmen. This permitted them to accumulate money rapidly, while simultaneously learning Western business methods. The result was a new social and economic type in China, the wealthy man actively and entrepreneurially in charge of his fortune.

The comprador was indispensable to his commission house. Multilingual and especially proficient in the pidgin English that served as lingua franca in treaty ports, he was interpreter, treasurer for Chinese accounts, and head of the Chinese staff. All local hiring and firing was done by him. In addition, he was the firm's principal source of information about Chinese markets and crops. He solved the endless problems caused by China's irregular weights and measures and its— to Westerners—still less predictable business ethics. Finally, he either directed or assisted in all the firm's market operations. "It would be easier," said Augustine Heard, Jr., "to tell what the comprador did *not do* than what he did." A poor or negligent comprador could be the ruin of a foreign commission house.

Although the web of treaties and special privileges continued to grow well into the twentieth century, finally to be abolished only in 1943, American commission houses in the treaty ports began to decline in the 1860s. The American Civil War dislocated trade and finance somewhat, but there were deeper systemic reasons that had a greater role. Improvements in transportation and communication reduced the need for independent judgment at the China end of the trade. Early in the century, a good voyage from New York or Boston took almost four months; the clipper ships of the 1850s cut the time to about ninety days. By the late 1850s, however, P&O steamers were running between London and Hong Kong in under sixty days. Through telegraph service was inaugurated between Egypt and India in 1865; and by 1871 this line had been extended to Hong Kong. This meant that principals in New York or London henceforth could make their own decisions. With the telegraph, moreover, there came English banks and the telegraphic transfer of funds. As a result, carefully nurtured relations with London banks, which had once been special assets, declined in value as principals turned directly to the banks themselves to finance operations in China. Of all the former activities of the commission houses, only brokerage was still in much demand by the 1870s; and that did not produce sufficient profits to warrant the continuation of such large establishments.

Survival in the new conditions of the late nineteenth century required investment. Firms that traded on their own account could still prosper, and so could firms that put their own capital into the development of industry or infrastructure in China. With one exception, this was not a road the American commission houses chose to take. As Albert Heard said, the point of doing business in China for them had always been to generate profits that could be transferred back to America. The ideal was to make a quick windfall in China and then invest it in a more secure field closer to home. For example, John Murray Forbes, instead of reinvesting in the China trade, put his fortune into the development of railways in the American Middle West. Others turned to textiles, steamships, and, somewhat later, telephones and electrical equipment. This made such good economic sense that the great hong merchant Houqua arranged for Forbes and John P. Cushing to invest in the United States some of his profits from the Chinese side of the trade as well.

Disinvestment of this sort occurred principally for three reasons. The first was that, legally and politically, the United States was a safer place in which to make long-term investments. At the same time, the American economy offered more attractive prospects for growth and development. For many reasons, there was no equivalent in China of the railway, steel, and electrical booms that made handsome returns for late-nineteenth-century investors in the United States. Finally, the rise of Chinese competition made even the established forms of commerce a risky and unremunerative field for foreign investors. By the second half of the century, compradors who had learned the techniques of Western business were organizing the trade on their own terms. All along, many compradors had maintained independent firms of their own while nominally working as employees of a Western house. As early as the 1850s, it had begun to occur to some of the foreigners that the comprador was actually the principal in much of their trade, and they his agents for dealing with certain aspects of the operation. Already controlling the sources of supply and the channels of distribution, Chinese availed themselves increasingly of the new financial and communication facilities in the treaty ports, and simply squeezed the life out of all but the most firmly entrenched foreign houses.

In the final analysis, therefore, the principal achievement of the nineteenth-century China trade was to generate capital for investment in American domestic development and to transmit to a new group of Chinese entrepreneurs some of the techniques and attitudes that underlay the dynamism of Western economic growth.

The one significant exception to the rule that Americans did not invest their own capital directly in the Chinese economy during these years was the brief involvement of Russell and Company and Augustine Heard and Company in steamboat operations on the Yangtze (Yangze, or Chang Jiang) River and a few coastal routes. Westerners obtained the right to navigate the Yangtze and travel in the interior of the empire by the Treaty of Tientsin, which Great Britain and France extracted from China in 1858. (The imperial government had second thoughts about this and refused to ratify the treaty until after an Anglo-French army captured Peking and burned the summer palace in 1860.) Heard's, which was feeling the decline of its commission business, got off to a fast start in the new field by placing the first commercial steamer of any nationality on the river. But Russell and Company quickly surpassed them with a larger fleet. By the late 1860s, Russell's Shanghai Steam Navigation Company had beaten all its major competitors; and between 1867 and 1872, the SSNC enjoyed a near monopoly of steam navigation on the Yangtze. For fifteen years, it was the largest ship line in China.

Steamships had a major developmental and modernizing impact upon the Chinese economy. For one thing, they were the cutting edge of modern mechanized industry. "As late as 1880," writes Kwang-ching Liu, the leading authority, "there was still not a mile of railway in China, not a single machine-driven spindle or loom. But, as of the same date, the three leading steamship companies in China already owned a total of forty-two ships." Such companies also showed the way to mobilize capital and deploy entrepreneurial techniques appropriate to modern industrial enterprises. The SSNC, which for several years in the 1860s was the largest public joint-stock company in China, was capitalized almost wholly from treaty port sources; and its largest single bloc of investors was Chinese. Many of these were former Russell compradors. Coming in as "friends and constituents" of Russell and Company, they permitted Russell's to manage the SSNC while actually owning less than one-third of its stock. In return, the Chinese got a new and profitable form of investment outside the reach of official squeeze. Later, when Li Hung-chang (Li Hongzhang) organized a Chinese steamship line to compete with Russell's, it adopted many of the SSNC's financial and operating procedures.

In these and other ways, the steamer business was more integral to the Chinese economy than the old commission house trade had been. As part of its bid for Chinese capital, the SSNC built wharves in the Chinese city at Shanghai and elsewhere, not just in the international settlement. This brought it not only capital but freight essential to the company's survival. The growing number of ships on the river periodically created a problem of excess capacity. By lowering rates, a company with convenient wharves could pick up not only freight for the import-export trade but sizable quantities of Chinese produce and manufactures for domestic consumption. This was part of Russell's success. By the 1870s, most of the freight on its steamers, whether intended for international or domestic commerce, was being shipped on the account of Chinese merchants.

Like the commission houses from which it sprang, however, the American steamship business on the Yangtze was soon caught between superior British capital on the one hand and rising Chinese competition on the other. In 1874, after only two years of competition, Butterfield and Swire's new China Navigation Company was able to force the SSNC to enter a pooling agreement to divide the Yangtze trade equally. Within one month of its signing, the first two steamers of Li Hung-chang's Chinese government–sponsored China Merchants' Steam Navigation Company appeared on the river. Against such competition, Russell's could not hold out for long. In 1877, it sold its fleet to the Chinese. Shortly thereafter, Russell and Company itself vanished from the scene.

(4)

Evangelism: The Search for Souls
in China

ALONG WITH COMMERCE, a second persistent characteristic of the American–East Asian relationship has been evangelism: evangelism in its pure sense, the search for Christian converts, but also evangelism in its wider expression, that complex of humanitarian efforts undertaken by the missionary movement. In the early nineteenth century, the search for profits and the search for souls might proceed in close tandem. One need only recall the indefatigable Reverend Dr. Gutzlaff, an American of Prussian birth, handing out Bibles (ca. 1838) from one side of an opium smuggler along the South China coast while the crew unloaded their illicit cargo from the other side of the ship. But merchants and missionaries were eventually to part company and even disdain each other.

The role of the Christian missionary movement in the shaping of modern East Asia has yet to be probed in depth. But enough is now known to conclude that the missionary impact was heavy in China, Japan, and Korea—though not always in realms central to the movement's aims, or in ways its members might have expected. And enough is also known to conclude that Americans, particularly American Protestants, who were in the forefront of the movement, wrought important results not only in Asia but also among their countrymen back home.

From the earliest years of the republic, the sense of religious mission burned strong among Americans. First with the "heathen" of their own land—the American Indians—then in the Near East, and soon after in the Pacific islands and China, Americans pioneered not only

44

in preaching but simultaneously in teaching and healing—as evangelists, educators, doctors, and nurses sent abroad under the sponsorship of Protestant churches and institutions. (American Roman Catholics were to enter the China mission field much later, after World War I.)

In dealing with such missionaries in Asia, one deals with a larger subject: the export of a fairly comprehensive ideology, also the export of Western learning. For these sojourners abroad were not just passive cultural intermediaries; they were, rather, conscious agents of change, of radical transformation. They came to Asia *to do something to* Asia and Asians, to reshape foreign societies. Inevitably, then, their presence created a far greater clash than did that of the traders. American and Asian merchants found they needed each other—they shared a common profit motive. But there was no such common denominator between missionaries and the local inhabitants.

The missionary record in China is important for a number of reasons. First, missionaries composed the largest group of Americans with whom Chinese came in contact prior to World War II and the stationing of U.S. troops there. Their presence was therefore significant in the development of Chinese perceptions of Americans.

Furthermore, as the largest group of Americans who experienced China directly between 1842 and 1942, these people became prime communicators of the one civilization back to the other. It was largely through their eyes, ears, and words that their countrymen at home came to know China. Simultaneously, through the myriad small-town collection plates that contributed to their support, they created a bond of special China interest among churchgoing Americans. It became customary for individual congregations to "adopt" missionary families—to help underwrite their salaries; to receive from them reports and newsletters; to hear from them in person on their (usually) septennial year-long furloughs; and to send them on lecture tours of other towns and states. Through letters, tracts, books, and speeches, Americans learned more of China from missionaries than from any other single source prior to the coming of sound films and television. Out of such communication grew widely shared national perceptions. Central to them was, inevitably, a hope to help change China—from authoritarian and backward and heathen, to Jeffersonian and progressive and Christian.

At its best, the American view of China that the missionaries helped create could be scholarly, dispassionate, and compassionate. Churchmen such as Samuel Wells Williams and Kenneth Scott Latourette were to help found modern Sinology in America. But at its worst, the perception of China that was instilled by the Christian practitioners could be self-righteous, narrow, condescending, and culturally insensitive.

Missionaries were of further significance because, unlike most Western traders and diplomats, they sought to work in the Chinese hinterland. As China was forced wider open after 1860, missionaries gained access to the massive expanses of village China. Here, through evangelism and education, they were exposed to two key elements in Chinese society—to the peasantry and to young people—in a period of increasing ferment. They gained thereby a unique insight into China beyond the treaty ports. And, equally important, rural China gained a view of the intruders.

Most significant of all, the missionaries were inescapably catalytic agents. In what they believed, brought, represented, and did—in their multiple, activist foreignness—they posed the sharpest challenge of all to the traditional Chinese order.

Missions operated within a very constricted but gradually widening context: first, the Canton system, prior to the Opium War; then a small-scale treaty system after 1844, with access restricted to five new ports; and finally, after 1860, a much loosened treaty system that permitted penetration of the hinterland.

Under the Canton system, the British had, as usual, led the way, thanks to the arrival of the London Missionary Society appointee Robert Morrison in 1807. Gentry hostility eventually forced Morrison to move to Malacca (near present-day Singapore), where he founded an Anglo-Chinese school and translated the Bible into Chinese. (One later graduate of that school, Yung Wing [Rong Hong], became the first Chinese to study at an American college and received his B.A. from Yale in 1854, then returned to China and a successful entrepreneurial career; this Sino-American tradition of so-called returned students was to flower fifty years later.)

In 1830, the first American churchmen arrived in Canton under the auspices of the American Board of Commissioners for Foreign Missions (ABCFM), an ecumenical enterprise that eventually became an arm of the Congregational denomination. These pioneers were David Abeel and Elijah C. Bridgman. They and their successors were to find the climate inhospitable to the aims of evangelism. It was eighteen years before the Congregationalists won their first two Chinese converts. Yet shortly after Abeel and Bridgman, came an energetic American physician, Peter Parker, a graduate of Yale, who established China's first eye clinic in Canton in 1834. Also an appointee of the ABCFM, Parker launched a tradition of medical missions that would produce as one of its many outgrowths the Rockefeller-funded Peking Union Medical College in 1913, said to be the finest teaching hospital east of Boston and west of California.

It was under the unequal treaties, however, and especially after 1860 (treaties which some missionaries helped to negotiate, thanks to their knowledge of the Chinese language), that the foreign presence had real impact. Permitted now to travel, live, and hold property outside the Western-controlled enclaves, churchmen found new opportunities not only as dedicated believers in the "Christianizing" of China but also—it must be stressed—as a protected elite. For the new treaties granting unlimited access also guaranteed immunity from Chinese law under the provisions of extraterritoriality. They thereby bestowed on these foreign sojourners an automatic upper-class status, a cocoon of inviolability. Nor was it a status that could be shaken off even if one rejected it—as some, in much later decades of nationalist ferment, sought to do. For their peaceful invasion of the Chinese countryside had been won by force of arms. And their presence had behind it the flag of their nation and the threat of arms in the protection of their rights. Missionaries could renounce their consuls, but consuls—and eventually their gunboats—could not abandon the missionaries, for the prestige of the state was at stake.

Not that most missionaries would reject their special status, especially in the years prior to World War I. Indeed, even as enlightened a missionary-scholar as S. Wells Williams welcomed the use of armed force in the effort to persuade Chinese to become their better selves. "I am afraid," he wrote in May 1858, "that nothing short of the Society for the Diffusion of Cannon Balls will give them the useful knowledge they now require to realize their own helplessness." A month later, with more violence in the offing: ". . . we shall get nothing important out of the Chinese unless we stand in a menacing attitude before them. They would grant nothing unless fear stimulated their sense of justice, for they are among the most craven of people, cruel and selfish as heathenism can make men, so we must be backed by force if we wish them to listen to reason."

A final important ingredient in the context of mission activities—beyond the Canton and treaty systems—was what must be called the Chinese anti-Christian tradition. For American Protestants were late arrivals in an ongoing religious probing of Chinese civilization by European Roman Catholics since the early seventeenth century. Roman Catholics of various religious orders had, in fact, made what seemed like substantial progress in the cultivation of the Confucian aristocracy, until the ill-fated "Rites Controversy" of 1715, in which syncretism (i.e., a compromise that could have allowed a special blending of Confucianism into Chinese Catholicism) lost out to purists in Rome.

One result of Catholic successes had been the alienation of the Confucian scholar-officials (or gentry), whose primacy seemed threatened. The outcome of the Rites Controversy turned the imperial court against the foreigners. Christianity was soon banned, and virtually all of the missionaries were sent packing.

Although it is estimated that some 150,000 Chinese Catholics were still privately practicing their faith in 1800, a strong anti-Christian tradition was also alive in the nation; and much anti-Christian literature survived, fueled by gentry hostility. That tradition was resuscitated in the ensuing decades by several factors. First, Western governments, traders, and missionaries all seemed to the Chinese to be intermeshed in the Opium and Anglo-French wars of the 1840s and the 1850s; missionaries were therefore part and parcel of the barbarian threat. Second, the century's major upheaval, the Taiping Rebellion, was led by a curious mystic named Hung Hsiu-ch'uan, (Hong Xiuchuan) who claimed to be the younger brother of Jesus Christ, and had put together a pseudo-Christian ideology that made the missionary offerings even more repugnant to the gentry. (Hung, whose movement also failed to win missionary support, had come by his visions through Robert Morrison's translation of the Bible.) Finally, after 1860, the missionaries posed a more visible and widespread threat to the gentry as protected rivals in the hinterland, bearing a distinctly heterodox message.

Little wonder, then, that the missionary presence in the last forty years of the century provoked a strong anti-Christian reaction. Over 240 anti-Christian riots are recorded between 1860 and 1899. And at the century's close came the mission movement's—and the West's—most serious and devastating challenge, the Boxer Rebellion, during which over 200 missionaries and about 30,000 Chinese converts were killed.

So much for the context of American missionary activities in the nineteenth century and halfway into the twentieth. What can one say in retrospect about the aims of the movement?

One central aim, of course—from earliest times and throughout, even as late as 1950—was evangelism, pure and simple: the preaching of the Gospel, under Christ's dictum and St. Paul's example, to all people everywhere. Two slogans were to characterize the American mission effort: "The Evangelization of the World in This Generation," and—more explicitly—"China for Christ." What was envisioned was a gargantuan task: the saving of China, soul by soul. The enterprise was inherently individual-oriented, emphasizing each person's individual worth. It was focused on salvation; and salvation would be achieved through evangelism and conversion. Although other aims coexisted or evolved over the years, evangelism remained the vocation of large numbers of missionaries; and among many of them there persisted a "fundamentalist" tendency, a stress on personal faith and a literal interpretation of the Bible.

The fundamentalist outlook survived well into the 1940s. One of its chief manifestations was the international but British-sponsored China Inland Mission (CIM), whose appointees were given no salaries, since "God will provide"; their hospitable Chinese neighbors, honoring Confucian precepts, seldom let them go hungry. Also present were more bizarre manifestations of Christianity's pentecostal wing: for instance, a notable and formidably large American female practitioner in Nanking in the 1930s who never bothered to learn Chinese, since she was convinced that she had "the gift of tongues" and that if she spoke loudly enough to Chinese, they would get the message. To beggars she would shout, "You are *dirty!* Go home and *wash!*" At which point they would flee, recognizing a demented foreigner, and she would rest her case. Such people contributed to the negative, or at least comic, stereotype of the missionary back home.

The viewpoint of the Christian evangelist in China is vividly communicated in the words of a besieged but undaunted late-nineteenth-century fundamentalist: "The street chapel is the missionary's fort, where he throws hot shot and shell into the enemy's camp; the citadel where he defends the truth; the school, where he teaches the A. B. C of heaven; the home, where he loves to dwell; the altar, upon which he is laid as a living sacrifice; the church, in which he worships; the throne, on which he rules the minds and hearts of the heathen;

the happy land, where he enjoys communion with his Maker; the hill
of Zion, where he sings sweet songs; the gate of heaven, where the
angels ascend and descend."

Evangelism, then, was strong and sustaining stuff. Yet, simultaneous
with evangelism, and increasingly powerful in its impact, was a second
aim: emphasis on good works, on improving the conditions of the sick,
the poor, and the oppressed. No doubt humanitarianism was bluntly
viewed as a route to evangelical success. To get at the soul, treat the
body. But the tradition was also an old one, and the original injunction
was Biblical: "By their fruits ye shall know them." After the turn of
the century such efforts would become part of the "social gospel" movement. But they were also present from the beginning, as one sees in
the example of Dr. Peter Parker.

Medicine came first and early, the healing of the sick, and eventually
the training of Chinese doctors and nurses—medical education. As
the hinterland was opened, missionaries sought to treat other highly
visible afflictions: blindness, infanticide, opium addiction, and foot-bind-
ing of women (a custom aesthetically appealing to traditional Chinese,
but one that had the effect of crippling the women for life). Out of
such concerns evolved the early creation of orphanages and institutions
for the blind, and ultimately China's first institutions for the education
of women.

In later decades, it was the missionaries who would convey to China,
through translations and also teaching, the expanding corpus of Western science and technology. Here was a central area of special need,
since the scientific revolution had bypassed Chinese civilization.
Though the scientific genius was never absent in China and would
one day resurface, the communication of Western learning was sometimes an uphill battle. As late as the 1930s, for instance, a missionary
scientist once tried to train his community's Chinese servants in the
rudiments of modern hygiene, specifically about the disease-carrying
filth of the common housefly. Slides were shown of the fly magnified
several thousand times, to gasps of horror from the audience. At the
end, however, the servants' leader had the last word: They all now
understood, she announced, why the Americans made such a fuss about
flies, since flies were so big in America. Chinese flies, on the contrary,
were small and harmless. (That same scientist once ordered a laboratory
table to be built by the local carpenter along the lines of a careful
perspective drawing. The carpenter looked dubious but said he would

try. A week later the table appeared, a tired parallelogram, with the back legs shorter than the front legs, since the craftsman had *built* it in perspective.) Such were the hazards of East-West communication.

It was, however, in the realm of communication— in education, the transmission of knowledge—that the mission movement developed its third and most potential aim. And it was here that the missionaries were to achieve their greatest impact: by 1925, a high-water mark, over 300 Protestant middle or high schools, with an enrollment of nearly 26,000 students, and sixteen colleges and universities.

Education was initially an outgrowth and extension of evangelism. The path to conversion usually lay through an acquaintance with scripture. Yet the Bible remained sealed to those who could not read. So one prerequisite to conversion was literacy; and literacy meant schools, with Morrison's Bible as the test.

In the nineteenth century, such schools—at the elementary, middle, and collegiate level—were few and far between. The route to power and privilege in China remained the study of the classics and the multiple hurdles of the examination system. Only toward the century's end did Chinese desire for Western learning coincide with the mission movement's new vigor after 1890. With the abolition of the examination system in 1905, mission institutions proliferated and were besieged by applicants. And with the dynasty's fall in 1911 and the creation of a republic, the promise seemed very great for the Western educational enterprises.

A fourth and final aim of the missionaries was a broad-gauged effort to improve the circumstances of life in village China, also in the new urban slums. In the 1920s and 1930s, the various denominations and such ecumenical enterprises as the YMCA and YWCA participated in major social welfare endeavors that culminated in the "Rural Reconstruction Movement." The ingredients of this effort were not new. Indeed, they had been presaged in the medical and educational aspects of the earlier mission record. What was moderately downplayed in these later reconstruction programs was pure evangelism. The prevailing guideline was now the "social gospel."

When one considers, then, the several aims of the missionaries in China (and elsewhere), one views a very multifaceted enterprise—a complex cultural export from its earliest days, a miniature of what would be President Truman's Point Four or President Kennedy's Peace

Corps of the post–World War II era. Yet it must be remembered that in China every American missionary wore and spoke and carried aspects of a civilization radically different from that of the Chinese; that every missionary also bore an alien religious and secular ideology; and that, because of the buffer of extraterritoriality, missionaries did not need radically to adjust to the society they had penetrated.

So much for missionary aims. What of the problems they faced?

First and foremost, they shared with other foreigners a vast ignorance of China—though some who came as teachers would become, through immersion, solid scholars of Chinese civilization. Many, "called" to the China service through inspirational religious conferences back home, arrived as innocents abroad, barely aware of the tasks confronting them or the history of the people to whom they had pledged their careers. Many, in the late nineteenth and early twentieth centuries, would come from pietistic small-town Midwestern and Southern communities, trained in church-sponsored colleges. Many of the evangelists lacked much formal education, so they often arrived ill-prepared. And yet, unlike the traders and men of commerce, they tended to make heroic efforts to speak and even read the Chinese language; communication was central to both teaching and conversion. And through learning the language they learned much more of the culture than their commercial and diplomatic fellow countrymen.

Another problem they faced was the real rigor of life, especially in the hinterland. Despite extraterritoriality, the foreigner living outside the treaty ports was constantly subjected to danger from bandits and rebels in the declining years of the dynasty and the warlord era that followed. Health, too, was endangered; families would be struck down suddenly by untreatable diseases, especially in the oppressive heat of the Chinese summer. And a further danger came from the hostility of the locals—both gentry and peasants—in many parts of the country. One graphic account, written in 1905, suggests the dimensions of the hardships:

> We were mobbed in the fu [provincial] city, mobbed in the district cities, mobbed in the large towns. We got so used to being pelted with mud and gravel and bits of broken pottery that things seemed strange if we escaped the regular dose. . . . We went out from our homes bedewed with the tears and benedictions of dear ones, and we came back plastered over, metaphorically speaking, with curses and objurgations from top to bottom. It went badly with our chapels that we rented.

They were often assailed; roofs were broken up, doors were battered in, and furniture was carried off.

One result of such hardships was the missionary tendency to live Western-style: in compounds surrounded by high walls. Since servants were cheap and allowed parents more time to pursue their calling, servants abounded. And the dangerous summer months of heat, humidity, and disease were endured by spending them in cooler climates— in mountain resorts or perhaps by the sea. Another result, however, was renewed dedication to the tasks at hand. The rigors were a testing, and some fled home permanently in illness and defeat. But many more stayed, despite lootings and even loss of life, relentlessly persistent to win "China for Christ."

A further problem that confronted the movement was that of translation, of the transmission of Christian ideas and terms into the Chinese language and outlook. There was, for instance, no Chinese equivalent to the Christian concept of "sin." As for "God," different Christian sects adopted different Chinese terms, none of them entirely precise. Sectarianism itself, it should be noted, was to pose an increasing problem; for by 1890 there were already nineteen Protestant denominations at work in China. Despite an ecumenical movement in the 1920s (and the founding of the interdenominational National Christian Council), Roman Catholics, Eastern Orthodox adherents, and others remained active rivals to ecumenism, confusing the would-be convert. No wonder that it would be asked from time to time among Chinese whether Christ had been an American or something else; a Southern Baptist, Episcopalian, or what?

Though cited earlier, gentry hostility must be reemphasized in this listing of problems. Protestant Christianity, an individualist ideology that preached the primacy of faith and personal loyalty to scripture, was in fundamental conflict with Confucianism. Rekindling China's leftover anti-Christian tradition, local and regional scholar-officials were often able to play upon peasant suspicions of the unsettling foreign presence. Anti-Christian placards, the fuel of riots, bore traditional allegations about the evil things that transpired behind the Westerners' compound walls: the extraction of eyeballs from orphans for the magical creation of silver, a multitude of sexual perversions. Out of the gentry's fanning of the suspicions of the populace came such outbursts as the Tientsin Massacre of 1870, in which twenty-one foreigners, including ten nuns, were killed, and, later, the Boxer Rebellion.

Perhaps most frustrating of the problems missionaries faced was the mystery of Chinese non-receptiveness. In conversions, at least, the mission movement was a disastrous failure. One deals here with an unresolved subject, the Chinese approach to religion. Except for the contrapuntal themes of Buddhism and Taoism—which had, of course, enduring significance—Chinese Confucian orthodoxy was this-world, not other-world, in its orientation. It emphasized one's behavior in the here and now—veneration of one's ancestors also, but minimal interest in any afterlife. Preachments about sin and salvation seemed to fall on deaf ears. Missionaries and scholars eventually diagnosed a phenomenon called Chinese "syncretism"—an apparently casual will-ingness to blend together several "faiths" rather than remain zealously true to one alone. It was possible for a Chinese Christian convert to burn incense to his or her ancestors, offer prayer sticks at Buddhist temples, pause reverently at Taoist roadside shrines, follow the pre-cepts of the sage Confucius—and also be a practicing member of a Christian denomination. What seemed bafflingly characteristic was a disregard for metaphysics, a zest for the here and now, and a boundless capacity to absorb credos and forms of worship. To more rigid Western-ers, the combination could be exasperating.

In due course, at a glacially slow pace, conversions did occur. By 1889 there were 37,000 Protestant communicants in China; by 1905, 178,000. But, with notable exceptions, the nature of the converts posed a difficulty. The nineteenth-century missionaries had, inevitably, their greatest successes with the lower orders of Chinese society—the poor, the rejected, and those in trouble. Such converts—often dubbed "rice-Christians"—could cause a church much trouble. An out-group, their tendency toward misbehavior further complicated their status as West-ern protégés; and they often brought their elite protectors into judicial interference in their behalf. One result was the further alienation of Chinese authorities.

A deeper level of difficulty surrounded the American missionary's self-definition. He or she carried the national emblem in color, clothing, customs, and passport. Yet how American—as opposed to universal—should one be and act on behalf of the Christian enterprise? How Western, again, as opposed to universal? After the American civil war, how Northern as opposed to Southern? And throughout, how Methodist or Baptist or Presbyterian or Episcopalian? Roman Catholics, once on the scene again, fared better; their church was, by claim, universal and encompassed all nations and regions.

Missionaries were also periodically perturbed by problems of ambivalence. However little they might know of China at first—and however obdurate and backward the Chinese might seem—Chinese culture, ethics, and even religions had a powerful attractiveness to those who were intelligent and sensitive. Despite the tyranny and corruption of officialdom and the poverty and misery of the masses, Chinese civilization had grandeur and subtleties that could enthrall the Western visitor. How might it be best improved without destroying it? Should one try to convert the leaders or—soul by soul—the masses? The Taiping Rebellion's pseudo-Christian ideology was examined but rejected by the missionaries; seventy years later the conversion to Christianity of Generalissimo Chiang Kai-shek (Jiang Jieshi) was welcomed by many. But the hardest question was to be posed by those other would-be transformers of Chinese society, the Communists, who shared many missionary objectives in the uplifting of the masses but disdained God and religion.

Perhaps suggested in the foregoing discussion was the general problem of missionary exasperation. China seemed so promising but was so resistant in delivering on its promise. One need only cite the Reverend Arthur H. Smith (1845–1932), the most widely read missionary publicist of his day, who used the following chapter titles in his classic 1890 description of Chinese ways and Western frustration: "Face," "Economy," "Industry," "Politeness," "The Disregard of Accuracy," "The Talent for Misunderstanding," "The Talent for Indirection," "Flexible Inflexibility," "Intellectual Turbidity," "The Absence of Nerves," "Contempt for Foreigners," "The Absence of Public Spirit," and "Conservatism." Dr. Smith went on to catalogue virtues as well as shortcomings, but the prevailing tone was exasperation.

The aims, then, were multiple, and so were the obstacles. What can one now say of the missionary record against this dual background? We deal here with a population of American Protestant workers that rose very slowly in the nineteenth century, that numbered only 200 by 1870; that reached 1,000 by 1900; that hit a peak of 5,000 in 1925, just prior to the turmoil of the Nationalist Chinese northward march; and that never again, from 1930 onward, totaled more than 3,000. The Great Depression, World War II, and the Chinese civil war all helped to reduce the effectiveness of the mission enterprise.

In the realm of pure evangelism, the results have already been suggested: only 178,000 Chinese converts to Protestant Christianity by 1905; 360,000 by 1920; and 536,000 by 1936. So the impact of the missionaries was not in numbers of converts. There were, of course, a few spectacular successes. Sun Yat-sen (Sun Zhongshan), the nominal leader of the republican revolution and the republic's first president, was also nominally a Christian. So, eventually, was Sun's ultimate successor, Chiang Kai-shek, who converted to his wife's Methodism early in the 1930s. Madame Chiang's brothers and brothers-in-law, who held high posts in the Kuomintang (Guomindang) government, were also Christians. And so, among Chiang's many opponents, was the flamboyant warlord Marshal Feng Yu-hsiang (Feng Yuxiang), who gained special notoriety by allegedly baptizing with fire hoses entire battalions of his troops.

But it was in other realms that the missionaries left a more enduring record. Already by 1905, before the abolition of the examination system, they had founded six institutions of collegiate rank, including the only places where Chinese women could receive higher education. After that year, Western-sponsored education burgeoned at all levels. Such institutions were inevitably uneven in the excellence of their academic offerings. But they were best, and most sought after, in the natural sciences, in mathematics, and, of course, in the history of the Western world.

The most successful Chinese graduates of these colleges or even middle schools often won grants to study at American colleges, especially after the American government "remitted" the "indemnity" extracted from China after the Boxer Rebellion and applied the funds to fellowships. Alternatively, until World War I, many sought advanced study in Japan, the modernized society closest to home. Meanwhile, in China itself, institutions such as the College of Agriculture of the University of Nanking (Nanjing) pioneered in agricultural education and the study of land usage in an overwhelmingly rural nation. Nanking University received assistance from Cornell; and similarly, other mission colleges sometimes developed special relations with institutions in North America: Yenching (Yanjing) University with Princeton and Harvard; Ginling College for Women with Smith. Yale University sponsored, from 1901, four educational institutions, including a middle school, hospital, medical school, and a nursing school in Changsha, Hunan; and it participated in a consortium-sponsored university in

Wuhan. Oberlin and Carleton colleges did similar work on a lesser scale, sending out students as teachers of English.

The heyday of the mission educational effort was the two decades between 1905 and 1925. Thereafter, although this work continued and sometimes even expanded, the anti-foreign and anti-mission content of Chinese nationalism and Chinese communism produced severe constraints. Even so, the graduates of Western-sponsored institutions—sometimes converts but more often not—gravitated to positions of leadership in successive Chinese governments.

There was, it must be noted, an important adjunct and precursor to the establishment of schools and colleges in the missionary record. That was the role of missionaries as communicators through the translation of Western knowledge into the Chinese language. And its greatest effect was felt in the late nineteenth century, before Western-educated Chinese could translate for themselves. It was in the unpretentious magazines and books published by missionaries that Chinese seekers often found their best source of Western learning in the late years of the besieged and decaying dynasty.

From 1833, the very earliest American Congregationalist, Elijah Bridgman, was able to offer articles in Chinese on the steam engine, world geography, and—for those who cared—George Washington, in a newsletter he printed in Canton under the title of *Chinese Monthly Magazine*. Far more significant, in the later decades of the century, was the work of Young J. Allen of Georgia. In Shanghai, China's new commercial hub, Allen published in Chinese *The Globe Magazine*, a weekly from 1878 to 1888, and a monthly from 1889 to 1907. This journal had a great influence on its readers well beyond the treaty ports. It brought to them contemporary Western knowledge of physics, mathematics, education, social welfare, and nineteenth-century European history. Its impact was increased after China's humiliating defeat by Japan in 1894–1895. In the desperate national search for an "answer" to China's weakened condition, the *Globe*'s circulation rose to 30,000. Without doubt, Allen's efforts contributed to the abortive Chinese "Reform Movement" at the end of the century. Also highly significant in the last half of the century were the translations by the American missionary John Fryer at the Shanghai Arsenal; Fryer's works became science texts for a new generation of Chinese.

A further portion of the missionary record relates, of course, to the sphere of medicine, medical education, and public health. Here the American contribution was substantial and, ultimately, paramount among Western efforts. Peter Parker's Canton eye hospital ultimately led to the creation of Peking Union Medical College and three other noted medical schools. By 1876, the missions had founded sixteen hospitals and twenty-four dispensaries. And by 1925, there were 301 hospitals and nearly 500 dispensaries throughout the nation. There was no other field in which Western learning could produce more dramatic results. Yet the medical and public health problems of village China remained staggering; and the graduates of Western medical schools tended to turn their backs on the hazards of rural life and choose instead more comfortable urban careers.

Evangelism, education, scientific study, and medicine were destined to bring Christian missionaries face to face with the intractable problems of social welfare: the conditions of the whole person, mainly the villager but also, increasingly, the inhabitant of the urban slum. From earliest times, missionaries had fought against infanticide, footbinding, female slavery, concubinage, and oppression of the poor by landlords and tax collectors.

But not until the 1920s and 1930s did the mission movement extend its attention from conversion, medicine, and education more frontally against the economic and social conditions that caused brutal oppression of the individual peasant or worker. Here, with Christian Chinese pioneers, missionaries helped strengthen the rural reconstruction movement. But here, too, they ran head-on into two substantial problems: the political and economic entrenchment of the Chinese upper classes of politicians, bureaucrats, and landlords; and the political and economic challenge from other would-be changers of the human condition, Marxist revolutionaries, who were willing to use violence to create a new society. In the former group they found a massive obstruction; in the latter a rival and well-disciplined ideology that denied the missionaries' central thesis, the existence of a Christian god.

Balanced conclusions about the China missionary enterprise are still difficult to formulate. Overseas evangelism always had its critics back home; and in the years since World War II, such criticism has gathered strength even within church groups. Was it not arrogant and presumptuous to try to inflict one's religion, ideology, and culture on others—in particular on civilizations far older than that of America? Much sharper, of course, has been the critique by Chinese, whether Confucianists, Nationalists, or Communists. For the Communists, after

1949, the missionary offering in all its aspects was denounced and dismissed as simply "cultural imperialism." For some time to come, the issue will be clouded by polemics.

Yet a tentative appraisal is nonetheless possible. Such an appraisal should note at the outset that the missionary movement was a reasonably accurate reflection of certain positive aspects of American society: of the national zeal for education, for the provision of community services in medicine and nursing, and for increased social justice. American ideals, applied at home through gradualism and pluralism, were at the heart of the overseas effort.

It should further be stressed that the missionaries played a central role in the shaping of the American view of Asia in general and China in particular. They were interpreters of China to Americans. And they were sometimes, though by no means always, important participants in the creation of American policy toward China. Although the point can be overstated, one cannot overlook the diplomatic roles played by such diverse churchmen as Peter Parker (appointed United States Commissioner in 1856), S. Wells Williams (Secretary of Legation for periods of time), and John Leighton Stuart (Yenching University president who became the last American ambassador to Nationalist China on the mainland). Nor can one overlook the profound impact of such writers as missionary Arthur H. Smith, missionary daughter and wife Pearl S. Buck, and missionary son Henry R. Luce.

As previously noted, the mission movement was—unbeknownst to its members—a privately sponsored model for later American government efforts to help reshape developing societies on a worldwide basis under secular auspices. Point Four, foreign aid, and, especially, the Peace Corps all borrowed heavily from the missionary example.

No appraisal would be complete without underscoring once again the role missionaries played as largely unwitting catalytic agents within a continuing process that can be loosely called the Chinese revolution— a process of volcanic upheaval that began in the 1840s and continues to this very day. By the knowledge that they brought with them, and simply by their presence in China, missionaries unquestionably hastened the breakdown of the old Chinese order and helped to kindle Chinese nationalism in all its many forms.

Finally, and largely through their educational efforts, missionaries became major contributors to the creation of a new Chinese elite in the era after the collapse of the Manchu empire. They also became, thereby, major contributors to important echelons of leadership on both sides of the Formosa Strait—the bifurcated Chinese revolution, in both Taipei (Taibei) and Peking.

In retrospect, their China effort, though on the face of it a total failure—China was *not* won for Christ—had mysterious qualities of success. China was, in fact, transformed through their help. But the transformation was not of their design.

(5)

The Opening of Japan

DURING THE SIXTEENTH CENTURY, Japan's so-called Christian century, Westerners had first come to Japan. We are unsure of the year; it was 1542 or 1543. The Portuguese and the Spaniards sought to plant their faith, as well as to enrich their purses by bringing Japan into continuing commercial relationships with the Western world.

The Iberians brought firearms, sponge cake, and gonorrhea to the Japanese; but the chief legacy of the Iberian intrusion and the ensuing cultural encounter was intense fear in Japan: apprehension about the subversive impact of Christianity, a foreign faith which the Japanese worried could shatter the new and fragile political unity of their island world.

So under the Tokugawa seclusion edicts enacted early in the seventeenth century, the practice of Christianity was forbidden. Japanese could not travel abroad legally, ocean-going ships were not permitted to be constructed, and foreigners were allowed access to Japan only on Japanese terms. That meant no priests, no proselytizing, and no scripture.

Ultimately, among Westerners, only the Dutch stayed. They were regarded as safe by the Japanese, because their interests seemed to lie largely in their account books, their guilders, and their schnapps. They did not try to convert anybody. Nonetheless the Japanese watched them carefully.

From the mid-seventeenth century to the mid-nineteenth century, Dutch trading activities were confined to the tiny football field–sized

61

artificial island of Deshima in Nagasaki harbor. There, a handful of merchants spun out a lonely existence, enlivened by an occasional shore revel in a brothel, or by the annual arrival of a trading ship from home.

The Chinese were the only other foreigners regularly permitted entry to Japan. To the Japanese, the Chinese traders were a source of information about the outside world, including the West, with Chinese translations of some of the Western classics providing the Japanese with a relatively easy way to penetrate the mysteries of Western culture, easier by far than Dutch, which seemed like such a barbaric tongue. Westerners knew little or nothing of this cultural flow, and they were not inclined to learn anything from the Chinese. The Dutch said little about Japan; they wanted no interference with their trade monopoly. And so Japan virtually sank out of the consciousness of the West.

As for the Japanese, the two and a half centuries between the seclusion edicts and the arrival of Commodore Perry saw the blossoming of a new political order in the form of the Tokugawa state. Historians subsequently used the phrase "centralized feudalism" to describe it. The protagonist was the shogun, nominal deputy of the Emperor, de facto chief executive power of the land. Vying for real power with the shogun and his court were the great lords of the realm, the daimyo, tied to the shogun by pledges of fealty. The warrior class, of whom the shogun was foremost, perennial aristocrats in the Japanese political world, became during this period salaried bureaucrats; and long years of peace ossified their military skills, although not their interest in military affairs.

Confucianism in its later—Sung (Song) dynasty—definition was intellectual cement for the society. Japan in the Tokugawa period was essentially secular; the vitality of Buddhism had faded. The values Confucianism placed upon a hierarchical ordering of society, on literary education, on loyalty, and on filial piety were generally accepted by the Japanese.

But Japanese Confucianism put loyalty to one's lord above obligation to one's family. And, also unlike China, learning was not standardized by the demands of an examination system. In Japan, hereditary authority stood unchallenged by any theory of rule by merit.

The political success of the Tokugawa system was demonstrated in its creation and its maintenance of effective national unity, a political framework encouraging a thriving commerce, bustling cities, and a culture which extended down to embrace the masses, at least within the cities and towns. Probably no other society in world history has been able to match this Tokugawa achievement of sustaining order at home and remaining at peace abroad for a period of more than two centuries.

But by the early 1800s, success had wrought failure. Political triumph stimulated a growth in wealth ultimately corrosive to the political order which had made it possible. The state saw no means of taxing the new wealth; it remained largely in the hands of the people who had earned it, the merchants. The result was hardship for the nominally privileged. The samurai, political functionaries, lived on fixed stipends in an inflationary era. Thus the samurai enjoyed power (and responsibility) but had no money. Merchants had money but no power. The result was profound unease. And the Confucian classics and works of statecraft had no answers for such problems.

Small wonder then that scholars were stimulated to look into the pre-Tokugawa past for inspiration for solving the problem. The study of Shinto, that core of native beliefs which predated Buddhism and which implicitly focused on the Emperor, revealed no place for the shogun.

And centers of potential subversion lay within the great states of Satsuma and Choshu in western Japan. These had been the last to yield to the Tokugawa house early in the seventeenth century, and memory of defeat rankled within them even in the mid-1800s. With foreign ships appearing more and more frequently in Japanese waters, menacing the security of the Japanese world, and the Tokugawa seeming hesitant and unable to cope, the whole edifice shuddered.

When Commodore Matthew Perry and his American squadron appeared in 1853, Japan's strategic position was still quite strong, thanks to the geographical isolation of the islands. The power of Western military technology, although increasing very rapidly, was not yet so great as to be overwhelming. Perry's smoothbore short-range artillery, although it could have played havoc with the coastal rice traffic, was otherwise probably not much of a threat to the Japanese. Japanese solid shot could have caused heavy damage to the wooden-hulled American ships, had these moved close enough to the shore to fire their own artillery with any hope of hitting anything.

Moreover, to travel the vast spaces of the Pacific from the underdeveloped western coast of the United States took two months, a long time for supply or reinforcement. And the United States, with 25 million people in 1853, was less populous than Japan, which had 30 million. It was by no means possible, therefore, for Americans to bring to bear upon the Japanese any overwhelming military power. The force they wielded was more psychological than anything else. But the appearance was overwhelming.

Fortunately for the Japanese, their nation was then of minor interest to any of the Western European powers. Great Britain was, for example, fairly well preoccupied with India and China. And chasing pirates off the coast of Borneo was higher on the list of Admiralty priorities than sending a Royal Navy squadron to carry out negotiations with the Japanese. It was the Americans who were the first to do so.

What of the Russians? They had begun to push eastward across the Urals in the late sixteenth century, about the same time as Japanese authorities were wrestling with the question of whether they should continue to tolerate the preaching of Roman Catholic missionaries from Europe. Moving across the great wastes of Siberia, aided by firearms, the paucity and disunity of the opposition, and the convenience of the great river systems, imperial Russian power flowed, reaching the shores of the Sea of Okhotsk in 1637. The Russians established a thriving fur trade, began the painfully slow building of a thin chain of strategic forts and trading posts across the immense landscape, and established a modus vivendi with the Ch'ing empire.

By the mid-nineteenth century, just after the opening of Japan, the Russians, through exercise of diplomatic skills of the highest order, persuaded the hapless Manchu to cede the coastal provinces of Manchuria, enabling the Russian empire to become a major Pacific power. Even earlier, Russian activity had spilled over into Alaska and northern California. Yet these were territorial overextensions from which the Russians ultimately retreated to the Asian mainland. Northern Asia alone was more than enough to digest. And Russian naval power in the western Pacific was as hampered as the American by its distance from home base, by its remoteness from the core of the people and the wealth and power of the homeland. Although as interested in Japan as the Americans, the Russians arrived there third, following the British. It was the Americans, then, who took the lead in "opening" Japan to the West.

Easing the way to China was important to Americans. Acquisition

of California in 1848 brought Asia closer; and on the San Francisco–
Shanghai great-circle route (Shanghai was beginning to replace Hong
Kong and Canton as China's major gateway to the maritime powers),
Japan was the place to stop. Steamships, with their inefficient engines,
burned large amounts of coal, of which Americans thought Japan had
quantities. It seemed selfish—almost immoral—for the Japanese to continue to seal themselves off from the West and from international commerce, which the Victorians viewed as "the handmaiden of civilization
and progress."

Beneath all the other motives was simple American curiosity.
Perry's expedition was not simply an armed force or an embassy; it
was also a scientific enterprise. The Americans wanted to learn all
manner of things about exotic Japan.

Japan could provide coal, safe harbors for trans-Pacific steamships,
and a possible field for Protestant missionary activity. Moreover, in
the cold waters of the northern Pacific, Americans were working the
richest whaling grounds in the world. But those men who had experienced the misfortune of shipwreck on Japanese coasts frequently found
themselves very badly treated. Here then was a constituency clamoring
for a treaty with the Japanese. A treaty could provide humane treatment and safe haven for unfortunate whalers.

None of these motives obviates the fact that China seemed more
important to Americans than Japan did. This was to become a continuing problem in the relationship. Whereas in the case of the American
relationship with China the initiative was taken by private hands—
merchants and missionaries, with the diplomats following behind—
with Japan the United States government took the initiative. Private
individuals could get nowhere and there were no foreign coattails to
ride on, as there had been along the China coast. The American government sought to break the impasse with the Japanese by sending out
a naval expedition, and Commodore Matthew C. Perry, the most distinguished senior officer in the American Navy at that time, was chosen
to head it.

No one appreciated a joke less than he did, one of his seamen
ruefully remarked of the commodore. Short-tempered, immensely
self-confident, commanding of figure, with a taste and a talent for
self-dramatization, Perry, unlike so many of his professional contemporaries, was entirely at ease with the new era of steam power and
shell-firing guns. He was by temperament and by experience well

suited to command the Japan expedition, which was to be the final task of his career.

Although Perry had not sought the appointment, wanting to command the Mediterranean squadron instead, he accepted his assignment with great conscientiousness. In the long run he was content, and he would consequently write to his wife that his first visit to Japan in 1853 was "one of the most important events of modern history."

At Perry's behest, agents combed the bookstores of New York and London so that he might read and study what was known to the Western world about Japan. He traveled to the whaling port of New Bedford in order to interview people there who knew firsthand the winds and the waters of the Japanese archipelago. There were large holes in Western knowledge of Japan; and by the time of Perry's arrival, the Japanese already knew far more about the United States than Americans knew about Japan. They had been reading about the West since the sixteenth century. Here was the beginning of a serious and continuing gap in knowledge between the two nations, a major element of that relationship.

Perry landed inside Tokyo Bay at Kurihama in 1853. He vowed when he left, after delivering a letter to the Emperor from President Fillmore requesting a treaty, that he would return the next year with a large squadron.

The Americans were active and noisy visitors—bellowing at the Japanese when their small picket boats bobbed too near the black ships. "Face" and security both demanded the maintenance of an adequate distance. On Sundays at morning prayer, the massed voices of hundreds of sailors would roar out hymns, resounding grandly over the water to the ears of the curious Japanese. The commodore kept the gunners at work firing salutes, both loud and smoky, designed not only to impress the Japanese but also to sustain American morale. And he was determined to keep his men busy.

Eating and drinking became an important part of the unfolding diplomatic ceremonial, with enormous alcoholic consumption marking the encounter between the two cultures. The Americans attempted to slake Japanese thirsts with champagne, Madeira, cherry brandy, and punch, with whiskey available by the barrel. Americans found their guests enthusiastic and undiscriminating. One Japanese visitor sampled everything, finally even downing a bottle of salad dressing.

Entertainment by the Japanese was highlighted by a series of exhibition matches of sumo wrestling. The Americans offered a performance by the "Ethiopian" Band of the U.S.S. *Powhatan*, which provided accompaniment for a minstrel show in blackface. At the end of the evening, one tipsy guest warmly embraced the great commander in chief himself, nearly crushing his splendid new gold epaulettes as he did so. The Americans surrounding expected an explosion of temper; instead, the commodore simply said, "Oh, if he will only sign the treaty, he may kiss me."

The experts who accompanied the commodore on the expedition, most well known of whom was scientist Dr. James Morrow, prepared lengthy reports for the United States Congress on what they had observed of Japanese mineralogy, ornithology, ichthyology, botany, and so forth. The United States was still, of course, pre-eminently an agricultural nation, and American farmers were always eager to know about new seeds and plants. The opening of Japan exposed to the West a new world of flora and fauna.

The "Japan pea," or soybean, excited enormous interest, and a number of other vegetables and fruits were introduced to American palates. Flowers came as well, such as the Japan lily and the anemone japonica. Japan clover, *lespedeza*, enriched the poor soils of the American South, and it spread rapidly.

In fact, what is interesting is the speed with which these new plants took root in American soil. By 1858, it was reported that Japanese varieties of yew, dwarf cypress, and juniper were already widespread in the United States. The botanical impact of the cultural encounter was therefore virtually immediate, although some of these new species may have come to America from Japan via China, prior to the Perry expedition. The commodore brought home three Japanese spaniels, similar in appearance to the King Charles variety. And Japanese ornamental fowl appeared also in America. The Frizzle or Crisp-Feathered Bantams were described as "like the inhabitants of their native country, a very singular race of fowls."

The expedition occasioned the exchange of presents, a custom of which Americans would find the Japanese exceedingly fond. The Japanese gifts to the Americans—silks, brocades, porcelains, lacquerware, and objets d'art—displayed the aesthetic achievements of Japanese culture, but they were in the aggregate somewhat disappointing to the Americans, who grumbled to themselves that they had not got more.

The Americans, with their gifts, chose to emphasize the technological feats of their culture. Those several items which made the greatest hit with the Japanese were Colt revolvers from Hartford, Connecticut, which the Americans delighted in demonstrating by frequently firing into the air; a functioning telegraph, which was immediately set up and put into use by the Japanese; and a quarter-size steam locomotive, tender, and passenger car with 350 feet of track. The samurai, with swords at their sides, clambered to the roof of the miniature passenger car, where they sat, apprehensive but entranced, kimonos fluttering in the breeze, as the train went round and round at the great speed of twenty miles per hour.

In his treaty, Perry exacted a Japanese agreement to care properly for American castaways, and to open as ports of refuge both the fishing village of Shimoda at the tip of the mountainous Izu peninsula and the town of Hakodate in the far-off northern island of Hokkaido. Furthermore, Americans gained the right to maintain a consul at Shimoda. Nothing was said in the treaty about trade, although Perry had raised the question in his talks with the Japanese.

But Japan was "opened." Perry had ended sixty years of spasmodic and, for Americans, highly unsatisfactory contact with the Japanese. To the Japanese, the barbarians were still restricted to remote and insignificant places in the empire. Yet as the implications of the Perry treaty sank in, many Japanese thought the shogunal authorities had betrayed the nation. And the Americans began to chafe under Japanese reluctance to fling wide the gates. But each side thought at the beginning that it could congratulate itself for having got more than it had given.

Little was in fact settled. Only after the first American consul, Townsend Harris, slowly, skillfully, and painfully worked out the details of a commercial treaty, signed in 1858, could it be said that relations were fully established.

The other Western powers, led by Great Britain and Russia, were quick to secure the privileges enjoyed by the Americans. The Harris treaty and successive agreements drew upon precedents established by Western diplomacy with the Chinese: a fixed tariff on goods imported into Japan, extraterritorial privileges whereby foreign nationals were subject only to their own laws and their own courts, and the "most favored nation" clause whereby one power would automatically receive any additional privileges wrested from the Japanese by any other power.

Having no fleet upon which to call for support, Harris nonetheless artfully used the threat of Britain's Royal Navy against the Japanese, telling them that if they refused to cooperate with the Americans they would find the British even more obdurate and demanding.

The period of 1858 to 1868 was a decade of disquiet for the Japanese leading to a profound change in government, and for the foreigners in their midst it was also a time of turmoil. Violence and bloodshed, assaults, murders, bombardments, and indemnities characterized the relationship between Japan and the Westerners as the Japanese struggled to order their own house while facing the increasing menace (as they saw it) of the predatory West.

Why did the Japanese see a threat and respond so successfully to it—in contrast, say, to the Chinese or the Koreans or other Asian peoples? There was in mid-nineteenth-century Japan already a substantial intellectual capital for investment in a modern state. Literacy was widespread, comparing favorably with that in Western Europe or America. Respect for education and intellectual curiosity were strong. A trained and sophisticated body of government functionaries already existed, ready for transformation into modern officials. A powerful and successful merchant class had developed the institutional framework of modern capitalism. And Japan's farmers were sufficiently skillful and industrious to produce the surpluses needed to finance the factories, the ships, and railroads necessary to carry the nation into the era of steam and iron.

Japanese had a strong sense of national identity, based upon cultural, linguistic, ethnic homogeneity, and given form by the imperial institution and by Shinto. Sensitivity toward and appreciation of military science characterized the samurai leadership of Japan. Their sense of the vulnerability of the nation was very great, and many of them were ready to look beyond the gun to the making of it, and all that meant in terms of social change. They were prepared to forge ahead to make the necessary changes.

Men around the shogun and lesser officials too were aware that the system was in precarious balance. The shogunate, with all its economic difficulties, now had to face the consequences of its incompetence in fulfilling its military mission, the defense of the realm, which was its very *raison d'être*. Once people began to question that, the end of the entire edifice was not far away.

In 1867 and 1868, this is exactly what happened. With the leadership of samurai from Satsuma and Choshu and the ardent cooperation of some of the nobles at the imperial court, the shogunate was overthrown and the Emperor "restored" to power. The old order crumbled. Under the name of the young Meiji Emperor, Japan embarked upon an era of startling change.

Japan took its place within the international community at a good time. The Western powers were not then interested in building territorial empires in East Asia; and by the time that they were, in the 1890s, Japan was already well launched. The Japanese had been able by then to build the rudiments of a war machine and of the foundries, arsenals, and schools necessary to nurture and sustain it.

Part of the genius of Meiji leadership was recognition of the need for such industry, and a thirst for the ideas which made it possible. A heavy governmental role characterized Japan's effort at modernizing, with the establishment of pilot plants in key industries: iron and cement, cotton and silk textiles, steamship lines. Remarkably, all this was achieved without foreign capital. The acquiescent farmer carried most of the burden; from his sweat came the necessary tax revenue to capitalize new and growing industry.

Happily, raw silk provided a ready source of earnings from foreign exchange, and the Japanese were quick to standardize skein size and establish quality control. Because of Japan's geographical and cultural isolation from other modernizing nations, the leadership was not obliged to cope with a revolution in popular expectations. The peasant expected to work hard for little return, and he did. As the old saying went: The peasant is like the sesame seed; the more you squeeze, the more you get. The Meiji government was ready to squeeze hard.

Although the Japanese got along essentially without foreign capital, they did not hesitate to seize the opportunity to exploit foreign knowledge by sending students abroad, mostly to America, and by hiring foreign experts to come to Japan to teach and to consult. This flow of people and ideas was scarcely unique in the second half of the nineteenth century between the industrial powers and many of the nations of that vast crescent known now as "the developing nations," stretching from the Ottoman Empire to Japan. But the Japanese were uncommon in their determination and their success in keeping the foreign experts away from the levers of power, from the making of policy. The foreigners were "on tap, not on top." Since they were paid by the Japanese government—and very handsomely—they were appreciated and they were well used. Indeed, some of the experts felt embittered that they were so systematically stripped of their specialized knowledge and then ruthlessly cast aside.

Japanese exploitation of foreigners and foreign sources of information can only be described as eclectic. In what was, by contrast with present times, a non-ideological world, the Japanese could take advantage of the latest ideas and techniques. And so they turned to what they believed was intrinsically the best source for each: to the British for advice on building and training a navy, a lighthouse network, a mint; to the French for army matters (until after the Franco-Prussian War, when they turned to Germany) and the drafting of codes of law. To the Italians they looked for help in fine arts and architecture; to the Germans for medicine and the brewing of beer.

The Japanese were all for public education, but for reasons quite unlike the American. They saw it as a resource strengthening the state rather than as a means of encouraging democracy. The Japanese were enormously attracted to the utilitarianism of the Protestant ethic, regarding it then as important in American life. The Empress was so taken with Benjamin Franklin's moral maxims that she composed odes to twelve of them. The Americans were probably the most important foreign influence on the grassroots level, a result of the leading American role in public primary education.

The texts and readers used were American ones in Japanese translation; most foreign teachers of English were American rather than British. English became the most popular foreign language for the Japanese student, and almost everyone struggled with it, with generally indifferent results. The Japanese took over American words rather than British ones. Thus they Japanized "truck" instead of "lorry," "elevator" instead of "lift." Baseball took hold, and all its vocabulary was taken over, to be pronounced in a Japanese way.

Best-remembered of the American visiting education experts was probably David Murray of Rutgers College, who for five and a half years, beginning in May 1873, was consultant to the Ministry of Education, helping to plan everything from curriculum to school architecture. Murray, with a positive image of the American "schoolmarm" in his mind, lauded the merits of women as teachers. And education for women was an American recommendation to the Japanese. Schools and colleges for Japanese women sprang up as they were doing at the same time in the United States.

The Japanese knew that the Americans were then pioneering in the development of horse-drawn agricultural machinery, and they were eager to begin developing agriculture in Hokkaido. Virtually unpopulated by Japanese in 1868, Hokkaido was highly vulnerable to Russian or other foreign penetration. The Japanese were mindful of what had happened to the Maritime Provinces in the Ch'ing empire, just across the Japan Sea.

But only with exposure to the legalism of the Western world did the Japanese become fully aware of the weakness of their position. Even the sovereignty of Hokkaido was not clearly defined. The island was potentially rich, and the Japanese were eager to exploit its resources.

This northern island presented problems—the climate, for instance—not dissimilar to those facing Americans in moving into their West. Hokkaido even had its "Indians" in the persons of the Ainu, a primitive aboriginal group which had over the centuries steadily been pushed north, and finally, their numbers rapidly dwindling, out of Honshu into Hokkaido.

Sapporo blossomed as the island's new capital city, its streets laid out in a rectilinear pattern like that of any town in the American Midwest. The Japanese began to grow and eat Concord grapes and McIntosh apples. Today, Hokkaido yields wheat, corn, and oats; its landscape, laced with stone walls and dotted with dairy cows, red barns, and silos, is reminiscent of Wisconsin. All this is a mark of the counsel and work of such men as Benjamin Smith Lyman, General Horace Capron, Edwin Dun, William Smith Clark, and other American experts—precursors of the twentieth-century Point Four program.

Capron, former Commissioner of Agriculture for President Grant, came to Japan for four years to advise on the overall settlement and progress of Hokkaido. Other foreigners envied his handsome annual salary of $10,000 in gold, in addition to housing, subsistence, and transportation. The Japanese found it hard to pry the elderly Capron loose from the comforts of Tokyo, but then they themselves did not then (or later) much fancy the bitter Hokkaido winters either.

Clark, president of the Massachusetts Agricultural College in Amherst (now the University of Massachusetts), advised on the founding in 1875 of a similar institution in Sapporo, what is now Hokkaido University. Although in Japan for only a few months, he was remembered for his forceful, energetic, and enthusiastic Christian character. He would take his students on long tramps through the woods, lustily singing and talking all the while. Today a stone monument stands outside Sapporo with his terse parting advice inscribed. "Boys, be ambitious!" it says. His actual words were reportedly, "Boys, be ambitious in the service of the Lord!" but the Japanese chose to shorten the message.

The Japanese needed knowledge of Western languages in order to gain direct access to Western learning, to open the West to Japan. Missionaries arriving early, like Guido Verbeck in 1859, found English teaching a useful way to support themselves while becoming acquainted with the people, the culture, and the language of their new environment. In fact until 1873 they were forbidden by Japanese law to proselytize the faith. Some remained teachers, enjoying the prestige of that calling among the Confucian-oriented Japanese, and finding their students more receptive to learning English than to submitting to catechism. The Japanese were so eager to learn that they were prone, in the early days, to hire any available foreigner to teach, accepting any native speaker of English as a competent teacher of it. Beachcombers, wharf rats, and barflies would find themselves standing before a blackboard, addressing a roomful of earnest and attentive pupils.

Outstanding among the teachers were Verbeck, William Elliot Griffis, and James C. Hepburn. Verbeck, an immigrant to the United States from the Netherlands, found Dutch, the Western language then most widely known to the Japanese, helpful in his early years at Nagasaki, where he taught several of the men who became important Meiji leaders. After the restoration, he was called to Tokyo, serving there as a school principal and political adviser.

Like Verbeck, Dr. Hepburn was a missionary, but he spent most of his time teaching and practicing medicine at his Yokohama clinic. His name is immortalized by the fruit of still other activity: a commonly used romanization of Japanese.

William Elliot Griffis was more important to Americans than to Japanese. After teaching in Japan for several years, he came home to write *The Mikado's Empire,* "perhaps the most widely read American book on Japan for a quarter of a century or more," other books, a large number of articles, and to lecture widely on Japanese affairs. He was regarded as one of the nation's leading authorities on the subject.

But most famous among all these American teachers in Meiji Japan was Lafcadio Hearn, a man of many nationalities. Hearn married a Japanese by whom he had several children, took a Japanese name, dressed in Japanese clothing, lived, worked, and died in Japan—without ever learning the Japanese language. True, most American teachers did not, but few were as steeped in Japanese culture or as fond of it as Hearn. His romantic and sentimental interpretations of Japanese culture colored the view of Japan of many Western readers.

On the opposite pole to Hearn was Edward Sylvester Morse of Salem, Massachusetts. Zoologist, ethnographer, archeologist, collector, artist, and lecturer, he was a man of prodigious energy and formidable talents who was as drawn to the practicality of Japanese life as Hearn was to its mystery. Morse went to Japan on a shell-collecting expedition; he was an authority on brachiopods. The Japanese grabbed him to teach zoology at the newly organizing Tokyo University. Living in the capital for two years, Morse kept an enormous copiously illustrated journal of his life there. His curiosity was insatiable. His open and hearty manner invited friendship; and in his long daily walks through the city and the nearby countryside, he tried to observe and record in words and pictures every detail of how the Japanese lived and worked. Insofar as he was able, he collected tools and other objects in daily use. His *Japanese Homes and Their Surroundings* was an immediate success and remains in print. Eventually he published a condensed version of his journal, calling it *Japan Day by Day*, which is one of the classic accounts of life in Japan by a foreigner.

Back in the United States, Morse was a popular lecturer. Not only did he speak well, but he could illustrate what he was saying by rapid chalk sketches on a blackboard; and as a tour de force he could simultaneously draw two different pictures, one with each hand. For the American public, Morse did much to spread knowledge of Japan and appreciation for its culture; and his collection, housed at the Peabody Museum of Salem, where he long worked, is an extensive and invaluable store of objects in common use in a Japan now long gone, and even in Morse's time rapidly disappearing.

There was also Ernest Fenollosa, again from Salem, a friend of Morse's and, like him, a professor at Tokyo University. It is curious that Salem, famous earlier for its commercial importance in the China trade, should later play in this way an important part in the cultural interaction between the United States and Japan. Like Morse, Fenollosa was a man standing between the two cultures, interpreting each to the other. Originally a teacher of Western philosophy, Fenollosa came to be known best for his work as collector, critic, and historian of art. For him, what began as an interest became a vocation and a passion.

Westerners at the time knew very little of Japan's higher art. But they had been powerfully attracted to the exoticism and superb workmanship exhibited in the minor arts and "curios," as they called them: lacquer- and metalware, porcelains, pottery, and woodblock prints. Westerners knew virtually nothing of Japanese sculpture or painting. And the Japanese were at the time uninterested in their cultural past. Fenollosa began looking and buying, like all the tourists, but with the help of some knowledgeable Japanese friends, he was initiated into appreciation of Sesshu, Kano, and the great masters.

Traveling to the most remote country temples, Fenollosa found masterpieces of carving and painting, sometimes untouched for years, buried in dust, cobwebs, and mouse droppings. Neglect, decay, and even discard was the alarming pattern of what the Japanese were permitting to happen to their artistic heritage during the 1870s and early 1880s. In the enormous zeal for modernizing and for things Western, the glories of the past seemed in danger of being swept away and forgotten.

For a collector, opportunities were fantastic. Fenollosa himself amassed a priceless group of paintings, eventually acquired by Boston's Museum of Fine Arts, making it pre-eminent in the field. But the American's enthusiasm was generous and infectious; he did much to persuade the Japanese of the importance of preserving and cherishing their aesthetic tradition. He spoke widely; he organized study groups to revive interest in Japanese art; he helped organize the Tokyo Art School; and he was instrumental in the taking of a national census of important works of art.

Ultimately, Fenollosa became the Western world's leading authority on Japanese art, and although his competence was profound, it was never narrow. His background as a philosopher was too strong for that, and he developed a great vision of a coming cultural fusion of East and West for which art would be simply the prelude.

A friend of Fenollosa and of Morse was the rich and eccentric Dr. William Sturgis Bigelow. Trained as a surgeon, Bigelow disliked medicine and gave it up for photography, travel, art collecting, and the practice of Tendai Buddhism. Edith Wharton dismissed him as a man "whose erudition . . . far exceeded his mental capacity." Yet, as a propagandist he had some importance in American life. Bigelow spent the years 1881 to 1889 traveling and studying in Japan, and he returned to Boston eager to share his great interest in Japanese civilization. His circle was a distinguished one. Henry and Brooks Adams, Isabella Stewart Gardner, Henry Cabot Lodge, and Theodore Roosevelt were among his friends. At his epicurean summer retreat on the remote island of Tuckernuck, west of Nantucket, house guests (gentlemen only) could swim, sail, sunbathe, enjoy an excellent table and cellar, browse in their host's 3,000-volume library, discuss Buddhism—in short, do whatever they wished, conscious that there was only one rule in that household: dressing for dinner was obligatory.

For his cremation, to the embarrassment of his family, Dr. Bigelow directed that he be dressed in the robes of a Buddhist priest. Half of his ashes conventionally repose alongside the remains of other Boston Brahmins in Cambridge's Mount Auburn Cemetery. The other half were taken out to Japan, where they rest next to the remains of Ernest Fenollosa at Miidera, a temple above the shores of Lake Biwa.

As Americans and Japanese discovered each other, neither culture was immune from faddism. Education Minister Mori Arinori proposed that the Japanese abandon their language for English. Another high official suggested a program of intermarriage, Japanese males with American females, in order to increase the size of the Japanese people by selective breeding. Many Japanese proposed that Japan should become Christian en masse.

In Japanese cities, the domestic architecture of the Meiji period provides a useful tangible symbol of what was happening. Those people who could afford it built a Western-style house, wing, or room in accordance with their circumstances, furnished it with overstuffed chairs, sofas, antimacassars, and overladen tables. This was only for show, for entertaining guests. Real comfort was still to be found in kimono, not Western clothing, on tatami mats, not in chairs. Behind the facade, the Japanese clung to their customary way of life.

Difficulties of cross-cultural understanding were exemplified by attitudes toward nudity. Western ladies found it upsetting that laborers in Tokyo's torrid summer heat stripped down to their loincloths. And every Western traveler wrote indignantly about the Japanese custom of mixed bathing.

The Japanese authorities pressuring foreign diplomats to amend the unequal treaties earnestly sought to convince the Westerners that Japanese were fully as civilized as they. Laborers were directed to put on more clothes, and an order went out to all public bathhouse keepers that bathers were to be segregated by sex. There already were separate entrances for men and women. Hoping to humor the foreigner, the bathhouse proprietors then stretched straw ropes across the large tubs so that the sexes would bathe entirely separately.

On their part, the Japanese were astounded by Western decor, which, in the houses of the rich, commonly included nude statuary openly displayed. And European-style clothing for women, which would on the most formal occasions leave the arms, the shoulders, and the back of the neck utterly exposed, seemed grossly indecent. Ballroom dancing, in which gentlemen would clasp these half-clad ladies and "hop about," as one diary described it, was simply breathtaking in its outrageousness.

As the foreigners persisted in refusing to amend the unequal treaties (real success with this did not come until 1894, when, at the opening of the Sino-Japanese War, the British yielded to Japanese pressure), the Japanese cared less about literal Westernization. Instead, they began searching their own traditions for the possibility of using old values to support the new nationalism, coming to the realization that modernizing might indeed be possible without Westernizing. Fenollosa, Morse, and other Western agnostics had already suggested that Western civilization was not a seamless political whole, that Christianity, for instance, need not be part of it, since it was quite possibly inconsonant with modern science.

In their late nineteenth-century proselytizing, the Christian missions in Japan aimed not at the poor and the fringes of society but at people of education, leaders in Japanese society. Christian missionaries played a large role in nineteenth-century Japanese education. And although the numbers of their converts did not equal the percentage of the population won by the Iberian missionaries of the sixteenth century, they were highly successful in winning substantial numbers of samurai intellectuals.

The result was a small but strong, fiercely independent Japanese Christian church, considerable respect for Christians throughout society, and—after the early 1870s—no anti-Christian sentiment of any significance (despite earlier intense hatred of Christianity). Christianity in Japan provided a sense of social mission, an opening wedge for socialism and internationalism, and a more liberal alternative to national orthodoxy. All this is vastly different from the story in nineteenth-century China.

The nineteenth century was, after Commodore Matthew Perry and Consul Townsend Harris, an era of amiability in American-Japanese relations. There were no real problems to argue. The sinews of an important economic relationship between the two countries were already taking form. By the turn of the century, American trade with Japan surpassed that with China. American desire for Japanese silk made Americans Japan's most important customers, which, for other reasons, they remain today.

The shadows still lay ahead. Racism was largely unstated; tensions over immigration, commerce, and geographical expansion were yet to flame. The United States, preoccupied first with the Civil War and later with the winning of the West, had no so-called policy toward Japan. Americans still had little interest in the world of the western Pacific.

Nor was Japan ready to move beyond its island chain, until the conflict with China erupted in 1894. The Japanese found the Americans somehow to be less predatory than the Europeans. Both disliked Europeans. Americans viewed Japan's growing success in constructing all the apparatus of a modern state as gratifying, and rejoiced in having contributed to it. The Japanese saw no loss of honor in assuming the role of the student in the relationship.

(6)

Immigration: The Yellow Peril

PERHAPS THE MOST EMBITTERED and embittering aspect of American–
East Asian relations has been the immigration of Asian people to the
United States. In our own century, the most vexing questions of this
sort have had to do with the treatment of Japanese and Japanese-
Americans on the Pacific Coast. There, after four decades of hostility
and discrimination, tens of thousands of innocent American citizens
of Japanese descent were interned in concentration camps during
World War II. In the nineteenth century, however, there were too
few Japanese in the country to attract much attention. As late as 1900,
they numbered only 12,000. Chinese, of whom more than 100,000
lived in the United States prior to the mid-1890s, were the heart of
the matter then. Resented as few other immigrants have ever been,
the Chinese were grossly mistreated.

Any sovereign nation has, of course, the right to determine for
itself whom it will allow to enter its territory and on what basis it
will permit them to live there. There is nothing inherently unjust—
although there is something ungracious—about wishing to restrict immigration; and Chinese are by no means the only nationality ever to
be the targets of an American nativist movement.

But the case of the Chinese in the nineteenth century stands apart
for several reasons. One of these is the severe and blatantly discrimina-
tory character of the legislation enacted to control Chinese immigration. Taken together, congressional acts of 1882, 1888, and 1892
suspended all new immigration of Chinese laborers, prevented the
naturalization of Chinese already living in the United States, limited

and later barred altogether the re-entry of Chinese laborers formerly residing in the country, and required that Chinese alone among the residents of the United States must register themselves and at all times carry identification papers containing a photograph.

The courts provided no relief from this legislative onslaught. In 1871, the United States Supreme Court had upheld a California state law declaring Chinese ineligible for citizenship; and in 1893, in the case of *Fong Yue Ting v. United States,* the Court ruled that the federal government could deport Chinese aliens by an administrative act, without having to go to court or show just cause. The stringency and comprehensiveness of these restrictions were literally unprecedented in the history of American immigration.

Then, too, the Chinese deserve special attention because of the extraordinary violence directed against them. Nineteenth-century America was a crude and violent place for many people; but no other immigrant group endured such furious, sustained assaults as these quiet, hardworking people from across the Pacific. Late nineteenth-century attacks upon Chinese are startling to us now not only because of their scale—eighteen lynched in Los Angeles in a single riot in 1871, twenty-eight murdered and three hundred driven out of town at Rock Springs, Wyoming, in 1885, to take just two examples—but their ferocity, as well. Frequently, Chinese were not simply shot or lynched, but dismembered, disemboweled, battered to death, or burned alive.

This is especially notable because it occurred while the United States government, with the support of its people, was insisting upon the right of American citizens to travel, trade, evangelize, and live securely in China. The official faith, one recalls, was that the encounter of East and West across the Pacific would elevate decadent China and fulfill the destiny of American civilization. That Americans should have clung to such a pretension while brutalizing the Chinese who lived among them seems, at first hearing, a dreadful, vicious irony. In fact, however, there is a clue here that helps to explain the reception given to Chinese in the United States.

In the beginning, such attitudes arose from a conflict between different values within American culture. Long before any Chinese lived in America, ideas about them had been transmitted back by Americans who had visited their country. These reports were often contemptuous.

As we have seen—and as Stuart C. Miller demonstrates at length in *The Unwelcome Immigrant*—they portrayed a people who, with some exceptions, were weak, cowardly, cruel, deceitful, superstitious, and unfeeling. Accordingly, many Americans were predisposed to dislike Chinese and oppose their immigration or citizenship—even before any had arrived.

From another perspective, however, the alleged deficiencies of the Chinese simply confirmed the American sense of mission. The moral and cultural foundation of the American presence in East Asia during much of the nineteenth century was the concept of a westward course of empire. The visible sign of this was thought to be the increasingly liberal, republican, and humane character of civilization in each of its westward appearances, starting from China and culminating in the United States. Reports of the decadence of the Chinese people could be seen as evidence supporting this concept.

If one believed, therefore, that the renovation of China was essential to the realization of America's own promise, the present degradation of the Chinese was a spur, not a barrier, to increased contact between the two peoples. The question was simply on which side of the ocean this contact ought to take place. Conceivably, it might start in the United States, on Americans' home ground, and then spread more effectively to China. This was, in fact, the conclusion of many people, notably the Reverend William Speer, an author and missionary to China who began his ministry among Chinese immigrants in California. To Speer, the presence of limited numbers of Chinese in the social, legal, and institutional environment of American civilization provided a laboratory in which to prepare for the greater challenge across the Pacific. This, among other things, made Chinese immigrants welcome.

The problem with the debate between opponents and proponents of Chinese immigration was that, while one emphasized the present degradation of the Chinese and the other looked to their future promise, both agreed that the Chinese had to change. Americans simply could not conceive of a relationship in which Chinese would be left alone to live and adapt as they might wish in this country. From the beginning, Chinese were under a special obligation to shape up.

The first major encounter with the Chinese as a people rather than an idea occurred in California beginning in 1848. This was the time of the gold rush, and Chinese labor played an essential role in the extraordinary growth that followed during the next two decades. Chinese built the most difficult and backbreaking parts of the Western railroads; the special tax that Chinese paid as foreign miners provided almost half of the state revenue of California for many years; Chinese agricultural workers raised much of the food that was consumed in California; and Chinese laborers performed most of the really odious, underpaid manufacturing work in industries such as textiles, clothing, shoes, and cigars. Much of this was work that others would not have taken even if the Chinese had not come. There is compelling statistical evidence that, at least until 1870, Chinese did not take any significant number of jobs from Americans and did not depress wages in the industries in which Americans chose to work.

Although the Chinese came at a time when the regional economy of the American Pacific Coast needed their labor and could absorb it, that is not basically why they came. They crossed the Pacific for reasons that were both more grandiose and more elementary.

Grandiose because the tales of wealth in California that were current in China were enormously exaggerated. One widespread rumor had it that in California there were vast hills of gold, in which all one had to do was dig a hole and walk away rich. The characters used to write "San Francisco" translated as "Old Gold Mountain."

Elementary because, had it not been California, it would have been someplace else for the Chinese. These were people who *had* to leave their traditional homes. The "push" factors behind their emigration far outweighed the "pull" factors drawing them specifically to the Golden Gate.

The Chinese who migrated to California in the nineteenth century came from the Pearl River Delta near Canton. This was a region that had been racked by various forms of economic distress and social and political disruption for years. As a result, there had developed a well-established pattern of migration from rural villages to places where money could be made. California was only one of these places; there were other target areas all over Southeast Asia, in parts of Latin America, and in some of the cities of China itself.

Wherever they went, the pattern was the same: men—particularly young men—left, and their families remained at home in the Delta. This meant that the emigrants had little if any real commitment to the places to which they migrated. They went to make money that could be sent home to support their families; and they had every intention of returning home themselves, once enough money had been accumulated. They were not immigrants in the usual sense therefore. Like the American missionaries in China, they were *sojourners,* people who meant to take up temporary residence in a foreign country but not remain there permanently.

A would-be sojourner too poor to survive in his home village needed help to leave. To obtain a small amount of credit, a ticket to the United States, and a channel for transmitting his earnings back to the family in China, the sojourner indentured himself (contracted his labor in advance) to a labor agent or a merchant. This credit-ticket system, as it was called, had two significant effects.

The first of these was to put the Chinese sojourner almost completely under the control of his creditor. Beyond the contractual obligations of debt and indenture, sojourners were dependent upon the good will of their merchants and labor agents for many important things. Prior to 1860, when emigration from China was still technically illegal, a sojourner wishing to return needed the patronage and protection of someone bigger. Even after the legal difficulties in migrating to and from China had been cleared up, a sojourner still needed the approval of his creditor to buy a steamship ticket for the return voyage. Steamer companies depended upon Chinese merchants for much of their traffic in freight and eastbound immigrant passengers; and in return for this business they agreed to sell westbound passage only to those Chinese who possessed a permit certifying that their debts had been paid and their contracts worked out to the full. But the ultimate element of control was the existence of families at home in the Pearl River Delta, within easy reach of the creditor or his agents. They were, in effect, hostages to the compliance of their menfolk in America.

The merchants and labor agents cemented this control at the American end by enmeshing the sojourner socially and culturally in a community they dominated. This community had a physical geographic core in the form of the Chinatowns that began to appear here and there. The largest and most famous of these was the one in San Francisco. The community also had a more amorphous network of linkages such as kinship groups, secret societies, district companies, and the like, which organized the lives people led within the perimeters of Chinatown. The sojourners, for the most part, entered this community willingly. They did so partly because, coming from many of the same places, they already had links upon which the societies in American

Chinatowns could build. Moreover, Chinatown and its network of link-ages met a vital need in their lives.

The ocean crossing that most of these men endured had much in common with the middle passage of the old African slave trade. The ships were likely to be aged vessels that could no longer make their way in more honorable and profitable trades. Within them, immigrants traveled in the most wretched conditions imaginable: densely packed into poorly ventilated spaces, herded into confined areas where they could be segregated and controlled, deprived of access to the decks and the open air. Food was meager and sanitation terrible. Some of these ships, stinking and disease-ridden, reached San Francisco with only half to two-thirds the number of living bodies with which they had started from China.

Sojourners disembarking after such a journey found themselves suddenly in the midst of a totally new and very strange place, where almost nobody spoke their language and virtually everyone did things differently than they. The societies and associations established by the merchants provided at least a moderately supportive environment, based upon familiar ways and a common language.

The second effect of the credit-ticket system was to skew American perceptions of the Chinese, so as to make the latter appear a threat to free institutions. Coincidentally, few parts of the United States were more sensitive to questions of this sort than California, which even then seemed to many people the cutting edge of America's future. In the excitement of the moment, proud Californians fancied that they could be to America what America was to the world: the model of a republican commonwealth. This idealized view of California's sig-nificance to America and the world raised the stakes in the debate over Chinese immigration. In effect, it put the Chinese under even greater pressure to Americanize themselves.

In a sense, California's destiny to be the prototypical republican empire increased the attractiveness of the Chinese. Their labor was building this future. Moreover, the belief that they had chosen to come—Californians were ignorant of the desperate circumstances that actually pushed sojourners out of their homeland—gave substance to America's claim to be a cultural beacon to lighten Asia's darkness.

The challenge to acculturate the Chinese thus became a welcome test not only of the universality of American civilization, but also of Californians' mettle as its exemplar. From the very beginning, Chinese were welcomed to California both by the employers, provisioners, and transportation interests that hoped to profit from them, and also by educators, missionaries, and humanitarians wishing to do something good for them.

But if California was a model in the making, it followed from this that the tolerable margin for error there was very small. Looked at in this light, several aspects of the Chinese immigration seemed more like a threat than a constructive challenge. One of these was the indenture system. By the second half of the nineteenth century, few Americans knew or cared that large numbers of white people had come to the American colonies in the seventeenth century as indentured servants and had then gone on to work off their indenture and become free laborers. As the nature of the credit-ticket system became clearer, the analogy that most often occurred to Americans was Negro slavery. Here, after all, were large numbers of non-white people, being imported under contract in the most appalling conditions, living in a dependent relationship in segregated communities, and working (often in gangs) under manifestly exploitative conditions. The threat implicit in this analogy was that before California could realize its potential it might be submerged in the kind of racial, social, and political conflict that was at the very moment tearing the eastern section of the country apart.

The analogy between Chinese indentured labor and Negro slavery caught on at least partly because it complemented the racial attitudes of the white population. California was intensely color conscious. In the 1850s, for example, the state was both anti-slavery and anti-Negro. A sizable portion of its population had migrated from the South to escape from a biracial society, and free blacks were just as unwelcome to such people as slaves. Moreover, like almost all other whites in the West, Californians had strong feelings against Indians and Mexicans. Opposition to still one more alien race easily pierced the veneer of cosmopolitan idealism. As the San Francisco *California* explained it: "We desire only a white population in California."

What clinched the case against the Chinese was their refusal to acculturate to the norms of American society. This refusal sprang from their identity as sojourners. Why should people who simply wanted to make some money and go home—people who, in addition, worked unusually long hours at prearranged jobs and lived (in compliance with everybody's wishes) segregated in a community of their own—

adapt to the culture of their host society? Why should they convert to Christianity, change ethics, clothing, food, recreational activities, or, for that matter, learn English?

Neither their jobs, their housing, nor their friendships required it. Yet to most Americans the Chinese were acceptable in the long run only as objects of reform. By rejecting acculturation and reform, they defined themselves out of American society. Once this had happened, Chinese lost their protective cover and were perceived as something akin to a snake in the garden. If degradation and enslavement were irredeemable, they had no place in the great republican experiment.

This is evident in the changing image and reputation of Chinatown. In the early years of the immigration, San Francisco's Chinatown was seen by whites as one of the jewels in the city's crown. A populous community of Chinese seemed to epitomize the economic and cultural vitality of the city and the state. It was a sign of cosmopolitanism, a symbol of California's imperial promise.

Soon, however, it was discovered that Chinatown was a sewer of disease, exploitation, and immorality, insulated against reformist interference by a degree of segregation that approached separatism. Thereafter, Chinatown became a target of nativist attacks and the chief source of evidence used to disparage the Chinese people. Instead of color, variety, and promise, descriptions of Chinatown from the late 1860s on emphasized things dark, dangerous, and mysterious. They spoke of hideous overcrowding; of disease, stench, and idolatry; of opium and prostitution; of vermin and people who ate dogs and garbage; of secret societies, tong wars, and barbarous ritual murders.

Little understanding the irrelevance of acculturation to sojourners, Americans concluded that Chinese were choosing a life of degradation. This perception of a separatist community that preferred degradation confirmed all the worst aspects of the long-standing image of the Chinese people. In doing so, it shifted the moral burden for the existence of poverty and disease from the inequities of American society (which, after all, could have paid Chinese laborers higher wages) to the racial character, as critics would have put it, of the Chinese themselves. As Chinatowns spread across the country, even reformers recoiled. Perhaps the only unsympathetic chapter in Jacob Riis's moving description of the plight of New York City's poor, *How the Other Half Lives,* is his account of the Chinese.

In sum, the irrelevance of acculturation to Chinese aims, and the resilience of their existing social and cultural practices, changed the valuation some Americans put upon their alleged "inferiority." No longer a curiosity, an inconvenience, or a constructive challenge, such "inferiority" became a judgment on the Chinese and a threat to the American future.

This was the first important criticism of the Chinese in California. Although it has racist overtones, it is curiously abstract to our minds today. It came from well-to-do—and often well-meaning—people concerned more for social order and republican institutions than for jobs, people who had no desire to murder the Chinese. But these relatively tame views were picked up by blatant racists and demagogues in the following years and used to rationalize and legitimize—to put on a higher moral plane—the kind of vicious gut hatred of Chinese that did lead to exclusion, discrimination, and murder.

The key to this development was the economic change that came over California in the late 1860s and early 1870s. As the mining boom and the construction of the original railway trunk lines passed their peak, the supply of really disagreeable work declined. California's economy was in flux, and wage levels, even for Chinese, began to rise. For the first time, Chinese became direct competitors with native white laborers for some jobs. This trend in the state economy coincided with the onset of a major depression throughout the United States in 1873, which limited opportunities for everyone.

In these new conditions, Chinese were no longer economically necessary to California. Yet they continued to come. Even though large numbers of sojourners were starting to return to China by the decade of the '70s, more than twice as many newcomers replaced them. Between 1868 and 1877, 60,000 Chinese left the United States and 130,000 arrived.

As economic conditions worsened, many Californians turned to the Chinese as scapegoats. The Burlingame Treaty of 1868, which had been sought by the United States and negotiated for the Chinese government by an American citizen, Anson Burlingame, assured both Chinese and Americans the right to migrate to each other's country and to travel, live, and become naturalized citizens there on the same basis as immigrants from most-favored nations. Burlingame and Secretary of State William H. Seward apparently intended these provisions to strengthen the position of American missionaries in China and at

the same time guarantee a steady supply of cheap labor for the development of the American West. In the latter respect, the treaty was out
of date practically from the moment of its signing. Willfully inferior
Chinese now seemed a threat to the livelihood of American citizens;
the new emphasis was not upon the value of their labor but the amount
of American wealth that drained back to China through them. This
was estimated to be between $5 million and $15 million a year. At a
time when all immigration was being questioned, recalcitrant Chinese
who refused to identify with their new home seemed the most offensive
immigrants of all.

Unable to prevent their entry, opponents took to violence and legal
harassment. In San Francisco, for example, a variety of laws were passed
to discriminate against Chinese. One taxed laundries that delivered
by foot at four to seven times the rate for laundries that delivered
by carriage. Another required that the queue be cut off any Chinese
who went to jail. A third, the Cubic Air Ordinance, required a minimum of 500 cubic feet of living space for each adult in residential
buildings. Enforcement of this ordinance in Chinatown led to the arrest
of so many people that the jails were soon found to be violating the
ordinance!

Legal discrimination against the Chinese had begun almost as soon
as the first sojourners arrived, but this type of misappropriation of
the law to harass and abuse was new. Originally, the goal had been
to prevent the Chinese from misusing certain American institutions
people assumed they would not understand. Many well-intentioned
whites supported this early form of discrimination, hoping that in time
Chinese might acculturate themselves sufficiently to warrant political
and legal equality. "China boys," wrote the San Francisco *Alta* in 1851,
"will yet vote at the same school and bow at the same altar as our
countrymen."

Along with the racial, cultural, and economic considerations men-
tioned already, the main reason legal discrimination took a vicious
turn was that the Chinese were ineligible for American citizenship.
State and federal officials had ruled this almost from the first; and in
1871 the United States Supreme Court upheld them. Since few Chinese
intended to remain long in the United States, ineligibility for citizenship might seem a relatively unimportant form of discrimination. In
practice, however, it placed Chinese in a uniquely disadvantageous
position. Most besieged ethnic, racial, and economic groups in Ameri-

can history have defended their interests by developing a bloc vote and winning a voice in the political process. Chinese alone among immigrant groups were prevented from doing this. By eliminating even the possibility of their voting, the bar to citizenship rendered them political nonentities, dependent upon the good will of others.

The dynamic of California politics, which rewarded bloc voting, additionally penalized the Chinese. The Republican and Democratic parties, closely matched in the state, bid high for the swing votes that could make the difference between them. Ordinarily, the parties had to weigh the gains against the losses in this competition, bearing in mind the risk of alienating some voters by identifying with others. The Chinese issue was particularly attractive in this respect, because almost all the votes were on one side. In the absence of political clout on the Chinese side, the contest between the parties magnified the power of anti-Chinese zealots and promoted the passage of extreme measures. Once established in this form as a staple of California politics, harassment and exclusion of Chinese soon won support in Washington as well. A succession of relatively close national elections attuned congressional and national party leaders to the importance of pivotal state issues; and as the parties fought for California's electoral and congressional votes, the Chinese once again were losers.

For this and other reasons, Chinese who left California found that a highly critical image had preceded them to other parts of the United States, legitimizing, if not actually creating, opposition to their presence. This was painfully ironic, because as Chinese began to leave California—and as new Chinese immigrants arrived on the East Coast—the credit-ticket system of indentured labor and the sojourner mentality declined in importance. Greater distances stretched the control apparatus of merchant creditors increasingly thin; while, simultaneously, Chinese in the interior of the country and on the Atlantic seaboard found the goal of returning to China less realistic and often reconciled themselves to remaining in the United States. This strengthened their interest in acculturation. In the case of Chinese outside California and Nevada, therefore, the slavery analogy, the critique of cultural separatism, and the revulsion against Chinatown that lay at the heart of the negative image were often irrelevant.

There, as in California, however, the image gave meaning and context to an increasingly bitter economic competition. In the eastern and southern sections of the United States, employers used Chinese as low-priced strikebreakers; and in the Pacific Northwest and the Rocky Mountain states, Chinese competed directly with whites for jobs in mines and construction camps. There were even plans to transplant whole colonies of Chinese from California and the Philippines to work plantation-sized units in the South. Little came of these plans: California Chinese refused to go, and those from the Philippines soon quit the plantations and took up fishing and small-scale farming on their own. In the meantime, however, the analogy to Negro slavery had been strengthened and a dramatic illustration given of the potential for Chinese to invade labor markets in many parts of the country.

In retrospect, one can see that opposition to the immigration and residence of Chinese in the United States peaked with congressional passage of the Geary Act in 1892. Apart from slavery, the most pervasive metaphors used by white Americans to describe Chinese had always emphasized their vast numbers: "flood," "wave," "horde," "host," "swarm," "invasion." "The magnitude of the possible inflow," wrote an author in the *North American Review* in 1886, "is appalling." The actual Chinese society in the United States, however, was almost wholly male. Given the anti-miscegenation laws of the time, it could not even maintain its existing numbers without fresh immigration. The legislative ban upon the new immigration of laborers and the re-entry of former residents meant that Chinese no longer had a future in America. Indeed, during the decade of the '90s, as the new restrictions took hold and sojourners continued to leave, the Chinese population of the country declined by more that 15 percent. Animus against them declined more slowly. But the urgency went out of the issue for most Americans once it became clear that there would not be a flood.

As this happened, a new pluralistic tolerance toward Chinese began to appear. Very much a minority viewpoint, this was nevertheless significant, because it took the place of the essentially intolerant, patronizing sympathy that had characterized earlier support for them. The effect was to put the encounter upon a more realistic, less emotional basis and relieve the Chinese of the special demands for change and acculturation that had so long dogged them.

The domestic roots of this pluralism included a sense of embarrassment over the outrageous treatment of Chinese, the location of an economic niche in which their labor fit usefully and non-competitively, and a growing recognition that the Chinese were little different from other immigrant groups in the nature of the problems they posed for American society and culture. Moreover, as time passed, the distastefulness of the whole subject, which had long denied Chinese a constituency among American whites, worked to their advantage. Persistence and quiet industry in the face of barbarous treatment eventually won them a grudging respect here and there.

All the more so as it became clear that there was a place for their labor in the American economy. The worst discrimination and mistreatment of Chinese occurred during the period when they were a trump card in the hands of American employers: cheap, hardworking labor, available in volume through middlemen who guaranteed their performance. By the end of the century, two things were happening to make this a less threatening prospect to white American workers. Growing numbers of Chinese were moving into fields such as farm labor and domestic service, which native Americans disdained. At the same time, Chinese who competed directly with white laborers for jobs in factories began to raise their wage demands, thus reducing the likelihood that their employment would lower the standard of living of other working people. As this was recognized, the Chinese appeared to fit the norms of American immigration better and lost something of that special character that had made them seem worse than others.

American foreign relations in the Pacific region, especially those with China itself, encouraged this re-evaluation of the Chinese. For roughly two decades after the Burlingame Treaty, American interests in China had been minimal. The decade of the '90s was a turning point, however. New forms of American economic interest began to be expressed; and, as we shall see, exports to China increased dramatically. In the meantime, acquisition of Hawaii and the Philippines gave the United States its first real strategic and geopolitical stake in Asia. Finally, reformist measures by the imperial government and the rise of republican sentiments outside it renewed Americans' sense of China's potential to change for the better.

The point here is that as the American stake in China grew, the valuation placed upon the Chinese people improved. Private interests wishing to sell, invest, convert, and reform in China chose to emphasize the potential of its people; the United States government, seeking a role in the Asian balance of power, undertook to encourage what it thought constructive there. In other words, the tone of the Sino-American encounter became more positive. A new respect was voiced in some circles for the Chinese literary tradition and the examination system by which civil servants were chosen. Other aspects of Chinese society came in for similar praise. The agricultural pattern was called Jeffersonian by one well-meaning commentator; another claimed, in the classic tradition of upgrading the national status of American immigrants, that a Chinese had discovered America! All of this rubbed off, at least a little, on the hapless Chinese living in the United States.

By the early twentieth century, the American attitude toward Chinese had come almost full circle. As the number of Chinese living in America declined, the governing consideration once again became the American image of the Chinese in China. A growing sense of the promise there, linked with uneasiness over the militarization of Japan, shifted American sympathies toward China in its dawning republican era. Now a new mythology began to take shape. Presidents Roosevelt, Taft, and Wilson—each in his own way—fancied the United States to be China's protector against rapacious imperialists and its appropriate model for modernization and reform. Nevertheless, neither Chinese nor Americans even forgot the naked hostility of the decades between Burlingame and Roosevelt, when the illusion of benevolence was stripped from America's westward course of empire.

(7)

Roots of American Expansionism

THE UNITED STATES has always been an expansive, assertive nation. From its earliest days, founding fathers such as Franklin and Washington conceived of it explicitly as an empire—a "rising empire," as Washington put it in 1783—with an inherent right to expand wherever its destiny or needs might direct.

For roughly the first century after independence, this expansion took two forms. The first, westward movement across the continent, was pivotal: it both expressed and fueled the dynamism at the heart of American society. The result of this was the vast nation of almost incalculable resources, with its imagery of individualism and struggle, that we know today.

The second, overseas commercial, cultural, and evangelical expansion, was peripheral in every sense. Such expansion had its uses: supplying certain specific lacks, providing a market of varying importance for excess agricultural production, and venting some of the most grandiose and least realistic psychological drives of the society. Moreover, it affected the history of certain other peoples, notably the Japanese. With the exception of the large export trade in Southern cotton to Great Britain, however, it was relatively unimportant to the development of the United States. Expansionism, even imperialism, was in the genes of American civilization. But until well after the Civil War, it appeared that a maritime empire of the British or French type was not.

Late in the nineteenth century, this began to change. By then, it was becoming clear that the continental limits of the United States had been reached with the Gadsden Purchase of 1853 and the acquisition of Alaska in 1867–1868. Enormous possibilities for growth and development remained within the country's existing boundaries, but henceforth there would be no more new expansion into contiguous territory. No one but buccaneers wanted to annex more of Mexico; and the rise of Canadian nationalism combined with the power of the British fleet to block expansion to the north. Only the ocean frontiers remained open.

So, with the renovation of the United States Navy, the annexation of the Philippines and Puerto Rico, the promulgation of the Open Door notes, and the appearance of big-power diplomacy under Theodore Roosevelt, America turned its expansive energies toward the overseas world.

This new stage of American expansionism differed from its predecessor in more than geographic focus. It had a character of its own that reflected important changes in the domestic society, economy, and politics of the country.

The most obvious of these changes was the elimination of slavery. Between roughly 1820 and 1865, few Americans had recognized that expansion was an issue in its own right, with moral and constitutional consequences of the first order. Instead, expansion had been subsumed under the debate over the extension of slavery and the maintenance of a balance of power between slave states and free. Proposals to annex new territory turned principally upon such considerations as whether the land in question was suitable for plantation slavery and whether its organization as a state would augment the Northern or the Southern voting bloc in Congress. With the end of slavery and its especially rigid type of political sectionalism, expansion was debated on its own merits for the first time since the days of Thomas Jefferson.

More subtly, the experience of the Civil War and Reconstruction changed American attitudes toward two closely related moral questions that arose inescapably in connection with territorial expansion: whether, to be true to its origins and principles, the United States must respect the inherent sovereignty of other political societies—their right to create, by revolution if necessary, a government of their own choosing; and whether it was justifiable morally for the United States to extend its sovereignty over others by conquest.

Prior to the Civil War, most Americans were sympathetic toward nationalist revolutions—especially if the nationalists were white, republican, and respectful toward the rights of property owners. In the 1820s, for example, popular support for the Latin American revolutions against Spain compelled John Quincy Adams and James Monroe to abandon diplomatic discretion and promptly recognize the new republics to the south. In 1848, sympathy for revolutionaries in Hungary and elsewhere in Europe was so widespread that American politicians such as Daniel Webster and Stephen Douglas competed to identify themselves with the issue.

This kind of identification with nationalist revolutions was inevitably a constraint upon American expansion, although, to be sure, it did nothing to save the American Indians. In the popular and political mythology of the time, America's continental expansion was conceived of as an "empire for liberty," an "extension of the area of freedom." This is a faith impossible to reconcile with the dispatch of over half the United States Army several decades later to extinguish the independence of the Philippines, seven thousand miles away.

In the interval, however, the Civil War had changed Americans' attitudes toward revolution, conquest, and political self-determination. Whatever else it may have been, the Civil War was plainly a forcible denial of the South's right to self-determination. To justify to themselves the fratricidal horror of one of the most murderous and destructive wars in modern history, Americans had to conclude that the right to revolution and self-determination were not absolute—that they were, in fact, less important than the unity of an existing nation, the continuity of institutions, and the rights of an oppressed minority. Moreover, to explain to themselves what General Sherman was doing in Georgia, they had to concede the legitimacy of wars of conquest.

The result was the shattering of what had been one of the nation's central myths. Americans emerged from the Civil War hardened to mass violence and alienated from the revolutionary tradition. More than that: they emerged with a growing sense of identification with the great monarchical empires of the age. When Polish nationalists revolted against Tsarist tyranny in 1865, a conspicuous body of American opinion—liberal as well as conservative—backed the Russians. America, said Herman Melville approvingly, stood before the world with "law on her brow and empire in her eyes."

Concomitantly, the international competition for empire changed between the middle and the end of the nineteenth century. In the era of Manifest Destiny, when the United States annexed Texas, California, and Oregon, the Western world's conception of empire was in flux. Since Adam Smith and the American Revolution, mercantilist colonial empires of the seventeenth- and eighteenth-century type had been largely repudiated as expensive, inefficient, and corrupting. Although commercial (and even territorial) expansion continued, there was a relative hiatus in the conquest of new colonies. Symptomatically, our term "imperialism," connoting a dynamic, aggressive, exploitative process, did not yet exist. The word itself first obtained currency later in the century as a sarcastic description of the posturing of Napoleon III.

By the final decades of the century, on the other hand, imperialism in the modern sense had become normal for the major Western powers—and even Japan. In the thirty years between 1870 and 1900, European nations acquired sovereignty over one-fifth of the earth's land area and one-tenth of its population. This was an intensely self-conscious process on the part of the various governments, and it was accompanied by the appearance of both popular and theoretical literature celebrating conquest and expansion as measures of national greatness. This gave American thought about overseas expansion a competitive impetus and a focused intensity lacking in the earlier part of the century.

Symptomatic of the shift outward in America's imperial vision was the appearance of a new group of American explorers on the last remaining frontiers of the inhabitable world in Asia and Africa. The great explorer-scientists of the nation's first century—men like Meriwether Lewis and William Clark, Zebulon Pike, Jedediah Smith, and the artist George Catlin—had challenged the mysteries and dangers of the North American continent. They were the pathfinders, the botanists, ethnographers, and skirmishers in the vanguard of the continental empire. After the middle of the nineteenth century, once the continent had been subdued, they gave way to more prosaic and systematic types, the forerunners of the scientists and bureaucrats in the United States Geological Survey.

Their true heirs in the later part of the century operated overseas, where both the personal challenge and the need for an American reconnaissance still survived. As the United States turned outward, certain of these men emerged as public authorities—"experts" or "professionals" according to the vogue of the era—on the only really promising parts of the world in which imperial expansion could still be undertaken.

William Rockhill, author of the first Open Door note, came to the State Department by way of the French Foreign Legion, a cattle ranch in the Rockies, and an almost unique scholarly mastery of inner Asian languages, history, and religion; but he won the critical backing of Theodore Roosevelt, Secretary of State John Hay, and the Adams brothers because of his published accounts of two remarkable explorations he had made in Tibet and the interior of China. (Rockhill's expeditions were notable for many reasons, not least because, though six feet three inches tall, red of hair, and prominent of nose, he had successfully masqueraded as a Chinese on one of them.)

By the same token, Dean C. Worcester, member of the original five-man investigatory commission sent to the Philippines in 1899 and later Secretary of the Interior there until 1913, had trekked through the interior of many of the archipelago's islands on a biological expedition for the University of Michigan earlier in the 1890s. An unfortunate choice in many respects—erratic, truculent, alternately paternalistic and contemptuous toward the Filipino people—he seemed, nevertheless, to be indispensable: the only American civilian to be found who knew what the islands were like outside the principal cities. George Kennan (a distant relative of the scholar-diplomat of our own day) began his career as a critic of Russian autocracy and popular analyst of political, diplomatic, and strategic trends in northeastern Asia after a spectacularly daring surveying trip across Siberia.

Romantic and often psychologically bizarre individualists, such men were seldom successful as policymakers or administrators. The empire outgrew them rapidly; and well before World War I their day had passed. For a time, however, they were important enabling agents. In retrospect, one recognizes them to have epitomized a transitional stage in the outward thrust of American energies beyond the continent.

The most important change underlying the creation of what many people have called America's "new empire" appears, on the surface, to have been economic. One of the most dramatic developments in the United States between the middle and end of the nineteenth century was the emergence of an industrial, urban economy. In one sense, this was a success story: industrial development and technological innovation brought with them profits, employment, and greater productivity. The face of the nation changed, for the better, many people felt; and by the turn of the century, there was genuine pride in America's identification with progress, its achievement of first place among the industrial powers of the world.

On the other hand, industrialism and urbanization caused terrible, soul-racking problems. Major depressions struck the country in 1873 and 1893, and there was a serious recession in the mid-1880s. Contemporaries said that half the years between the Civil War and the Spanish-American War fell in either a depression or a recession, and that 95 percent of all capitalists went bankrupt sooner or later. Partly for this reason, employers drove their workers hard and paid them little. It was the era of ten-hour days, six-day weeks, unsanitary buildings, and dangerous machinery.

Even Herbert Spencer, advocate of Social Darwinism and the survival of the fittest, recoiled from the "repulsive" pollution and stench of the American factory. "Six months residence here," he said after viewing the Carnegie steel works in Pittsburgh, "would justify suicide." The normal wage for unskilled laborers in such places was between $1.25 and $1.50 per day. When there was work to be had, that is. At its worst, the unemployment rate during the depression of the 1890s reached 20 percent, and for the whole period 1893–1898 it averaged more than 9 percent. For those out of work, there was no insurance or public welfare.

These dilemmas of poverty, failure, unemployment, and insecurity were intensified by the social environment in which they occurred. Influxes of immigrants and rural Americans overtaxed the facilities and political institutions of the cities. In the two decades between 1880 and 1900, for example, the population of New York City grew from roughly 2 million to 3.5 million; Chicago tripled in size; Detroit, Cleveland, and Milwaukee doubled. The population density of the tenth ward in New York in 1898 was 747 people per acre, probably the highest in the world at the time.

In the face of such an explosion, housing and public services lagged far behind the need for them. As late as 1900, two-thirds of the streets of Chicago were unpaved; most of the streets of Baltimore and New Orleans and over one-third of those in Philadelphia, St. Louis, and Atlanta lacked underground sewers; better than half the streets of Atlanta had no water mains. The inevitable effects of such conditions were aggravated by the inexperience of most of the newcomers with the requirements of life in cities, or America, or both. Vice, corruption, violence, and exploitation rose; and public health plummeted. At the turn of the century, rural death rates in the United States were 20 percent lower than those in the cities. When New York introduced effective street cleaning and garbage collection in 1895, the death rate there fell 27 percent within two years.

Americans of many motives and persuasions agreed that the malfunctioning of the economy, the demoralization of the cities, and the corruption and ineffectuality of government cried out for rectification. Eventually, broad alliances would be struck between them to attack specific issues under the banner of progressivism. The earliest attempts to deal with such problems, however, were primitive and fragmented. Among them, two stand out, Populism and expansionism. Where the former looked to internal purification as a remedy, the latter sought an external escape.

The new expansionism of the 1890s arose at least partly because many people blamed America's economic troubles on overproduction. Too much investment in the industrial economy, it was said, had created excess productive capacity in relation to the purchasing power of the American public. The resulting failure of the American market to consume the output of its own factories, people concluded, lay behind the high incidence of depression and recession, the general decline of profits and price levels characteristic of the age, and the impoverishment of the working class. The more fearful of the nation's political and economic leaders worried that unless a remedy were found, American capitalism might destroy itself and produce a social revolution. Rather than encourage the government to intervene and redistribute wealth, so as to create a larger effective market within the country, they looked to increased exports to end the glut and keep up profits and employment.

The emphasis upon exports made sense, because by the last quarter of the nineteenth century, American industry had achieved sufficient maturity and efficiency to compete successfully with British and German rivals for the markets of the world. Apart from cyclical fluctuations, industrial exports had grown steadily since the Civil War; and by the end of the century several industries relied upon foreign sales for a significant part of their business. Exports of iron and steel, for example, took between 7 and 15 percent of total output, depending upon the year; exports of agricultural implements and machinery sometimes as much as 16 percent. More than half of the illuminating oil refined in the United States and about one-quarter of the sewing machines made here were sold abroad. So was roughly half of the copper mined in this country. With examples like these in mind, it was plausible to suppose that, if overproduction were indeed at the root of the economy's troubles, the way out was to increase exports.

By the same token, some Americans hoped that exporting capital would relieve the pressure on the domestic economy. Investing in another country was much riskier, however, than simply trying to sell goods there. Its greatest appeal—and that a rather desperate one— was to minor leaguers in the financial world who could not compete at home with the likes of Morgan, Harriman, Henry Lee Higginson, or Kuhn, Loeb and Company. Consequently, while verbal speculation flourished over such esoterica as Chinese and Russian railways, relatively little actual investment occurred outside the North American continent and its adjacent territory. It took the recession of 1907 and the gathering attack on investment bankers in the progressive era to shake the faith of major European and American investors in the long-term attraction of the American economy. As late as 1900, there was still more than five times as much European capital invested in the United States as there was American capital invested in the whole rest of the world.

Those who argued for overseas markets did not necessarily want the United States to conquer and rule a great colonial empire on the Victorian model. Despite the lessons of the Civil War, many Americans still found that a course difficult to reconcile with their own constitution and Declaration of Independence. More important, however, the businessmen with most to gain from commercial expansion opposed anything, such as wars and colonies, that would increase the costs and power of government. It is true that those in the coal, steel, and armaments industries stood to gain from naval construction; and the makers of cheap clothing, blankets, and tents profited from increased recruitments. But for most businessmen, gains of this sort were more than offset by higher taxes, the disruption of commerce, dislocations in the labor and capital markets, and increased social agitation. In an age of depressions, living in fear of anarchy and socialism, they wanted less excitement and more predictability.

For the most part, therefore, the emphasis was simply upon using

American foreign policy to create favorable trading conditions. This took various forms, including improving the consular service, negotiating reciprocal tariffs, recognizing and supporting governments sympathetic to American trade, and building a navy competent to protect trade routes and overawe local troublemakers. The Open Door policy in China was the principal Asian expression of this emphasis in policy: a formal commitment by the United States government to the desire of business interests for what they called a "fair field and no favor."

By the same token, the territorial acquisitions of 1898 suited the needs of economic expansionists. Hawaii and the new protectorate in Cuba offered safe, attractive investment opportunities and valuable raw materials. Puerto Rico, Hawaii, and the Philippines established an American strategic presence along key trade routes. The Philippines had the potential to become the base of operations for American economic penetration of the Asian market, an American equivalent of Hong Kong.

It would be mistaken, however, to conclude from this that late-nineteenth-century American expansionism was wholly—or even primarily—economic in motivation. The returns are not yet in from the historiographical debate over this question. For every scholar who ranks economic causes first, there is another who finds the picture more complicated. No one denies that the condition of the American economy influenced the thought and action that led to expansionism. Indeed, the evidence is overwhelming that many people, including men of great political and economic power, sought expansion to relieve the pressure of overproduction. But the promotion of foreign trade and investment was not, *in itself,* the essence of the expansionism of this era.

For one thing, the fear of overproduction cannot successfully explain what was new in turn-of-the-century American expansionism.

Morally, politically, and strategically, the heart of the new expansionism was the acquisition of a large colonial empire, the projection of American military and naval power into Asia and Latin America on a permanent basis, and the deliberate emergence of the United States as one of the key forces in the international balance of power. The turn of the century was a transitional moment for America in all these respects. Where previously the initiative had lain with private interests, the government simply playing the role of a rather unreliable enabling agent, now *the United States government itself was the expan-*

sive force. This was the truly imperial dimension that changed not just the weight but the character of American intervention in the lives, the rights, and even the economies of other peoples. Without it, the pursuit of commercial advantage would have made only a diffuse impact upon the rest of the world. Yet, as we have seen, this went far beyond what business advocates of exports desired.

Moreover, a closer examination of economic conditions in the United States raises doubts even about the conviction behind the rhetoric of overproduction and expansionism. Both as an analysis of the economy and as a prescription for its future, the overproduction argument was wrong—and apparently was widely understood, or at least suspected, to be wrong at the time.

The industrial economy was not actually overproducing. Rather, it was making the wrong things in the wrong way and marketing and distributing them ineffectively. To be sure, consumption was low because of a lack of adequate purchasing power. But the biggest obstacle faced by American industry at the time was its lingering reliance upon growth industries of the past, such as railroads. The great markets of the future, whether for consumer goods or for heavy industries such as construction, were in the rapidly growing cities. Once industry reorganized internally and adapted its operations to this new prospect, the specter of overproduction passed.

Even if the country had been suffering from overproduction, imperial expansion in Asia would not have been a credible safety valve for the industrial economy. At the time of the Spanish-American War, 79.1 percent of American exports were agricultural rather than industrial. Although some industries, as we have seen, relied heavily upon foreign markets, most did not. In contrast to their British, German, or Japanese counterparts, American industries seldom exported as much as 10 percent of their output.

Moreover, American exports, such as they were, went overwhelmingly to Europe and to the rest of North America, not to the Asian and Latin American targets of the new expansionism. During the period between the 1890s and World War I, 60 to 70 percent of American exports regularly went to Europe and 40 to 50 percent of American imports came from there. By contrast, all the overseas territories of the United States combined—Alaska, Hawaii, the Philippines, Puerto Rico, and the lesser islands—took only 7 percent from exports and provided 9 percent of imports. In the whole period of 1890 to 1920,

China never took more than 3.5 percent of American exports and 1.4 percent of American foreign investment. Despite all the talk, when opportunities for major and potentially lucrative investments in China arose, they were neglected or ignored.

Although modern imperialism may well be related to the evolution of capitalism, it is clear that in the American case we have to look beyond economics to social psychology for a full explanation. The impulse to turn outward, which, as we have just seen, offered little realistic hope of curing the country's troubles, was part of a larger psychological struggle of the American people to understand the nature, limits, costs, and opportunities of their new urban-industrial society. People of our own time who have wrestled with the economics of nuclear power, particularly the difficulty of finding ways to use its extraordinary potential in ways that will not make everything worse, should understand their dilemma. Americans of that earlier time needed something constructive to do with the new capacities that were producing such ambiguous results in their factories and cities.

Expansionism in all its forms captured their imagination, because it offered a way to marshal the strength of the society and economy without intensifying their internal disarray. By projecting American power abroad, one might hope to achieve not only markets and a measure of relief from overproduction, but social discipline and a restoration of national purpose.

Consider, for example, the leading strategic architect of American expansion, Captain Alfred Thayer Mahan, the president of the Naval War College. In 1890, Mahan published an epochal book, *The Influence of Seapower upon History,* which established his reputation internationally and won him the ear of leading American politicians such as Theodore Roosevelt and Henry Cabot Lodge. Mahan approached foreign relations from two basic postulates. One was that the natural model for a maritime nation wishing to achieve greatness was eighteenth-century England. As we have seen, that was the era when England turned its energies definitively from continental rivalries toward the creation of a great maritime empire and the control of the seas. The second postulate was that the federal government, which had encouraged American industrial development, must accept responsibility for promoting overseas commerce as an outlet for domestic productivity.

Drawing upon both postulates, Mahan urged that the United States develop a battle fleet capable of controlling the trade routes in which Americans had a national interest—and support this fleet with strategically placed bases, stockpiles, and fortifications in the Atlantic, the Caribbean, and the Pacific.

His reasoning was that if America failed to avail itself of its power to expand, it would rot from within. Its people would lose the heroic virtues, the integrity, and the moral discipline that come from accepting great challenges. Simultaneously, the economy would stagnate for want of foreign markets. The societal result would be an erosion of both individual liberty and social order. As the authorities tightened their grip in an effort to retain control, the impoverished and culturally disoriented masses would move toward open rebellion and the imposition of socialism.

To a surprising degree, this complemented the views of leading social critics, such as Josiah Strong. A Congregationalist minister active in the Social Gospel movement, Strong wrote and lectured to a very sizable middlebrow audience during the late years of the nineteenth century. He was perhaps the leading contemporary intellectual heir to the romantic conception of a westward course of empire. But unlike earlier adherents to this idea, Strong was troubled by a gnawing fear that America's moment as the cutting edge of history was passing.

He based this conclusion partly upon the specter of overproduction, about which so many others were also concerned, but even more upon the deleterious moral effects he perceived in urbanization and immigration. Taken together, he argued, urbanization and immigration were destroying the character of American life. Poverty, discontent, intemperance, prostitution, violence, and disease were spreading through the cities. So were such alien growths as Catholicism and Judaism! In the wings, the socialists lurked, waiting to lure the growing legions of the ignorant and the disaffected with their specious pretension to "solve the problem of suffering without eliminating the factor of sin." What to do?

Strong's answer was that America must take advantage of new improvements in transportation and communication to lead the peoples of the world out of their isolation in separate national units and forge a common global society. We recognize this as economic and cultural neo-imperialism. In his own terms, however, Strong was talking about something spectacularly daring: freezing at least one of history's dimensions at the moment of American ascendancy. If, as he urged, the United States and Britain were to join in civilizing and Christianizing the world in their image, and if America were to use its immense resources to establish a global economy of mutually beneficial exchange with itself and its vast new industries at the center, conceivably there might be an American millennium. American energies and products would flow out into a receptive Westernized Protestant world—and in the process give new purpose, new scope, new character and discipline to life in this country.

Mahan and Strong, like the businessmen and government officials in search of foreign markets, speak to us (as they did to their contemporaries) from a position of classic ambivalence. They were talking with their backs to the wall about survival; yet they were also talking about a kind of millennium. They had come to the paradoxical conclusion that the United States was both very powerful and very vulnerable: that the nation had within itself the potential for successes of a magnitude that would alter the course of human history and greatly enrich the American people in the process, but that if this potential were not realized and fulfilled, then the very forces that had created it would dreadfully misfire. Overripe is the way the condition was often described at the time.

It is of the greatest importance for understanding American expansionism to realize that the strength perceived by such analysts was deployable only abroad, while the vulnerability was intrinsically domestic. They were not afraid of what any other nation might do to the United States, but they were critically concerned about what the United States might do to itself. At bottom, American expansionism in the 1890s was an effort to use the latent strength at the nation's disposal to dispel the vulnerability and anxiety it felt within.

(8)

The Philippines and the Imperialism of Suasion

ONE'S FIRST INCLINATION is to consider the Philippine Islands only a marginal participant in American–East Asian history. There are persuasive reasons for feeling this way. Geographically, the archipelago is literally marginal, or peripheral, to East Asia; ethnically and culturally, it belongs to Southeast Asia. Moreover, it came to prominence relatively late in the course of America's dealings with that part of the world and was always seen by most Americans as merely an adjunct to more critical involvements elsewhere. Seldom have the Philippines attracted much interest in their own right.

This is true as far as it goes, but fundamentally misleading. The real importance of the Philippines to the United States has been moral and exemplary, rather than strategic or economic. The American empire in those islands gives an insight into America.

The Philippines were the only place in Asia—indeed, the only place outside the Western Hemisphere—that the United States ever ruled as an imperial possession. Although a few elite Filipinos hoped otherwise, it was always clear to Americans that the inhabitants of the islands would never become citizens of the United States, nor the archipelago itself be brought fully into the union. The Filipinos and their islands thus became that rarest of phenomena under the republican form of government, subjects.

Sovereignty opened up the possibility for Americans directly to affect every aspect of Philippine public life. And this immense potential power was actually used in a variety of ways, from shooting revolutionaries and deporting political dissenters, to improving public health, building roads, establishing school curricula, defining political institutions and economic structures, and sanctioning power relationships within the society at large. With the possible exceptions of the occupation of Cuba early in the twentieth century and the occupation of Japan after World War II, there is no other instance of America's exercising such power over people recognized to be permanently ineligible for American citizenship and outside the protection of the Bill of Rights. There is literally no other case in which the United States exercised such power for so long a period of time.

The Philippines, then, were the place where the United States came closest to enjoying free rein to do whatever it wished with the lives of another people. This in itself made the Philippine-American encounter different in kind from the relationship between Americans and Chinese or Japanese. The insular empire in the Philippines revealed at its most unfettered the early-twentieth-century American style in dealing with less developed Asian societies.

The first Americans to visit these islands went as merchants in the 1790s, more than a century before the Spanish-American War. Spain, which had governed them since the sixteenth century, made it a policy to discourage foreign trade or settlement; and as a result, the earliest Philippine-American contacts were usually brief and clandestine. Vessels trading principally with some other part of Asia would simply call at Manila to try to fill out incomplete cargoes. The products of the islands were attractive in their own right, however; and in 1796 a vessel named *Astrea* opened a direct trade between Salem and Manila, exchanging hats, wooden compasses, and Madeira for sugar, indigo, pepper, and hides that had been produced in the archipelago.

This trade caught on. It spread from Salem to Boston and New York. By the turn of the century, although it was still technically illegal for foreigners to live or own property in the Philippines, there was enough business involved to make it worthwhile for several American commission merchants to establish themselves informally in Manila as agents for the trade. Eventually, in 1814, Spain reconciled itself to the new order of things and opened the port of Manila officially to foreign trade and residence.

These early American traders arrived at one of the great turning points of Philippine history; and by their presence and economic activity, they and their successors during the nineteenth century played a major role in creating social and cultural forces that ultimately undermined Spanish sovereignty. To understand this, one must first appreciate the philosophy and character of the Spanish empire in the Philippines.

The Philippines were unique in East Asia, because they did not have a highly developed civilization at the time of their original contacts with the West. When the Spaniards came to stay, in 1565, they found a society, economy, and culture that were locally oriented toward extended kinship groups called *barangays*. The people who lived in these communities were relatively peaceful in their relations with each other, literate in a variety of dialects, and talented at various crafts and skills ranging from metalworking to boatbuilding. There were networks of modest trade both within the islands and between the archipelago and Japan, Indonesia, and mainland Asia. But there was no superstructure of law or administration, no artistic or literary tradition of high culture, and no power of political or military organization adequate to resist a European army.

Even though the Spaniards were few in number, Filipinos (whom the Spaniards called *indios*) could not mount an effective resistance. By the end of the sixteenth century, Spaniards had overrun most populated parts of the archipelago, except for the mountainous region in northern Luzon and the Muslim (or Moro) strongholds in the south on Mindanao and its outlying islands. In the process, the Spaniards chronically disrupted the indigenous society and economy—by violence, evangelization, the introduction of a system of forced labor, the creation of quasi-feudal fiefdoms called *encomiendas,* and by depleting the food supply.

The effect was devastating. Witnesses reported that as a result of the Spanish presence, traditional patterns of authority were eroding, crime and disorder increasing, villages being abandoned in favor of a return to the safety of the hills. In some places, agriculture was deliberately neglected in hopes of starving out the Spanish invaders and the Chinese merchants who quickly followed in their wake.

Under the prodding of the clergy, Spain imposed a regime designed to protect the Philippines and the Filipinos against further destructive exploitation. It closed the islands, as a whole, to foreigners; and, within the archipelago, closed the countryside and the villages to all Europeans, including Spaniards, except for the clergy and a small number of governmental officials. There were complicated reasons for this. (It was, among other things, part of a power struggle between Spanish clergy and laity in the islands.) What matters for our purposes, however, is the effect: the Spanish policy of isolation—ironically akin to that in Tokugawa Japan—froze Filipino life midway through a period of acute disruption, throwing the society back upon its own badly battered cultural resources.

For the next 250 years, until the second half of the nineteenth century, Spain governed the Philippines through Spanish priests and the descendants of the traditional *indio* elite. As late as 1848, apart from a small military and naval contingent, only a few hundred Spanish laymen lived anywhere in the islands, outside Manila and its immediate periphery.

Early in the second half of the eighteenth century, however, the artificial isolation of the Philippines was pierced. Here, as in China, the British led the way. British forces occupied Manila between 1762 and 1764, and during their stay Philippine commerce was opened for the first time to Europeans from outside Spain. Confined to Manila and a few other cities by their own law, Spaniards had devoted their economic energies to the celebrated galleon that made an annual voyage to Acapulco and back. The galleon trade was essentially an exchange of Mexican silver for various Chinese and other Asian products amassed at Manila during the year. The Philippines were simply an entrepot, not the source of the wealth. The British, unlike the Spaniards, were interested in native Philippine products such as sugar and hemp. They continued to seek them out—bribing and smuggling where necessary—even after the occupation was over.

This started the commercial development of the Philippine countryside. In particular, it pushed up land values by making it profitable for landowners to specialize and produce for an export market. As a result, new wealth began to appear in the provinces, much of it in the hands of new men who were not part of the traditional elite. With this wealth came aspirations to lead a less parochial and specifically a more Westernized style of life.

This was the situation into which Americans projected themselves in the 1790s. They went to the Philippines seeking profits; but in the process they became, like the British, catalysts of social and economic change. The commission merchants who had established themselves illegally in Manila around the turn of the century put out connections

to the American firms doing business at Canton and eventually coalesced into two major trading houses—Russell & Sturgis; and Peele,
Hubbell & Company.

As Spain's own efforts at economic development lagged, these two
American firms and their British counterparts became the principal
dynamic element in the Philippine economy, the locus of initiative.
In the absence of modern banking and credit facilities, they not only
acted as commission merchants but as bankers, investors, shipping and
insurance agents, and landowners. By the middle of the nineteenth
century, Russell & Sturgis had come to play so pivotal a role in these
respects that it was commonly referred to in the islands simply as
"the great company."

For the American merchants and investors, these were highly risky,
precarious operations. Both the American firms eventually went bankrupt—Russell & Sturgis in 1876 and Peele, Hubbell in 1887. All but
forgotten by the time Commodore Dewey sailed into Manila Bay, they
had nothing whatsoever to do with the American decision to annex
the Philippines. For Filipinos, however, these powerful external stimuli
to commercialize, modernize, and secularize their society had a lasting
impact. They posed a direct challenge to Spain's continued insistence
upon isolation and its reliance upon indirect rule through priestly and
traditional leaders.

Had the Spanish government accommodated itself to change—for
example, by liberalizing and secularizing its administration, improving
public services, and recognizing that a new group of economic and
cultural leaders had replaced many members of the traditional elite—
it is conceivable that the Spanish empire might have survived in the
archipelago for decades more.

Instead, however, the Spanish community and the church-state
through which Spain ruled remained to the end the chief support of
the status quo and the foremost obstacle to change. As a result, reforms
that could have been dealt with under Spanish sovereignty—reforms
such as liberalizing the government—became fused with highly emotional issues of racial dignity and national pride that deepened Filipinos'
alienation from Spain.

So in the end, across the whole spectrum of reform and discontent,
advocates of economic development, improved government services,
racial dignity, class interest, and political or educational liberalization
all found in the Spanish regime a common target. The Spaniards be-

came for Filipinos what the Manchus were becoming for many Chinese.

Accordingly, in 1896, after years of unsuccessful reformist agitation by the economic and social elite of the islands, a group of urban lower- and lower-middle-class conspirators launched an armed rebellion under the leadership of a romantic figure named Andres Bonifacio. The organization he formed was named *Katipunan,* a Tagalog acronym. Bonifacio was a talented conspirator, versed in the writings of European social revolutionaries, but an incompetent general. He was replaced and eventually executed, after a shabby trial for treason, by Emilio Aguinaldo, a minor official from Cavite province who had enjoyed some success against Spanish military forces. After months of sharp fighting, Aguinaldo accepted a large payment from the Spanish government and retired to Hong Kong in 1897. But the social forces behind the revolution remained. When the United States declared war on Spain in 1898 and transported Aguinaldo back to the islands to help Americans destroy Spanish power there, the Filipino people rose anew and seized control of virtually the entire archipelago outside Manila on their own, before American ground forces could be deployed.

This posed a serious problem for American policymakers. At the outset of the war, the McKinley administration still had limited and uncertain goals in the Philippines. Its immediate aims were to attack and defeat Spanish military and naval forces and seize the city of Manila. As the seat of Spanish government in the islands, Manila would be a valuable bargaining chip in the eventual peace negotiations. Beyond this, many people felt that Manila would make an admirable base of operations for American naval and commercial activities in the western Pacific, an American equivalent of Hong Kong.

Certain individual exceptions notwithstanding, neither the administration nor Congress had originally intended to take the whole archipelago from Spain. Apart from Manila and whatever surrounding territory might be required to make the city defensible, the islands did not seem intrinsically attractive.

Even after Dewey's victory, on May 1, 1898, the initial response of the leading American expansionists remained guarded and ambivalent. Theodore Roosevelt came out briefly against annexation, arguing that the islands were too far away. Captain Mahan recommended taking Manila and possibly the island of Luzon, upon which it was located, but nothing else. Henry Cabot Lodge thought it might be well to acquire the whole archipelago, and then trade everything except Luzon to Britain for various Caribbean islands. The leaders of both wings of the Democratic party—William Jennings Bryan and former President Grover Cleveland—opposed taking anything at all.

Most of these people assumed that residual sovereignty and power in the Philippines would continue to be exercised by Spain, except in those places the United States either seized or acquired in the treaty. McKinley's original peace proposal, presented to Spain a month after Dewey's victory, was simply that Spain convey to the United States "a port and necessary appurtenances." Everything else, implicitly, was to be at Spain's disposal.

The astounding success of the Philippine revolution invalidated this assumption. Actual control of the islands outside of Manila and a few other spots was now in the hands of Filipinos. This raised vexatious questions as to what the United States should do. Nobody seriously thought that the Spaniards could reconquer the Philippines, but it was clear that if the United States recognized Spanish sovereignty there in the peace treaty, they would try. This would lead to a great deal of death, destruction, and political instability in the region, for which Americans would have to bear much of the responsibility.

On the other hand, nobody seriously supposed that an independent Philippine government could survive by itself in that age of high imperialism. In both Washington and London, it was widely held that if the United States should leave, Japan or Germany would move in; and the British, who would have found German control of the islands a serious threat to their own position in East Asia, informally urged the United States to keep the Philippines for itself.

There was a third option besides independence and outright acquisition. The United States could have recognized Philippine independence and then established a protectorate over the archipelago to warn off other foreign powers. This would have been acceptable to at least some elements in the Philippine revolutionary government; and it was actually recommended by a number of anti-imperialists in the United States Senate. But it was not a credible alternative in the eyes of the McKinley administration, because a protectorate of this sort would have left the United States responsible to other nations for the Filipinos' behavior toward foreign citizens and interests. Since the administration, like most Americans of the time, considered the

Filipinos a backward people likely to behave erratically or even violently to foreigners living among them, it did not want to accept such a responsibility. In the phrase of the time, it maintained that it would accept "no responsibility without control."

This lack of credible alternatives increased the administration's receptivity to frankly imperialistic, annexationist arguments. Acquiring the whole archipelago, it was said, would improve American trade and the American strategic position in the Orient; it would fulfill American obligations to international society and at the same time signal American arrival in the ranks of the great powers. By autumn of 1898, the administration had reversed its former policy and instructed its negotiators in Paris to get a treaty giving the United States sovereignty over the whole of the Philippine Islands.

In the meantime, an extremely ugly situation had developed at Manila. An American army had been dispatched to the Philippines even before news of Dewey's victory had been received. (The reasoning behind this was that the slow-sailing transports could be called back if Dewey had been defeated, but that the army would be needed promptly if he had won, in order to establish support facilities on shore and maintain an American presence.) This army, swelled by reinforcements, took possession of Manila from its Spanish garrison in August after a mock battle meant to save Spanish honor. Farcical in its theatrics, this arrangement nevertheless reflected certain realities: the Americans wanted Manila; and the Spaniards, realizing that they could hold out no longer, preferred to surrender to a white Western power rather than their own former subjects.

Predictably, this deal between Americans and Spaniards infuriated the Filipinos, who were at the time besieging Manila, which they considered the natural capital of their independent government. The result of the maneuver, therefore, was to place the Americans inside Manila looking out, and the Filipinos outside Manila looking in—the two armies facing each other with increasing hostility and suspicion across the cordon surrounding the city. As it became clear that the United States intended to take over the entire archipelago, tensions along this line rose to great intensity. Troops jeered at and baited each other; commanders on each side became convinced that the other was about to attack. The situation made an outbreak of actual fighting almost inevitable. On the night of February 4, 1899, two days before the peace treaty with Spain was ratified by the American Senate, a minor incident set off general firing between the two armies and quickly escalated into a full-scale war.

This war—which Americans then and now have called an insurrection, thereby evading the Filipinos' claim to be resisting a foreign invasion—was bound to be won militarily by the United States sooner or later. This was so partly because of the overwhelming strategic power of the United States, but more because of the weaknesses and inadequacies of the Philippine government. The latter was, after all, a new creation with only the most rudimentary administrative and financial machinery, headed by the increasingly dictatorial General Aguinaldo. It was being torn apart internally by regional, linguistic, religious, and class tensions.

Nevertheless, the disadvantages under which the Filipinos labored had their compensations; and these have given this vicious war—which was filled with the most dreadful atrocities on both sides—a special fascination ever since the Vietnam War. For one thing, the enormous imbalance in regular forces compelled the Filipinos, who would have preferred to wage conventional warfare, to adopt instead guerrilla tactics that proved far more vexing and punishing to the American invaders.

Concomitantly, the expendability of the central government and the diffuse character of social and political organization in the islands deprived Americans of convenient targets against which to use their admittedly overwhelming power. This sustained the spread of a guerrilla, or what in the future would be called a people's, war. In the circumstances, a conventional military victory could not by itself establish American control. It would still leave at the local level a combustible polity governable only by the recurrent, overt use of force. This was a higher price for empire than it seemed likely the American public would be willing to pay.

This was all the more true because the American empire in the islands had been politically vulnerable at home all along. Right from the beginning, there had been a strong anti-imperialist movement in the United States. It was a strange alliance of people who had little else in common. Some were idealists who thought that ruling another people against their will was incompatible with the tenets of America's own Declaration of Independence and that enslaving a colored people, in particular, was tantamount to repudiating the outcome of the Civil War. Others were isolationists who wanted to avoid involvement in the strategic rivalries of the western Pacific, or nativists and racists who didn't want Filipinos in the American electorate or labor force. Many of the anti-imperialists were simply Democrats who wanted to embarrass a Republican administration.

Whatever their motives may have been, they were a powerful political force. They came within two votes of defeating the peace treaty with Spain. A week after that, on February 14, 1899, they produced a tie vote in the Senate on the Bacon Resolution, which would have promised Filipinos full independence as soon as they could establish a stable government of their own. The Bacon Resolution was defeated only by the tie-breaking vote of the Vice President.

Formal anti-imperialism of this sort, associated with the Anti-Imperialist League, probably peaked during the presidential election in 1900. As the official movement began its long decline, however, there appeared in its place a mood less focused but more pervasive and ultimately more effective. It was, in part, a mood of apathy and disenchantment, rooted in the public's reaction to the length and ferocity of the Philippine-American war.

By the summer of 1900, two-thirds of the United States Army was engaged in the Philippines. The war there was proving costly both in lives and money, disgraceful in the atrocities committed by Americans, shocking as evidence of the intensity of Filipino opposition. It was impossible to ignore the reality that tens of thousands of Filipinos were prepared to die rather than be annexed to the United States. This took the bloom off the idea of territorial imperialism for many Americans whose original approach to the question had been romantic, idealized, or even simply casual.

Then, too, there was the international context. While the United States was bogged down in the Philippines, the British were similarly mired fighting the Boers in South Africa. Africa had just been divided among rival European empires; China seemed on the brink of a similar fate. War scares and alliance-mongering were in the air. This led many people on both sides of the Atlantic to re-examine imperialism. The result was a new form of anti-imperialism more sophisticated than that of the moralists and idealists, more comprehensive than that of the nativists and isolationists.

The classic intellectual formulation of this new anti-imperialism was John A. Hobson's *Imperialism: A Study,* published in 1902. An English "radical" economist, profoundly humanistic in his values, Hobson argued that the many groups that either benefited or thought they would benefit from imperialism were really only pawns of the world's finance capitalists. Having spoiled their own domestic markets by taking too large a share of corporate earnings for profits and reinvestment at the expense of wages, these investors were driven to use the power of the state to open safe, attractive new investment opportunities abroad.

Hobson's ideas—though not his great book, which caught on slowly in the United States—were well known in early twentieth-century America, even by arch-imperialists such as Henry Cabot Lodge. For most people who knew them, they too compromised the imperial pretension unfolding in the Pacific. They complemented and helped to shape a new moral critique of imperialism arising from the progressive reform movement in America.

Yet there were still many Americans who wanted not only to defeat the Philippine "insurrection" but also to establish a permanent and formal empire in the islands for the economic and strategic advantage of the United States and, conceivably, the benefit of the Filipino people. The cleverest tacticians among these remaining imperialists realized that they could retain the Philippines only if they defused the political opposition of Filipinos to American rule. In order to neutralize the political threat to imperialism at home in America, Filipinos had not only to be conquered but converted. This was the origin of what William Howard Taft called the policy of "attraction."

Attraction began as a tactic for pacification. Originally the carrot to offset the stick of military repression, it eventually superseded the military approach altogether as the principal American strategy for dealing with the Filipino people.

The policy grew out of the experience of the Schurman Commission, a body composed of three civilians (including Dean C. Worcester) and the ranking military and naval officers in the islands. Ordered by President McKinley in 1899 to gather information about the islands and to recommend policy, the commissioners held public hearings in Manila to solicit informed opinions. Because fighting was already in progress, however, the sampling of opinion that could be obtained in this way was highly unrepresentative: only persons inside American lines could appear to testify. What the commissioners heard, therefore, was primarily the opinion of conservative Westernized Filipinos, many of whom resented Aguinaldo's new prominence and feared that the revolutions against Spain and America might lead to social and economic agitation against their own interests.

Taken at face value, their testimony suggested the existence of a widespread desire in the Philippines for order, reform, and modernization—a secularized government, for example, more infrastructure, improved public education, guaranteed personal liberties, steps to encourage economic growth. This was a gratifying discovery for the Americans, because it implied that the interests shared by Americans and Filipinos might be more important than those which divided them. "The very thing they yearn for is what of all others our Government will naturally desire to give them," the commissioners concluded in their report.

As the Philippine-American war continued, the views of the Manila elite gained adherents in the countryside, as well. The advance of American troops into more and more provinces and the adoption of guerrilla tactics by their Filipino opponents spread violence and its accompanying social and economic dislocations into most parts of the archipelago. Provincial elites, who had once dreamed of dominating the revolution, found themselves instead caught in a cross fire between the United States Army and local guerrilla groups. So did many peasants. Reluctantly, growing numbers of people concluded that since the Americans could not be driven away, collaboration with them for agreed ends was preferable to a continuation of the fighting.

In this way, a structure of accommodation, or collaboration, emerged, linking the American government and the Filipino elite. The Americans needed the elite to mediate with the mass of the people; the elite needed the Americans to impose order and restore their leadership of society. By cooperating, each could achieve what neither could bring about alone.

The architects of the collaborative empire were William Howard Taft, on the American side, and a group of the Filipino elite who founded the Partido Federal late in 1900. Taft, the first civil governor of the islands, led a new commission to the Philippines earlier that year. Originally functioning as both the legislature and the executive, the commission took over the government of the archipelago province by province, as the Army progressed with pacification. It needed safe, talented, cooperative Filipinos through whom to work.

Active participation by Filipinos in their own government was a cornerstone of the policy of attraction. Over the years, the personnel changed, but the progress of political devolution continued. In 1907, only five years after the formal end of the Philippine-American war, an elected assembly was inaugurated. Nine years later, the Jones Act promised eventual independence at some unspecified date in the future. Although these developments moved faster and sacrificed more control than Taft and his colleagues had originally intended, they did disarm opposition to short-term American sovereignty. During the administration of Woodrow Wilson and his governor-general, Francis Burton Harrison, prominent Filipino politicians actually intrigued behind the scenes to slow the juggernaut of independence, lest the American military and economic presence be withdrawn too quickly.

Beyond this, the cement of collaboration was a number of shared interests in development and reform. Building upon the testimony before the Schurman Commission, the Americans inaugurated popular programs to modernize and extend public education, secularize the state, build roads and other infrastructure, and secure preferential access to the American market as a stimulus to Philippine agriculture. Many of these programs have since come under serious criticism: education for being irrelevant and denaturalizing, free trade for distorting the Philippine economy and making it dependent upon the United States. At the time, however, they won gratitude and support from most of the Filipino people, as evidence of American good faith.

The result was, in many respects, a success. Americans gained a governable colony that was never again an issue, let alone an embarrassment, in domestic politics; Filipinos achieved substantial control of their own development; numerous useful projects were undertaken cooperatively; and, not the least of accomplishments in a colonial relationship, both sides were spared the agonies of large-scale political violence. Between roughly 1906 and 1941, there was only one large-scale revolutionary outbreak, and that was directed against Filipino political and economic leaders more than Americans. As the original generation of American imperialists passed from power, even formal independence ceased to be an issue between the two peoples.

An internally autonomous commonwealth was established in 1935 (it could have come several years earlier but for bickering among Filipino politicians as to who should get the credit); and complete independence followed in 1946, making the Philippines the first major Western colony to reclaim its sovereignty. A tactical gamble initiated to pacify and retain the islands had, in practice, paved the way to national freedom.

But there was a hidden price for all of this. America's reliance upon collaboration and suasion to maintain its insular empire made the collaborators a privileged group. Positioning themselves between the two real loci of power and authority in the islands, the American government and the mass of the Filipino people, they became indispensable mediators. Since the only credible collaborators—the only people with the authority, outlook, and education necessary both to deal with the Americans and to deliver the allegiance of the people— were the members of the established elite, the imperialism of suasion thus became a bulwark of class interest.

Within the government, elite collaborators used their offices to frustrate Americans' occasional attempts to move beyond nation-building programs to a kind of reform that would have redistributed wealth and power. Outside, in the political life of the people, they used their role as spokesmen of the nation to identify themselves with popular issues such as nationalism and independence.

Given the general permissiveness of American rule and the confidence after passage of the Jones Act in 1916 that independence would eventually come, it required little heroism to lead an independence movement in the Philippines. Yet there, as in any other colony, nationalism and independence remained powerful emotional issues. Campaigning for independence and running against imperialism were easy ways for the elite of the islands to rally public support without having to address issues of social or economic equity that might have compromised their own interests.

Moreover, the elite said, the "discipline of the independence movement" required solidarity behind the nation's leaders. In this way, issues that were legitimate but remote from the daily lives of most Filipinos were manipulated as symbols to purge politics of its social and economic content.

Behind the facade of liberal devolution and developmental benevolence, America thus became a dual sanction for elite rule in its Philippine colony—buttress and target simultaneously. While protecting and institutionalizing the power of the Filipino elite, Americans also allowed themselves to be used as an external device for deflecting criticism of their regime. This led to a surrender of initiative and an evasion of responsibility by the United States without actually ending American intervention in Philippine life. The result compromised everyone involved, corrupting and vitiating Philippine public life, setting back many of the causes to which one side or the other was ostensibly committed, making a mockery of nationalism, and defining Philippine-American relations as an exercise in illusion. "Damn the Americans," said Manuel Quezon, Sergio Osmeña's successor as leader of the Nacionalista party and chief tactician of independence, "why don't they tyrannize us more?"

(9)

The Open Door

THE OPEN DOOR is one of the lodestones of American history. The most famous issue in American–East Asian history prior to World War II, it also ranks in the public mind with Washington's Farewell Address, the Monroe Doctrine, and the Cold War policy of containment as one of the pinnacles of American diplomatic history. Yet behind this well-known term there lurks a world of confusion, because over the years the Open Door has become mythologized.

The Open Door is, in effect, four separate things: 1) an *episode,* a set of events in Sino-American relations that gave their name to the period around the turn of this century; 2) a *doctrine* presented in a series of diplomatic notes that articulated the major American policy toward China in that period; 3) a *tactic* for bringing about the economic and cultural penetration of China at the lowest possible cost; and 4) a *concept,* an interpretive device used by historians to explain the expansionist aspects of American foreign relations everywhere, but especially in Asia.

The first of these—the episode itself—is the key to the other three. There would never have been Open Door notes—and hence, from the American perspective, no open door doctrine or concept—had not the course of events in China seemed to require a new and special American response. The need for such a response arose because during the 1890s, as American economic and evangelical interests in China grew, the environment there became more threatening.

The growth of American interests, though real, has to be kept in perspective: China and the United States were still, even at the end of the nineteenth century, very peripheral to each other's basic interests. To the Chinese, Britain was still the most important foreign power, followed more or less in order by Russia, Japan, Germany, and France. The British still maintained a powerful naval force off China's coast and on its inland waterways; they dominated foreign economic and political life in the treaty ports; and they took about 70 percent of all China's foreign commerce. The Chinese view of the United States, in contrast to the British and others, was that among barbarians it was relatively appealing, precisely because it was too weak and economically insignificant to pose much of a threat to them.

Realistically, China was no more important to the United States than the United States was to it. American exports to China during the 1890s peaked at a mere 1.1 percent of total American exports—half of this little trade coming from a single industry, cotton textiles. American capital investment in all of Asia amounted to only about one-eighth of the United States investment in Mexico alone. Moreover, 20 percent of all the capital Americans invested in China was in the form of missionary property, not a tangible asset.

But even people who understood how unimportant the China market actually was to the American economy tended to believe that it had a tremendous potential. China was, to their mind, the largest potential market in the world and certainly the last great untapped and undeveloped market for the kinds of manufactured products that the United States was then believed to be overproducing. During the 1890s, the actual statistics of Sino-American trade seemed to confirm this. The dollar value of American exports to China rose between 300 and 400 percent: in a typical year around 1890, the United States sold $3 to $5 million worth of goods there, whereas in a typical year around the turn of the century it sold $12 to $15 million. To the many people who were concerned about overproduction and the future of the American economy, this looked like the pillar of cloud and fire that might lead them out of their dilemma.

The steel and oil industries looked to China for just such relief. American steel companies, disturbed by the near completion of the basic trunk lines of the American railroad network, saw in the vast distances and the immense traffic potential of China a wonderful field for the development of railroads—and, therefore, a dynamic new export market for American steel. The Standard Oil Company—which had taken over huge new oil fields as they were discovered, in order to preserve its monopoly, seeing no likelihood that the domestic American market could consume all this oil—looked to China as a place to work off its oversupply of petroleum. Oil for the lamps of China was the cry. Of course, this line of reasoning appealed not only to industrialists and investors but to working people also, who saw exports as a stimulus to employment at home.

American missionaries found themselves in a similar situation. The actual record of conversions in China was paltry; and partly for this reason, China ranked well below India and the Ottoman empire as a target of the American missionary movement during most of the nineteenth century. But during the 1890s, China finally came to the fore, surpassing India in both manpower and budget. The statistics for all of this seem quite modest today. In 1890, there were about 200 American ordained Protestant missionaries in China, accompanied by a little more than 300 missionary women, working on a total budget of about $400,000 (gold) per year. By the end of the century, there may have been as many as a thousand American missionaries, operating on a budget of between half a million and one million dollars per year. Small though these figures are, they represented a significant commitment not only by the missionaries themselves and the various mission boards at home that sent them out but also by thousands of American churchgoers, who contributed to their support and followed their progress.

Symptomatically, when in 1900 the Boston *Herald* took a poll of five major occupational groups in fifteen cities, it discovered that clergymen were the most avid expansionists in every one of them. American churches were looking outward at this time; and, more than any other part of the world, China captured the imagination of their parishioners.

But as this sense of a great American potential in China grew, actual conditions in the empire seemed to turn against the United States. Under the treaty system that had existed since the middle of the nineteenth century, the Western powers had tacitly agreed that the simplest and cheapest way to exploit China while avoiding the risk of war among themselves was to prop up the central government of China and make it provide safe and suitable conditions for Western missionaries and businessmen. So long as the West remained powerful enough to force its will upon the central government, Western interests were best served by the existence of an effective central government.

That way, instead of having to deal with dozens of regional power brokers or, worse yet, fight each other for the very dubious and expensive honor of trying to rule parts of China, there was a single convenient source of central power with which all foreigners negotiated their treaty rights and to which all foreigners turned for the enforcement of those rights against Chinese challengers.

Hence one of the chief reasons the Imperial Maritime Customs Service collected customs revenues for the Chinese government was that the West wanted to be sure that China would have the funds it needed to survive and carry out its responsibilities to protect foreign interests. Reliance upon China's central government in this way set the stage for the use of the Open Door as a tactic. Since the most favored nation clause, included in major treaties with China, assured that all of the leading foreign powers would share the rights and privileges obtained from China by any of them, a door opened to one would let in all.

However humiliating it might be to have an open door imposed upon them, the Chinese could still incorporate the relationship with the West into their traditional world view. They knew—even if Westerners did not—that China was too large and populous a place to be conquered and ruled by a small number of foreigners coming from a distance of ten or twelve thousand miles. And they knew also that China as an idea—a civilization, an ethic—was too supple and resilient to be defeated by armored cruisers and marines. From the Chinese perspective, it was important that the foreign barbarians were coming to the Middle Kingdom to seek privileges of a sort the Chinese did not seek; and it was also important that the competing ambitions of such foreigners made them vulnerable to Chinese manipulation—to be played off against one another.

Beyond this, the leaders of China divided as to how to respond to Western encroachments. One group, complacent in the superiority of traditional Chinese civilization, felt that the West should be resisted both politically and culturally. The other group—the "self-strengthening movement"—believed that Western power was so real and threatening that at least the techniques and machinery of the foreigners had to be adopted in order to defend China.

Their assumption was that science, technology, and management skills were superficial, whereas literature, ethics, culture were fundamental. Thus one could borrow the former without endangering the latter—and, in effect, have the best of both worlds. Their doctrine was "Chinese learning as the fundamental structure, Western learning for practical use."

This self-strengthening movement appeals more to Americans today than the diehard conservatism of its opponents, but it was equally impractical. Experience soon proved the impossibility of separating technology and skills from the values and learning that had produced them. The self-strengtheners suffered greatly because their efforts were repeatedly sabotaged by the conservatives. But the self-strengtheners' biggest problem was the schizophrenic goal they set themselves. Every time they borrowed one thing, they created a need to borrow or know something else.

As a result, the introduction of modern railroads, steamships, telegraphs, and mines—which seemed so halting to the Westerners—seemed much more like a juggernaut to many Chinese. There was no place at which they could draw an effective line of defense against this cultural invasion. The more the self-strengtheners succeeded, therefore, the more they threatened and alienated many of their countrymen. Ironically, the biggest short-term impact of the self-strengthening movement may have been to increase resentment of the West and foster anti-foreign nationalism.

The ultimate test of the self-strengthening movement, of course, was whether it actually strengthened China. For people of that era, the verdict was supplied by the Sino-Japanese War of 1894–1895. In that war, which had to do nominally with the control of Korea, the new-style army and navy created by Li Hung-chang (Li Hongzhang), politically the most powerful of the self-strengtheners, was decimated; and Japan won an overwhelming victory. In retrospect, one can see the beginning of the end for the Ch'ing dynasty. As a result of the war, Japan imposed a huge war indemnity that strained the finances of the Chinese government and also demanded that China cede to Japan actual political control of a part of the empire.

Although the European powers were able to prevent Japan from taking over mainland Chinese territory in 1895, the victory of little Japan over giant China destroyed foreigners' confidence that the central government of China could survive much longer. This meant that the traditional open door tactic of relying upon the central government to protect and legitimize the Western position inside the country was vulnerable. So within two years of the time the European empires prevented Japan from taking any of China for itself, they began to protect their own future in China by dividing key parts of the empire into regional spheres of interest.

Beginning with Germany's seizure of a harbor in Shantung (Shandong) Province in November 1897, the four great powers of the day—Britain, Germany, Russia, and France—leased from China (sometimes at gunpoint) a number of at least potentially important seaports and secured exclusive economic privileges and defensive rights in the adjacent provinces. At the same time, the powers concluded non-alienation agreements according to which China pledged never to transfer control of the region in question to any third party. Essentially, these were claims by the sphere-holding power to take over the sphere outright if and when China should finally disintegrate.

By the end of 1898, Russia had a sphere in Manchuria, Germany in Shantung, France in the southern provinces, and Britain in the Yangtze Valley. Within each of these, the sphere-holding power was building fortified bases and giving exclusive railway and mining concessions to its own citizens.

So the rules of the game had plainly changed, and the traditional open door tactic of keeping hands off and relying on the imperial government to protect the interests of all foreigners in common was no longer relevant. The United States had to do something to protect its future in China.

This was not just an abstract or logical problem. Political pressure mounted on the McKinley administration from many sources. The American Asiatic Association, a business lobby, launched a successful publicity campaign that was picked up by newspapers and journals. Missionaries and their supporters warned in sermons and religious periodicals that the country would default on its Christian responsibilities if it were to abandon an active role in China.

Even the bureaucracy brought pressure to bear upon McKinley. His Minister to China, Edwin Conger, started from a position opposing spheres of any kind and evolved by early 1899 to a recommendation that the United States seize the whole province of Chihli (Zhili), including the city of Tientsin and the approaches to Peking, as the American sphere. The American consul at Amoy (Xiamen) wanted Fukien (Fujian) Province as an American sphere; the Navy wanted the Chusan (Zhoushan) Islands off the mouth of the Yangtze River.

President McKinley's problem was that there was almost nothing he could do either to get a sphere of interest for the United States or to prevent other nations from getting spheres for themselves. Either of these courses would have required that the United States have large amounts of credible military and naval power to lay on the line—whether against the Chinese, to get a sphere, or before the Europeans, to block the spread of spheres. In 1898, however, when most of the spheres were acquired, such power as the country had was tied up in the Spanish-American War. In 1899, when that war ended, a new one broke out in the Philippines, eventually, as we have seen, requiring most of the United States Army to defeat the Filipinos.

So in September 1899, hoping to head off the growing political and bureaucratic pressures inside the United States before they could escalate into a demand for something the country was literally unable to do, Secretary of State John Hay dispatched a series of almost identical diplomatic notes to each of the leading imperial powers having an interest in China. Taken together, these became known as the first Open Door note.

By then it was much too late to ask the Europeans to give up their existing spheres in China—too late even to ask them to allow equal opportunities for investment within their spheres. But, as we have seen, the opportunity to invest was much less important to American expansionists of this era than the opportunity simply to trade.

So the note conceded what was unavoidable and instead concentrated on preserving an open door for American commerce in the new spheres. It asked each sphere-holding power to treat the commerce of all nations the same way it treated its own commerce within its sphere, to honor the existing treaty rights that other nations had in that area, and to retain the Chinese tariff, collected by the Imperial Maritime Customs Service, with the revenues going to China rather than to the sphere-holding government.

This was, of course, a bluff. If any of the governments involved had said no, the United States could have done little in retaliation. Generations of American historians have criticized the Open Door note on just these grounds, arguing that it was unrealistic and, as a policy, vulnerable to the first nation that cared enough to stand up to the United States. The argument is true as far as it goes. One has to admire the shrewdness of the bluff. With a new base of operations in the Philippines, the United States didn't need a sphere in China, provided that America could still trade in other people's spheres. The

Open Door note thus targeted precisely the "bottom line" of American interest in China; and it did this in a modest and conservative request that other nations found almost impossible to reject.

We know that some of the sphere-holding powers wanted to say no, but none of them wanted to go out on a limb alone and reveal the full extent of its ambitions in the new spheres. Consequently, all the powers wound up giving at least conditional assent to the American request.

Whether or not this was a success for American China policy, it was certainly a *political* success for the McKinley administration at home in the United States. It quieted the demands for more decisive and risky actions.

In the meantime, just as the international environment in China seemed to be deteriorating, domestic events within China also began to threaten American interests. The anti-foreign feelings aroused over the years by the whole range of Western encroachments upon China— everything from railroads that desecrated graveyards to spheres of interest that humiliated the government—began to heat up during the late 1890s. Among the first Americans to feel this hostility were the missionaries.

A much higher percentage of missionaries than of traders or diplomats tended to live and travel alone or in very small clusters in the countryside and the cities of the interior, away from the relative safety of the treaty ports. They and their Chinese converts were usually the first victims of anti-foreign outbursts; and because of their sense of vulnerability, they quickly became agitated and demanded protection or retaliation whenever one of their number was harmed, or even threatened.

After the Sino-Japanese War, anti-missionary incidents began to rise. This provoked some concern among all the Western governments; but it particularly upset the American government, because missionaries were an unusually large part of the American interest in China, and, as we have seen, a growing part, with many supporters among the American public.

In 1899, this anti-foreign feeling boiled over in the form of the Boxer uprising. The Boxers were only one of several socially disruptive movements that arose at about this time in China, but of these they were the group that posed the greatest danger to the West. They were not, however, exclusively anti-foreign in their orientation.

The Boxers rose partly because of the decades of humiliation at the hands of Westerners, partly because of the dislocations caused by the limited modernization that took place under the self-strengthening movement, and partly because of a series of natural disasters culminating in a succession of acute famines that caused a mass migration of several million homeless and hungry people into the region around Peking. These were all signs, from a Chinese perspective, that the dynastic cycle was about to repeat itself and that the Ch'ing dynasty was nearing its end. So there was a powerful anti-dynastic as well as anti-foreign aspect to the Boxer movement. Indeed, many of the Boxers might have found this an almost meaningless distinction, since the Manchu dynasty itself was of foreign origin.

The imperial government decided to divert whatever threat the Boxers posed to the dynasty by joining the Boxers in a joint anti-Western movement. The government was well situated to do this, because it had just taken a reactionary turn for reasons of its own. Alarmed by the seemingly radical reform edicts of the Hundred Days in the summer of 1898, government officials and the military had supported a palace coup by the Empress Dowager that deposed the young Emperor and scattered or executed his liberal advisers. A movement to resist the West and drive out the foreigners complemented such actions.

Nevertheless, the alliance between the court and the Boxers was a desperate gamble. The Boxers proposed not simply to end cultural borrowing and drive out Western missionaries and businessmen; they intended to kill the foreign devils. Inevitably, therefore, there would be Western retaliation: foreign warships and armies would strike back. The historical record showed that while the West could not conquer or occupy China itself, Western power could reach and, if need be, destroy any of the major cities of China. In 1860, British and French armies had actually occupied Peking and burned the Summer Palace. Surely they could do so again.

The only additional defensive strength provided by the Boxers was the large number of peasants mobilized through the movement, the emotional fervor of those involved, and their faith (misplaced, as it turned out) that supernatural formulas would protect them against foreign bullets.

The court gambled on such poor odds partly for emotional reasons and partly because the alternative—siding with the West against a large part of its own people—was an even worse bet.

The government of China simply was not strong enough to defy its own people, once aroused. As the Empress Dowager herself put it: "China is weak; the only thing we can depend upon is the heart of the people. If we lose it, how can we maintain our country?" So in June 1900, the government allowed the Boxers to take over the streets of Peking. They shortly murdered two foreign diplomats, put the foreign legations under siege, and (surprisingly) turned back an international column of marines that attempted to fight its way up from Tientsin to lift the siege.

This made China once again a major problem for the McKinley administration. The turmoil in China not only endangered American lives and interests but renewed the threat of a European division of the empire. On top of this, 1900 was an election year. McKinley had to act decisively, lest the Democrats criticize him for neglecting American interests and lives. But at the same time he had to act in such a way as to avoid giving the Democrats the issue of militarism or imperialism with which to attack him.

For all these reasons, McKinley had to find a policy that would do four things: 1) save the lives of the Americans trapped in Peking and some besieged outposts; 2) protect the Open Door principle against renewed attacks by the other foreign powers once their troops intervened in China; 3) support the Chinese central government, lest China simply collapse from within and thereby necessitate further foreign interventions; and 4) satisfy American public opinion that he was upholding the national honor and interests without going farther on the route which had been taken in the Philippines toward formal, territorial imperialism.

McKinley's ideal response to this challenge would have been what the American tacticians in Vietnam, two-thirds of a century later, called a surgical strike: in this case, a unilateral American relief column that would fight its way into Peking, extract the Americans, and leave. This would have satisfied the need for action and the saving of lives without any explicitly imperialistic aftermath such as a colony or a protracted occupation. It would also have done the least possible damage to the Chinese central government and left America free to put pressure on other foreign powers not to enlarge their spheres of interest. But the idea was impossible; there was not enough American military and naval power available to undertake such a unilateral mission.

This meant that the United States would have to act jointly with the other imperial powers. As a minority of one in a group of six, the United States would run the risk of being drawn along by the others into something that did not suit the administration's interests.

So to establish the ground rules for the American involvement in the military expedition to Peking, McKinley and Hay issued a second Open Door note, declaring the purposes for which the United States was acting. This was a unilateral statement of America's own goals, designed primarily for domestic political consumption.

The United States was invading China, the note proclaimed, to restore order, defend legal rights under the treaties and international law, preserve the Open Door for foreign trade, and help to maintain China as a "territorial and administrative entity" (i.e., by sustaining the central government against both foreign pressures and domestic rebels, such as the Boxers). Unlike the first Open Door note, the second was not an attempt to bind other nations to a common position; it was simply an announcement of American motives and goals. The other powers recognized it as such, and, except for Great Britain, none of them even bothered to acknowledge having received it.

Almost immediately, a myth began to grow that the United States had committed itself in the second Open Door note to defend the territorial integrity of China. The American declaration, it was said, had prevented the other powers from going on to divide China among themselves once Peking had been occupied and the diplomats in the legations freed.

People who knew better, such as the State Department's China expert William W. Rockhill, encouraged the growth of this myth as a means of expanding America's role in the Asian balance of power. Soon the myth came to have a life of its own. Since the United States never did take a sphere for itself, and even went on to return to China a large part of the Boxer indemnity for use as a scholarship fund to educate Chinese students in American colleges, Americans came to see their country as China's special friend and protector among the Western powers.

Although not absolute nonsense, this image grossly exaggerated the reality of Sino-American relations. China escaped even greater dismemberment in 1900 primarily because the logistics were too complicated for the Europeans to manage. Governing all of China was beyond their capacities; they did not want to fight a war with each other over the division of spoils; and so, in the circumstances, continuing to operate through the central government of China remained the cheapest way to exploit the country.

For that matter, America's own commitment to the Open Door, while doubtless better from the Chinese perspective than a policy of seizing spheres, was hardly the disinterested act that the myth suggests. Given small American trade and limited American military and naval power, it suited the nation's interests to make as small a governmental commitment there as possible.

An open door for commerce and missionaries gave Americans everything they really needed at the lowest possible cost. Even the scholarship fund to educate Chinese youths in American colleges was less than perfect altruism. It was, among other things, an act of perhaps unconscious cultural imperialism: an attempt to entice and possibly bind the next generation of Chinese intellectuals and professionals to the United States and the American models they would learn there.

The diplomatic historians of a generation ago overlooked the shrewdness of the Open Door and concentrated instead upon the elements of mythology and bluff in the policy. Preoccupied with the idea of containment—both that of Japan and Germany in the 1930s and that of Russia and the People's Republic of China in the 1940s and 1950s—they criticized the mythologized Open Door policy for promising something the United States could not deliver: namely, a defense of China's territorial integrity and the containment of Western and Japanese aggression in China.

This critique underlay A. Whitney Griswold's contention in *The Far Eastern Policy of the United States,* still one of the most influential books on the subject, that American relations with China have been characterized by repeated cycles of assertiveness and withdrawal. Griswold's interpretation, in turn, influenced George F. Kennan's widely read study *American Diplomacy, 1900–1950* and Tang Tsou's *America's Failure in China, 1941–1950.* They agreed that the Open Door, unprofessional and unrealistic, had introduced into American China policy a chronic disparity between ends and means.

More recently, a new generation of historians has argued that the Open Door policy was a shrewd and realistic way to develop a form of imperial expansion that would be cost-effective for the United States. As a rising industrial power allegedly afflicted with overproduction and probably the world's greatest producer of agricultural surpluses, they argued, what the United States needed most from the rest of the world was markets—primarily for its economic output but also for its political and religious culture. Since the United States was a second-rate military and naval power until the eve of World War I, it was impractical to compete with the European empires for the conquest of colonies in which to develop these markets; and since most colonies lost money on a strictly governmental basis, it wasn't even good economics to develop a colonial empire. So an open door to trade and evangelization, with someone else paying the bills of government and taking the responsibility for keeping order, was the ideal setting for American expansion. This is what William Appleman Williams in *The Tragedy of American Diplomacy* called "imperial anti-colonialism."

Williams and his followers, in what is known as the Wisconsin school of diplomatic historians, contend that the Open Door notes in China arose from a specific historical situation but transcended it—that the notes articulate a broader American approach to the world and, for this reason, point to a concept or interpretive device that one can use to help understand generally American expansionism.

The Open Door has thus come a long way from its beginnings in the evolution under pressure of a long-standing Western tactic for dealing with China. The notion of an "Open Door empire" suggests, among other things, the degree to which twentieth-century America is the successor to nineteenth-century Britain as the leader of the Western challenge to East Asia. For what is "imperial anti-colonialism" if not a variant on what John Gallagher and Ronald Robinson, referring to mid-nineteenth-century British expansionism, termed "the imperialism of free trade"?

This debate among historians is instructive. It reminds us that nations with comparative economic advantage can afford to advocate an open world trading community. The imperial metaphor does scant justice, however, to the realities of the period 1898–1900, when the Open Door originally took shape as an ingenious and rather desperate response to a nation's military weakness and an administration's political vulnerability.

(10)

The U.S. and the Emergence
of Imperial Japan

JAPAN'S EMERGENCE as a regional power was slow but steady, almost as if planned. But the leaders of the Meiji government had no long-range blueprint; rather they saw themselves as simply struggling for the survival of their nation in a predatory nineteenth-century world. Their aims, at first extremely modest, expanded only with their successes. The tragedy of Japan's rise to power was that the success was so great that the aims swelled to unwieldy proportions. But in the early decades of the Meiji period (1868–1912), cool rationality prevailed; the chauvinists, the adventurers, were kept firmly in check. The Japanese risked little and gained much.

As early as 1871, the government's chief diplomatic aim was to amend (and eventually terminate) the unequal treaties. Not only were they viewed as a national humiliation, for the Japanese had learned that such relationships characterized European agreements only with states which they regarded as backward and inferior, but also there was the practical matter of the tariff. The low fixed tariff on imported goods not only laid bare Japan's infant industries to foreign competition but also limited the amount of governmental income which could be realized from customs revenues. Money as well as face was at stake.

The Japanese were quick to catch on to what "international" law, as defined by the Western powers, was all about; although that world was certainly very different from the Confucian order Japan had previously known. The Japanese busily translated and pored over Western legal texts and avidly sought out the wisdom of Western legal experts.

"Sent by God to help the Japanese" was one description of the

134

big and burly Vermont lawyer Henry Willard Denison, adviser and treaty drafter for the Foreign Ministry for nearly two generations (1880–1914). Denison was one of the least known but most influential of all foreign advisers to the Japanese government. Much of the diplomatic paper of the Meiji period reflects his hand. A private man, self-effacing and discreet, he was cherished by his associates, who were deeply impressed by his knowledge, his loyalty, and his passion for verbal craftsmanship. Denison drew the Ministry toward the Anglo-American standard of diplomatic practice, and his influence is one reason why so many Japanese diplomats consistently tried to maintain cordial relations with the Western maritime democracies when other segments of the Japanese government had grown hostile.

In retrospect, what the Japanese were able to accomplish during this era of national weakness, which lasted at least until the first war with China (1894–1895), is remarkable. Not only did they win agreement (1894) from the Western powers to amend the unequal treaties, but they were also able, largely through adept diplomatic maneuver, to round out and rationalize their geographical frontiers. They were quick learners.

To establish a buffer zone around the central Japanese islands, the Bonins, the Ryukyus, and the Kurils were annexed. These chains shielded the homeland from the eastern, southern, and northern approaches. The Japanese simply took over the Bonins and colonized them; the Kurils they got from the Tsarist government by ceding to Russia their interest in Sakhalin. The Ryukyus were a more complicated matter. These islands, culturally akin to Japan, enjoyed a fair measure of independence while giving allegiance simultaneously to China and to the lord of Satsuma. Acceptable though this arrangement might have been in the Confucian tributary system, it would not wash in the new Western international world.

When the Japanese mounted a punitive mission to Taiwan (Formosa) in 1874 in order to avenge the death of some unfortunate Ryukyuan sailors, they assumed a protective role and established the beginnings of a legal foothold in these strategic islands. Ultimately the Chinese were entirely excluded from any rights of sovereignty, and the Japanese absorbed the Ryukyus. The Formosan expedition also served to illustrate Japan's embarrassing maritime weakness. The Japanese were obliged to rely upon chartered foreign shipping to ferry their troops overseas.

Japan expressed similar interest in the Korean peninsula, long a tributary state of China, closed to all but Chinese contact prior to 1876. In that year, Japanese warships approached the island of Kanghwa, and Japanese diplomats forced the Koreans to sign a treaty covering diplomatic, consular, and commercial relations. The treaty challenged China's exclusive suzerainty over Korea and set into motion a Sino-Japanese rivalry for influence in the Korean court, which was settled only after China's defeat in the Sino-Japanese War two decades later, and ultimately by Japan's annexation of Korea in 1910.

Along with the diplomacy of securing the oceanic frontiers during the 1870s, '80s, and early '90s, the Japanese regularly put substantial sums into weaponry, the creating of a modern army and navy. They lacked the resources to build very heavily, and the armed forces remained modest in size. Although this seemed a hardship at the time, in the long run it was probably just as well, because military technology was changing so rapidly. A race was on between guns and armor. In shipbuilding, iron was giving way to steel; in ship propulsion, coal would soon yield to oil. The most powerful (and expensive) warship could become obsolescent soon after it slid down the ways. The times were good for letting others take the lead, because in the relatively open world of the late nineteenth century, technical information, even of a military nature, could generally be purchased.

Although the American naval officer Alfred Thayer Mahan wrote principally about Great Britain's maritime empire, his arguments seemed equally applicable to Japan, an island monarchy lying off the shores of the great Eurasian land mass. Mahan urged an aggressive rather than a defensive strategy, and he was convinced of the value of the battle fleet over commerce raiders, laying down the argument for what would emerge in the new century as a commitment to the dreadnought, the all-big-gun battleship, by the world's leading naval powers. At the time, Mahan was certainly one of the major intellectual American influences upon the Japanese.

Rivalry over Korea, the last of Confucian China's satellite states, led Japan and China to fight each other in 1894; for as the Japanese began to gain in self-confidence, the idea of Korea in potentially hostile hands was intolerable to contemplate.

In the war, which lasted only a few months, the Chinese were still using foreign military advisers. Their principal fleet was for all practical purposes commanded by a Prussian artillery specialist; and an American adventurer, an Annapolis graduate named Philo McGiffin, made himself conspicuous. Although the Japanese were still obliged to get all their larger warships from foreign yards, they were deploying them with no outside help.

Japan triumphed both on land and at sea, to the astonishment of virtually all onlookers, and the delight of most Americans. It was David against Goliath: Americans viewed the Japanese as embodying Yankee skill and energy in defeating backward, slothful, obscurantist China. The success of Japan's modernizing contrasted sharply with the spectacular failure of imperial China.

The most serious consequence of the war was the strong physical, financial, and psychological impetus it gave to Japanese empire building, to continental adventure. The large indemnity extracted from the Chinese seemed to mean that war in modern times paid—handsomely. Japan won all the rights enjoyed by the Western powers in China, becoming the first non-Western imperialist power. The Japanese annexed lush, undeveloped Formosa and its neighboring Pescadores (Penghu) Islands; and although they did not yet secure a toehold on the Asian mainland, they tried to do so on the Liaotung (Liaodong) Peninsula, where the important fortress and naval base of Port Arthur commanded the seaward approaches to Peking. Russia, France, and Germany, acting together in the Triple Intervention, forced Japan to relinquish Liaotung, to the rage and humiliation of the Japanese. Here was one seed of future conflict. Another was that the war intimately intermeshed the Japanese with the volatile politics of Korea, where, although China was now gone, Russia intrigued.

During the Boxer Rebellion, Japan intervened along with the Western powers and acted like a Western power, except that the Japanese soldiers did not loot. Their well-disciplined behavior was exemplary. Nearly half (8,000) of the rescue force (17,000) sent to Peking was Japanese.

For the United States in East Asia, the Open Door episode had been a turning point. In the decade after it, the outline of modern American–East Asian relations first became evident. For roughly the next half century, the principal encounter between East and West was to take place across the Pacific Ocean, involving the United States, Japan, and China. In that encounter, the United States, economically and militarily the most powerful nation in the Pacific world, characteristically poised itself between the real and present strength of Japan on the one hand, and the enormous but unrealized potential of China on the other. From time to time, America allied itself openly with one of them against the other, always faintly aware of the threatening possibility that someday they might ally with each other against the United States.

As recently as the late nineteenth century, this would have been an unimaginable pattern. Then the United States was a minor participant on the periphery of a great cultural collision between West European and East Asian civilizations. By the late 1890s, with the treaty system in place and the new European spheres of interest proliferating throughout China, it appeared that Europe had won this struggle for mastery and added China to its imperial system. The United States, for all its talk of a westward course of empire and a special need for China's markets, was reduced to issuing Open Door notes asking other nations to allow America equal commercial access to their parts of China. And Japan, which by its defeat of China in 1895 had initiated the competition for spheres, was confined still to island East Asia and the Korean peninsula. The main arteries of the East-West encounter remained the Sino-Russian land frontier and the British maritime route through the Indian Ocean. The Pacific was little more than a backwater, although Americans scarcely saw it as such.

The European position in China at that point looked stronger than it really was. The fleets and spheres of interest in East Asia were geographically the outermost extensions of European power; and both technologically and strategically there was a low ceiling to the commitment that any European nation could make halfway around the world. Not only was it costly, cumbersome, and risky to project power across such distances—with long and vulnerable lines of communication—but other places closer to home mattered more.

The Europeans, for all their panoply of power, simply did not have the strength either to govern China directly or to fight it out with each other for control there; nor, it seems, did they have the will. Even granting their technological and economic superiority, their success in China during the nineteenth century had depended upon two prerequisites. The first of these was the existence of a Chinese central government weak enough to be compliant to foreign demands but powerful enough to keep internal order without European garrisons. The second was the coordination of European power and policies, most of the time behind the lead of Great Britain.

By the turn of the century, neither of these could be taken for granted any longer. The Chinese imperial government, though more resilient than many contemporaries thought, was clearly tottering toward its fall; and in the offing there were nationalistic movements unsympathetic to special treatment for foreigners. Meanwhile, the age of British hegemony was passing. Seen in this light, the competition for spheres of interest, which looks like the culmination of European imperial aggression in China, was really the beginning of the end.

This passing of the European moment of ascendancy in East Asia was only starting at the turn of the century; full fruition came well after World War I, when the Europeans had exhausted themselves fighting each other on their home ground. Britain remained the leading foreign economic power in China—with, elsewhere in the region, the massive Dutch economic presence in what is now Indonesia and the French presence in the states of Indochina—until World War II ended the old order forever.

But decades before that, a power vacuum was beginning to open up in East Asia as the Ch'ing dynasty and British naval and mercantile supremacy started to weaken. Into this vacuum there moved three new powers: the rising empires of the United States and Japan, and China itself, which slowly and falteringly reclaimed its rightful role as one of the major participants rather than simply the object of the East-West encounter.

For Japan, the year 1902 and the signing of an alliance with Great Britain, the first such agreement on the basis of equality between a Western and a non-Western state, marked a real coming of age. The alliance made it possible for the Japanese to fight the Russians, knowing that if they did so and if another power were to join in to help the Russians the British would fight alongside the Japanese. Japan would not again be stripped of the spoils of victory. No Triple Intervention would be possible.

The Russo-Japanese War (1904–1905) has been upstaged by the cataclysmic World War I which followed so soon, but its intrinsic importance was very great, generating at the time a lot of literature—both eyewitness accounts and works of analysis. "A classic example of a conflict waged for purely imperialistic motives," William L. Langer later called the war. Neither of the belligerents, Japan or Russia, suffered the tread of an enemy foot; the combat ground was Korean or Chinese; and for the Koreans it was, of course, the second time in a decade they had to endure such an experience.

" 'Jap' the Giant Killer," as *Punch* put it, was again triumphant. The white man lost, which startled everyone, pleasing colonial peoples everywhere and imparting a global significance to the war. What Indian historian K. M. Panikkar has labeled "the Vasco da Gama era of world history" was brought to an end.

For Russia, war and defeat incited revolution, from which the regime recovered only with difficulty and temporarily. Military failure cut at the very core of Tsardom, for that regime had justified its harsh repressive character as the necessary cost for building a powerful military machine. A multinational empire was weakened; Poles and Finns hoped that they perceived imperial disintegration on the horizon.

For Great Britain, the later historian can see that Japan's annihilation of the Russian fleet at Tsushima Strait (1905) finished an era of global naval supremacy that started with Nelson's triumph at Trafalgar (1805). Japan would now assume the place of premier naval power in the western Pacific as Britain summoned home the scattered fleets, squadrons, and flotillas of the Royal Navy to guard against the growing German menace in the North Sea.

Japan, victorious but exhausted, had lacked the industrial or financial sinew to fight a protracted war or to pummel the Russians any more; but Japan now emerged a major power—not a great power, but a regional one. From the Russians Japan got southern Sakhalin, the Liaotung peninsula, control of the South Manchurian Railway, and a paramount position in Korea. In five years the Japanese would absorb Korea entirely, in an action which provoked not one protest anywhere in the world. Japan had become an imperial presence upon the Asian mainland, sphere unclearly defined, with fateful consequences.

When power balances change this dramatically, there is a tremendous potential for violence. The rising and declining powers must either work out an accommodation such as the Anglo-Japanese Alliance of 1902 or fight, as in the Sino-Japanese War of 1894–1895 and the Russo-Japanese War ten years later.

The new power balance put the United States in an anomalous and quite vulnerable situation. By the beginning of this century, the United States was the world's leading industrial power and potentially its greatest military and naval power. Its merchants, investors, social critics, and strategic theorists were calling for the use of that power to assert an American national purpose and interest in Asia. Its President, Theodore Roosevelt, was emotionally attuned to doing this— not only because, as someone has said, he was only really happy when engaged in a fight, but also because he believed that a constructive world order could only be achieved through the responsible and active use of national power. (Needless to say, Roosevelt's sense of responsibility in the use of power was not everyone's; but there is no question as to the sincerity of his desire to do, as he repeatedly expressed it, "our share of the world's work.") Intellectually, emotionally, and economically, Americans were primed for their moment of emergence as a great power in the vacuum that was then beginning to appear in China.

But in reality, in the short run the United States was unable to realize its potential power in Asia. This was partly a question of political will. The combined effect of the Philippine-American war (with its shameful atrocities), the widely publicized misconduct of American troops and missionaries in China after the suppression of the Boxers, and the new anti-imperialism in the English-speaking world was to sour both Congress and the electorate toward any further interventions in Asia. All too often, it seemed, intervention in Asian affairs led to expenses, deaths, and atrocities out of all proportion to any benefits obtained. It was evident that Asia was a theater of imperialist competition and rivalry, in which there were few, if any, cheap or honorable gains to be had. Accordingly, there simply was no broad or deep constituency in domestic American politics to support aggressive new initiatives there by the American government.

Moreover, in the short run, even if there had been a constituency and a will, the power itself would still have been lacking. By the turn of the century, it is true, the shipbuilding programs of the late 1880s and the 1890s had begun to pay off; and the United States Navy was increasingly large, modern and powerful. It had a superficially impressive record in the Spanish-American War, although the decrepitude of the Spanish squadrons and the appalling marksmanship of the American warships at Santiago detracted from this upon closer examination.

For all its growth and improvement, it was a navy with a long way to go. When Theodore Roosevelt became President, the United States was still inferior in battleship tonnage not only to Britain and the leading European powers but even to Japan.

An even more serious problem—since, in fact, the fleet continued to grow and modernize, quickly passing Japan and eventually becoming second only to that of Great Britain—was the dilemma of how to divide American naval power between two coastlines. To avoid the possibility of a piecemeal defeat, prevailing naval doctrine in these years prescribed that the main battle fleet be concentrated either in the Atlantic or the Pacific, not divided between the two. Since American interests were much greater in the Atlantic and the Caribbean, the fleet was ordinarily concentrated on the east coast of the country, leaving only a token American naval presence in the Pacific.

The full magnitude of the embarrassment this could cause the United States became evident only in the Theodore Roosevelt years. Although people had always recognized that the Navy would be at a serious disadvantage fighting in the western Pacific, thousands of miles from its principal bases, this had not been thought an insurmountable problem.

The tactical plan was that after fighting a harassing and delaying action, the Pacific squadron would retire to a fortified anchorage somewhere—at the turn of the century it was not clear where this would be, since neither Pearl Harbor nor Subic Bay had been developed as a major base at that time—to await relief by the main battle fleet from the Atlantic. Japan's success during the Russo-Japanese War in destroying first a major fleet in its fortified base and then a major fleet brought in from the Atlantic to replace it ended that illusion forever.

As a result, in 1905, amid all the rhetoric of expectation and greatness, the United States Army formally reconciled itself to losing the Philippines in the event of a war with Japan; and in 1906, the Navy consolidated its battle fleet by transferring the last American battleship from the Pacific to the Caribbean. Staff work begun in these years led in 1907 to the original version of "War Plan Orange" (a none too subtle reference to Japan), postulating an essentially defensive American role in at least the opening phase of any war with an Asian power.

As far as the deployment of real power in the western Pacific was concerned, therefore, there was neither the will nor the way. This was an inherently frustrating situation: that is, to be committed, at least rhetorically, to the ends which the United States denied itself the means to realize. All the more so because in the meantime the other great rising imperial power in East Asia, Japan, was actually expanding.

Japan was moving politically and militarily into Formosa, Korea, and, following the Russo-Japanese War, Manchuria; while, at the same time, it was expanding commercially. Japanese emigrants were settling in places such as Hawaii, Brazil, Peru, Mexico, and the United States, places Japan did not aspire to invade or govern.

The official position in Japan was that these were two completely separate accounts. Territorial annexation of Korea and Formosa reflected strategic and defensive needs; Japan was frankly pre-empting these regions on grounds of national security. Economic and human expansion, on the other hand, was felt to be largely apolitical, a peaceful and constructive attempt to promote progress and prosperity through open competition with others in international trade. Consequently, Japanese reasoned, the targets of Japan's economic expansion ought not to feel threatened or attacked. All Japan wanted in Hawaii, the Philippines, and the United States was what Americans wanted in China, an open door.

From the American perspective, however, the Japanese desire was in fact profoundly threatening. The same country that was pre-empting parts of Asia territorially was now challenging the United States culturally and economically across the Pacific. Japanese even had their own millenarian mythology to counteract the American talk of a westward course of empire. In the Japanese version, the original seat of civilization had been in Armenia and Persia. From there *two* streams of culture had flowed out in opposite directions: one culminating in what Uchimura Kanzo called "democratic, aggressive, inductive America" and the other in "imperial, conservative, deductive China."

> Grander tasks await the young Japan who has the best of Europe and the best of Asia at her command. At her touch the circuit is completed, and the healthy fluid shall overflow the earth.

To Americans, this was a completely alien, almost literally unthinkable concept. Nothing in the history of American thought or life had prepared them for the idea that Asian civilization might be the culmination of the human experience and that Asia might advance *eastward* across the Pacific to deal with the United States on *its* terms.

This was not just a rhetorical abstraction. Beginning in the 1890s, the waves of expansion radiating outward from the United States and Japan began to intersect each other at various points in the Pacific. When local American whites overthrew the Hawaiian queen in 1893 and set up an independent government of their own, for example, they felt it necessary, in order to protect and consolidate their rule, to restrict future Japanese immigration.

When the Japanese government, in turn, protested this by sending a cruiser, the McKinley administration responded by setting in motion the wheels that eventually led to formal American annexation of Hawaii in 1898. In the Philippines, as we have seen, Americans thought explicitly that if they did not annex the archipelago Japan might do so instead.

This is one of the reasons for the emergence of opposition to Japanese immigration in California at just this moment. Hostility to the Japanese rose contrapuntally as animosity toward the Chinese continued its relative decline. As in the case of the Chinese, part of the opposition was blatantly racist and part was based on misguided fears of economic competition.

The timing and rhetoric of the anti-Japanese movement suggest, however, that there was another dimension as well. Japanese first came to California in significant numbers as part of the broader pattern of expansion just described. But unlike the nineteenth-century Chinese, they came with the approval of their government; for California was one of the target areas of Japan's commercial and human expansion.

Americans refused to recognize the distinction Japanese made between economic and political expansion. They had resisted that expansion in peripheral places such as Hawaii and the Philippines, and they found it particularly threatening and offensive in their homeland. The subsequent limitations and prohibitions upon Japanese immigration, naturalization, and landholding, the boycotts, school segregation, and also personal violence against Japanese, reflected not only racism and economic anxiety but also Americans' traumatic psychological confrontation with the reality of Japanese power. The fears thus aroused at the beginning of the century culminated in the Immigration Act of 1924—which the Japanese deeply resented—denying Asians the right to enter this country and become citizens.

People who had thought of themselves as part of the cutting edge of history now found themselves challenged in a way and from a direction they had never imagined. The greater intrinsic power of the United States notwithstanding, Japan seemed to be realizing its potential as a great power in the Pacific ahead of the United States. For all the pretentious rhetoric of American expansion, *vulnerability* was for a while one of the key concerns of those Americans who actually faced outward across the Pacific.

This evolution of attitudes toward Japanese immigration closely paralleled a shift in the general American outlook toward Japan itself. During the late nineteenth century, there had been widespread admiration for Japanese modernization. Particularly by comparison with China, Japan looked like a model student. Even some European nations paled by comparison. During the Russo-Japanese War of 1904–1905, public opinion in the United States identified Japan as modern and progressive, Russia as decadent and barbarous.

But as Japanese military and naval power continued to grow, a counterimage started to emerge. There was increasing talk of Japanese militarism, warnings that the industrial and military technology of the West was being grafted onto an indigenous and very dangerous body of Asian values and mores. Even so relatively well informed and sympathetic an observer as Theodore Roosevelt began to speak ambivalently about the social and political effects of what he called the "samurai tradition"—and to speculate that in Japan Westernization was only a thin veneer over warlike values that, one suspects, both thrilled and repelled him.

Americans' ambivalence toward the emergence of Japanese military and naval power shows clearly in the attitudes of the war correspondents covering the Russo-Japanese War. Most coverage of the war was favorable to Japan. The courage, efficiency, and intelligence of the Japanese at every level contrasted dramatically with the corruption and incompetence of the Russian command and the confusion of Russian troops. Personally, however, some of the correspondents found Japan's victory over a white enemy very disturbing. Their own peripheral, almost parasitical role and their dependence upon the Japanese command for information and permission to move about intensified this reaction. Willard Straight, who became one of the architects of America's East Asian policy during the Taft administration, was a reporter for Reuters during the war. "For no particular reason," he wrote to a friend in 1904, "with no real cause for complaint I now find myself hating the Japanese more than anything in the World. It is due I presume to the constant strain of having to be polite and to seek favors from the yellow people." By the following year, the strain had become even worse. "The Japanese," he wrote, ". . . certainly seem very much less human than others. One cannot feel the individuality of the men themselves. . . . [Russians] are white, and that means much. . . . One recognizes him [a Russian] as a man, and the Japanese will have to change a good deal before they cease to cause one to look for the tail."

The Japanese, for their part, found Americans at least as aggressive and offensive as Americans found them—and, in many cases, for better reasons. From Japan's perspective, the American annexation of Hawaii and the Philippines was not a defensive response to Japanese expansionism but an egregious expression of a new American imperialism. That expansion violated what had seemed to the Japanese an implicit understanding that the two nations would behave differently from the Europeans in the Pacific expanses that lay between them, competing for economic advantage but not territorial domination. Feeling disappointed, even betrayed, Japanese leaders began to alter their evaluation of America, seeing it more and more as a political and territorial rival, one more Western imperialist interloper in Asia.

Beyond this, the Japanese public reacted very angrily to the American-mediated peace that ended the Russo-Japanese War. This was the treaty for which Theodore Roosevelt subsequently won a Nobel Prize. Genuinely desirous of peace, Roosevelt was nevertheless distinctly pro-Japanese; and Prime Minister Katsura Taro understood this. Both governments were aware that, although victorious, Japan was financially and militarily overextended and needed an early end to the war.

For his part, Roosevelt hoped that a peace that consolidated Japan's rule in Korea and its influence in southern Manchuria would draw Japan's expansionist energies onto continental northeastern Asia and divert the Japanese from the sensitive Pacific islands. Faced with an almost intransigent Russian delegation, Japan bowed to Roosevelt's counsel and compromised on a moderate territorial settlement without financial indemnity. Although this was not a bone of contention between the two governments, it did produce rioting in the streets of Tokyo, the alienation of some elements in the Japanese military establishment, and the fall of Katsura's ministry. As the sponsor of the peace talks, the United States was blamed by many Japanese for depriving them of the fruits of victory.

And discrimination against Japanese immigrants in California would continue to irritate relations between the two countries. All Japanese, even those who privately criticized the conduct of their countrymen abroad, resented the racism underlying their treatment.

During the first decade of the twentieth century, in sum, the strains of big power rivalry, exacerbated by racial tensions, visibly eroded the established framework of cooperative relations between the United States and Japan. Nevertheless, the growth of hostility between the two nations was held in check. There were several reasons for this.

One reason was that officials in both governments saw greater advantages in preserving Japanese-American friendship than in allowing the incipient drift toward antagonism to gain momentum. Both countries were still testing their wings in the geopolitics of Asia and the Pacific, and each found the good will of the other a useful support. Japan, for example, financed much of its war with Russia in American investment markets and relied on Theodore Roosevelt to help arrange a settlement before its own exhaustion and Russia's deep reservoir of reserves could compromise its success. The United States, for its part, remained acutely conscious of its strategic weakness in Asia and its need there for allies with real power. With Britain withdrawing from the region, Japan was the most attractive and credible Asian ally available, much preferable to Russia, for example. So there were important strategic considerations that argued for continued harmony. To this end, the Taft-Katsura conversations of 1905 and the Root-Takahira agreement of 1908 pledged the two nations to respect each other's interests in Korea and the Philippines.

Then, too, Japan and America were economically compatible. The United States was Japan's largest single export market; and although Japan was nowhere near as valuable to the United States, it was much the most important part of Asia both for American exports and for American investments. By the time of World War I, Japanese-American trade was more than twice as valuable as Sino-American trade, and American investments in Japan were 38 percent greater than in China. This mutually beneficial economic relationship served as a cushion that absorbed other types of tension or hostility.

Finally, both governments realized that there were constructive alternatives to the confrontation then emerging between them in the Pacific. America could cultivate its own garden—its vast domestic market, particularly in the rising cities of the era, and the rich opportunities in its new possessions—and Japan could direct its expansion onto the Asian mainland, away from California and the American islands.

(11)

The Path to Catastrophe

THE STRUCTURE OF ACCOMMODATION—which on the American side was largely the work of Theodore Roosevelt and his second Secretary of State, Elihu Root—was, in a way, a success. It bought time in which the United States and Japan could adapt to their new relationship. But it was too precarious to last for long.

One of the crucial underlying assumptions of the accommodation was that the China market was potentially big enough for everybody. Americans and Japanese would not have to play tit for tat on the islands and peninsulas of the Pacific or race each other to divide China, because there would be profits enough for everyone in the open door exploitation of the China market. This simply did not turn out to be true.

After a brief flurry during the Russo-Japanese War, American exports to China actually declined, until by 1910 they were down to less than 1 percent of total American exports. Japanese exports to China also declined, though not as steeply. They lost about 15 percent in value between 1905 and 1908. More important from the Japanese perspective were the successes of Chinese merchants and Chinese political endeavors in frustrating Japan's plans to develop a Manchurian sphere with Japanese immigrants. The absence of a China payoff in the short run for either Japan or America undermined relations between the two nations. Each blamed the other for at least some of its difficulties.

Japanese and Americans both assumed that China was an object with little or no initiative, which could be used, even manipulated, by dynamic outsiders with only minimal attention to whatever the Chinese may have wanted. The rise of nationalism in China invalidated this assumption. One symptom of changing China was the growth of anti-foreign movements, such as the 1905 boycott of American products and the 1908 boycott against the Japanese. Such movements contested the initiative of foreigners and to some degree constrained them and damaged their interests. A second symptom was the power of Chinese nationalists, often used inadvertently, to generate competition between Japanese and Americans for cultural and ideological influence over their nationalistic movement.

Many Japanese saw in the revitalization of China an opportunity to assert their cultural leadership in the Asian world; some drew analogies between Japan at that moment and the role of Greece in the Mediterranean world after its defeat of Persia. Here lay the roots of the Pan-Asianism which would in the 1930s find expression in the Greater East Asia Co-Prosperity Sphere, which was more than merely a Japanese rationalization. Many Asians, particularly young people, found themselves drawn to the ideal of a resurgent Asian civilization, guided by the one Asian nation that had proven itself to be an equal in war and in commercial competition with both traditional China and nations of the West.

Japan's aspirations in this respect conflicted with the American pretension to lead a westward course of empire and transmit Western virtues to the East. This idea was surprisingly important to Americans of the time, even those who—having never heard of the westward course of empire and being, therefore, unaware of their intellectual roots—would have used quite different terms to describe the idea. Not only did this seem good business, since presumably a Westernized China would be a better trading partner; it also struck many of them as something that involved survival in cultural competition. For those who feared that Japan had grafted Western technology onto Eastern values to produce a modern savagery, China was the last chance: an opportunity to start over again and do the job right, with the largest and potentially the richest and most powerful of all Asian countries as the subject. The birth of a modern republican China offered Americans an opportunity to transmit not just technical know-how but republicanism, liberalism, and what they—in their pre-Vietnam War innocence—would have called a Christian respect for the value of human life and the integrity of the individual. To enlist American support against Japan and other potential aggressors, Chinese leaders such as Yuan Shih-k'ai (Yuan Shikai), the warlord-president in the first years after the overthrow of the dynasty in 1911, often encouraged such ideas and so later did Chiang Kai-shek. But it is most unlikely that the Chinese believed any of it themselves.

China's new condition had enduring historical significance. For out of the combination of economic frustration, cultural anxiety, and geopolitical vulnerability there emerged the formulation—which lasted through World War II—that American *expansionism* and Chinese *nationalism* could fuse symbiotically to protect the interests of both countries and the future of civilization against Japanese imperialism. Needless to say, this greatly embittered Japanese-American relations.

Probably the greatest blow to the early-twentieth-century structure of accommodation, however, was the change of political leadership in the United States. Theodore Roosevelt and Elihu Root had understood the limitations of their deployable power and had responded to this geopolitically by placating Japan at the expense of China. This was the only realistic way to adapt American policies to the real balance of military, naval, and economic power in East Asia. Even during Roosevelt's own administration, however, this was severely criticized by younger foreign service officers such as Willard Straight and F. M. Huntington Wilson as an abdication of American responsibilities and a misreading of the future of Asia.

Roosevelt's successors, William Howard Taft and Woodrow Wilson, took their cue from his critics and denounced the realism of the Root-Takahira agreement as cynical and immoral. Their orientation was moralistic and economic rather than geopolitical. From that perspective, Japanese expansionism on the continent—specifically the annexation of Korea, the formalization of a sphere in Manchuria, and, later, the seizure of Germany's former sphere in Shantung during World War I, and the Twenty-One Demands made by Japan upon China in 1915—was both immoral and threatening to American economic interests.

So beginning in 1909, American policy toward Japan began to stiffen and become somewhat self-righteously judgmental, while American policy toward China became much more supportive and solicitous. This was a shift that made sense to the new architects of America's East Asian policy. The great stakes were now in China, they argued. It was too late to do much with Japan, and the United States should reorient its policy to the new reality and opportunity. The problem with this approach was that in the short run the only country in Asia whose trade really mattered or whose power could really hurt the United States was Japan.

American historians traditionally, and with reason, have distinguished the "dollar diplomacy" of William Howard Taft from the "missionary" or "moralistic" diplomacy of Woodrow Wilson. The fact is, however, that the world view of these two presidents was much closer in substance than their rhetoric suggested. The crucial distinction was that between them and their predecessor, Roosevelt.

In elevating economic interests and moral principles (theirs, not necessarily those of others then or later) above the pragmatism of geopolitics, Taft and Wilson shared a conviction that America's economic and ideological expansion would benefit the world, not just their country. Taft, it is true, emphasized commerce and foreign investment. In doing so, however, he sought more than simply profits. Like generations of Americans before him, he believed that honest trade was mutually beneficial and that the development of backward regions—their integration into the international economy dominated by industrial nations like his own—promoted progress. He literally could not imagine prosperity and republican self-government in Africa, Asia, and Latin America without large-scale intervention by the private sector of the developed economies. In explaining the principles of dollar diplomacy, he liked to make the point that dollars were more constructive instruments of American foreign policy than bullets.

Wilson preferred to emphasize morality and ideology. Peace, democracy, national self-determination, the fulfillment of God's will were his themes, not trade and investment per se. In practice, however, Wilson felt that America could meet its responsibilities to promote these goals only if its economy flourished; and, like Taft, he considered American economic penetration of less developed parts of the world a force for liberalization and modernization. The concept of a peaceful, orderly, liberal, and open world informing both his Fourteen Points and his blueprints for the League of Nations served, among other things, to outline an ideal economic environment for America's bankers and industrialists, now the most powerful in the world. It was "imperial anti-colonialism" and the "imperialism of free trade" all over again. Tactical differences notwithstanding, the Wilsonian vision of the world came to much the same thing as Taft's dollar diplomacy.

The crucial point is that while Theodore Roosevelt has richly earned a reputation for brandishing—and, in the case of Panama, using—a big stick, his conception of America's role in the world was significantly more discreet and self-denying than that of his successors. Conscious of his own and the country's limitations, Roosevelt respected the pluralism, the heterogeneity, of the world. He never dreamed, even in his most bullying and arrogant moments, that it could be made over in America's image. Not in his own lifetime. Taft and Wilson, taking a nominally loftier view of the possibilities of American foreign relations, imagined responsibilities that obscured the real distinction between American national interests, as perceived at the moment, and the progressive well-being of the world. In the process, the pluralism of Roosevelt's era gave way to a new sense of the universal applicability of American values.

This in turn led to an interventionist mentality more grandiose and self-righteous than anything that had preceded it. The imperialists of 1898 had lived in a world of checks and balances. Other powerful nations, along with a certain lingering ambivalence, had restricted their freedom of action. The moralists of two decades later, living in by far the richest and most powerful nation in the world, presumed a global sanction that justified intervention almost anyplace.

During the transition to this new attitude, the thrust of American relations with East Asia faltered. There were numerous false starts, such as the on-again, off-again support of the government for American railroad and lending projects in China; hints of confrontation, as in Wilson's personal decision to denounce Japan's Twenty-One Demands; and increasingly ambiguous and tortured rephrasings of the open door philosophy and the Root-Takahira allocation of spheres, as in the Lansing-Ishii agreement of 1917.

For as long as the United States remained only potentially a real power in Asia, the new rhetoric proved both ludicrous and highly dysfunctional. Without actually having sufficient weight behind it to accomplish anything tangible, it alienated Japan and misled the occasional Chinese statesman who took it seriously. The Twenty-One Demands were withdrawn, for example, not because of Wilson's wrath but because Japan's ally Britain objected and because there was domestic opposition within Japan itself.

By the end of World War I, however, the balance of forces foreshadowed at the turn of the century was finally coming into being. The

United States had become what it would remain for the next five or six decades—the greatest military, naval, and economic power in the world—and Japan had emerged as *regionally* the most powerful force in Asia. Outraged by the apparent failure of the Versailles Conference to obtain Japan's withdrawal from the former German sphere in Shantung, Chinese nationalists had held protest demonstrations in Peking in May 1919 in a portent of the stormy decade ahead.

To adapt to this new situation—and also to deal with the domestic political problems caused in many nations by debates over staggeringly expensive postwar naval budgets—the great powers, led by the United States, Britain, and Japan, met in Washington during the winter of 1921–1922. Although few foresaw it at the time, the outcome of the Washington Conference—the so-called Washington system of treaties to stabilize the arms race, to secure imperial possessions in Asia and the Pacific against each other, and to promote an open door for international trade in China—brought even closer the end of the European era in Asia.

Washington, and its London sequel (1930), may have successfully abated the costly arms race, but the conferences failed to bring any persisting sense of collective security. Many Japanese deeply regretted the loss of the Anglo-Japanese Alliance, now supplanted by the Washington agreements.

East Asia was still in upheaval, in large part because of Chinese nationalism, to which neither Japan nor America was prepared to accommodate fully. Each nation still suffered under the ethnocentric delusion that it alone was to be the savior of the Chinese. Yet the Chinese were "ingrates" in the eyes of Japanese and Americans both. To the American public in particular the Chinese revolution had gone sour. The Chinese seemed to persist in their failure to achieve a modern and efficient democratic political order, and the revolutionaries were speaking out in increasingly strident anti-Western tones. Chinese leaders, it appeared to Americans, had seriously compromised their ideals. Sun Yat-sen turned to the Soviet Union of V. I. Lenin for inspiration rather than to the America of Warren Gamaliel Harding. So China could not then capture the larger part of whatever good feelings Americans might have toward the people of East Asia.

While China receded in American favor, Japan gained, briefly, in a response which appeared almost rhythmical in its regularity. Japanese politics were changing, for the better it seemed to Western liberals. The apparatus of democracy put together by the Meiji constitution of 1889 was beginning to work. The Meiji oligarchs, one by one, inevitably dropped from the scene, leaving room for political parties and new power groups, such as urban salaried workers and businessmen, to come to the fore. As in America at the same time, the business of Japan seemed to be business.

After Washington, Japan voluntarily withdrew from the former German concession in Shantung Province and from Siberia, where it had sent an army during World War I. The Japanese parliament, the Diet, manifested greater self-confidence, even venturing to slash the military budget; and prime ministers were political party members with cabinets responsible to parliament. In 1925, all adult Japanese males became eligible to vote. Women with bobbed hair and lipstick, dancing the Charleston to the music of the Victrola, proclaimed a renewal of Japanese receptivity to the latest styles of America and Western Europe. "Cabaret culture," it was derisively called by disapproving older Japanese, who interpreted it as a sign of moral decay and the loss of good old values. Frothy and ephemeral, it carried a whiff of the feverish anxiety of Weimar Germany without Weimar's creative substance.

Frank Lloyd Wright's Imperial Hotel, completed in the early 1920s, provided a visual symbol of the growing cosmopolitanism of Tokyo. To the foreigner, it became Tokyo's best-known building. The Imperial, a bizarre architectural statement more Mayan than Japanese, became famous for successfully riding out the great earthquake of 1923 which leveled much of the Japanese capital. Wright, a collector of a huge number of hastily chosen Japanese woodblock prints (ukiyo-e), loudly proclaimed his debt to that artistic tradition, while not admitting any later influence of Japanese domestic architecture upon his work. He was too much of a nationalist—and egoist—for that. Wright saw himself entirely as the planter of modern architecture among the Japanese rather than the other way around.

Before the Pacific war—as the Japanese call that part of World War II in which they fought (apart from China)—Japan set the tempo and called the tune for relations with the United States. Japan acted; America reacted. America had been more satisfied with things as they were. Japan was not content; the Japanese were still looking for their "place in the sun." In the late 1920s, the spirit of the Washington

Conference faded and Japan became—in the American view—increasingly disruptive. Behind Japanese restlessness were two specific grievances: a resurgence of China under the Kuomintang (Guomindang), which endangered what Japan wanted there, and the effects of the world economic crisis.

With the death of Sun Yat-sen and the rise of Chiang Kai-shek, the Chinese revolution took on new form and showed new vitality. In fashioning a unified republican state, the Kuomintang seemed likely to be as successful as Sun Yat-sen had not. To the foreign powers with investments, concessions, and spheres of influence in China, Chiang's new power was threatening. Would foreigners be able to retain the privileges they were accustomed to enjoying? No power was more apprehensive than Japan. No power had such a large share of its imperial interests concentrated in China. For the Japanese the question was How far could they accommodate their desires to the demands of Chinese nationalism? And consistently they underestimated the strength of these demands.

At the same time, moving toward 1929, the world economic condition was not good. Japan depended more and more upon a healthy world market that would buy what Japanese factories made. For the vigorous and healthy pursuit of modern life, Japan's economy seemed to be increasingly precarious. The Japanese were a large, and multiplying, number of people, living on a narrow geographical and resource base, increasingly dependent upon the income from exports for survival. And in the years 1929–1931, the value of these exports plummeted by 50 percent, with a catastrophic impact on the lives of many Japanese. American women decided that in a depression silk stockings were a luxury. America slashed silk purchases; and in 1929 silk had been 83 percent of the total ($432 million) value of United States imports from Japan.

Japan had already, during the 1920s, suffered the lowest annual economic growth in its modern history. The Great Depression hit Japan as badly as any nation in the world; and, as elsewhere, it severely shook public confidence in capitalism, economic individualism, and parliamentary democracy. Even America, the great republic, embarked upon a new governmental policy of intervention in the economy which apprehensive critics charged was dangerous radicalism.

In bad times, people and nations look to their own interests. Many Japanese now felt that the world had shortchanged them; in the popular phrase of a later era, Japan was a "have-not nation." America and the Soviet Union had great land masses and huge resources; the Western European nations possessed their vast maritime empires. What did Japan have? Japan had arrived on the international scene too late to build an empire comparable to the others. And now foreign tariffs and foreign immigration laws reinforced the Japanese perception of the world as a cold and unfriendly place affording little room or comfort for Japan.

Americans, preoccupied by their own serious internal difficulties, were unconcerned about Japanese feelings. And they remained grossly ignorant of Japan, with little awareness of the major shifts in mood and policy taking place there. Cherry blossoms, Mount Fuji, and geisha were the unchanging American images. Few American newspapers retained correspondents in Tokyo, and among the usually young and inexperienced handful who reported from there, only one or two could speak or read any Japanese. What information was available to them was limited not only by their own lack of linguistic competence or knowledge of Japan, but also by Japanese unwillingness to provide it. Heavy censorship blanketed Japanese life just at the time Americans most badly needed the news.

Thus Americans back home had a very sparse diet of information. In the last months of peace, historian Ernest R. May concludes, the American public received no sense at all of what the Japanese were trying to convey—either of any desire to negotiate or warning of the limits beyond which Japan would not yield.

Parliamentary government in Japan began to disintegrate in the early 1930s. The public increasingly discredited the political parties as self-interested and corrupt. Violence erupted in public life, with "government by assassination" (the title of one of the few books in English on the subject, written by a British correspondent based in Tokyo) describing the spasmodic accretion of power by the military, particularly the Army, the most dynamic elite group in Japanese political life at that time. Japan's civil leaders seemed more and more reluctant to speak out against what was happening. And undoubtedly many Japanese were sympathetic to the trend of nativism, seeing the Army as the custodian of old values, of all that was pure in the Japanese tradition, of all that was imperiled by the changes of modern life.

Americans, knowing little of what was really going on, interpreted

Japan as having fallen into the hands of right-wing fanatics, of having become, like Germany or Italy, a totalitarian fascist state, bent on national expansion at all costs. Americans could therefore dismiss Japan as a nation gone amok, beyond reason, therefore beyond understanding. American historians of Japan are much more inclined to regard this period as an aberration in Japanese history than Japanese are, and more inclined to make moral judgments. What the Japanese are now apt to look back upon as folly, the Americans see as vice.

For Japan, policies of state in the 1930s and early 1940s proved as disastrous as those of the Meiji had been successful. The scale was larger but the intent perhaps not so different: the achievement of the independence and security worthy of a great power. Yet unlike many other nations at the time, Japan did not slip into dictatorship. No charismatic leader or monolithic political force emerged. No revolutionary mass party surged forward to grasp power. There was no Hitler and there were no Nazis. Even the Army and the Navy, holding more power than anyone else, disliking and distrusting each other more and more, were torn within by disputes, schisms, and factions.

No single dramatic incident catapulted Japan into a new political pattern; rather, it all happened by seemingly inexorable drift. Decision-making blurred and became more complex, more Japanese, one might say, a happening entirely in tune with the swing toward nativism pushed by the Army. The supple Meiji constitution remained the letter of the law, and represented the continuity of the formal government.

But the voice of the people was no longer heard in the way it had been in the 1920s. Real power fell increasingly into the hands of middle-level bureaucrats and officers. The military enjoyed and exploited their right of direct access to the throne and were in a favorable position to advise (and manipulate) the Emperor. The military exercised leverage over the Prime Minister and his cabinet through their power to refuse to supply their members to serve as Army Minister or Navy Minister. Without military support, a cabinet could not survive, a Prime Minister could not serve.

In 1931, after provoking an incident involving a railway explosion at Mukden (Shenyang) the Japanese Kwantung Army moved in force into the hitherto Chinese-occupied portions of Manchuria. In little more than three months Manchuria was Japanese; the Chinese hardly resisted. But Tokyo was left to make whatever explanations it could to whomever questioned the Army's action.

Storms of foreign criticism rallied popular support to the Army; the Japanese simply waved the flag harder. "Asia for the Asiatics," they proclaimed as they attempted to put themselves at the lead of a Pan-Asian, anti-Western, anti-colonial movement. But the Japanese remained their own most ardent admirers; other Asians were skeptical of Japanese idealism, prone to lump Japanese together with Westerners as part of the imperialist world they sought to resist.

In the building of what came to be Japan's new empire, Manchuria was not only the initial but also the prize acquisition. As large as Germany and France combined, Manchuria was rich both in the quality of its soils, with the promise of bountiful harvests, and in what lay beneath the surface of the ground. Anthracite and iron ore were there conveniently next to each other and in quantities not to be found in the home islands.

In its undeveloped and underpopulated state, Manchuria was as vulnerable to aggressive neighbors as Hokkaido had been seventy years before. Until the twentieth century, the Manchus, not themselves an agricultural people, had preserved their homeland from dense settlement. Even during the twenty years after their regime had disappeared and Chinese farmers had streamed over the frontier to open up the land, there was space for many more. The Japanese had already heavily invested in fortifying and developing the Liaotung (Kwantung) area with its naval base of Port Arthur and its great commercial port of Dairen (Dalian) and the strategic South Manchurian Railway. They felt the urgency of moving in and establishing themselves throughout the whole province before the Chinese had fully absorbed their own "last frontier." Although historically Manchuria had been autonomous, the Chinese now regarded it as an integral part of China, the "Northeast," they called it. For the Japanese the area would provide "breathing room," and an increment of strength enabling Japan to face China and the Soviet Union with greater equanimity. Manchuria seemed to the Japanese both a natural adjunct to the industrial base of the home islands and a power vacuum inviting penetration.

"Manchukuo," as the Japanese called it, sprang formally into existence in March 1932. It was a fictional state, whose titular leader was the last Ch'ing monarch, a frail creature who, with his court ladies and eunuchs, had been trotted out to provide some shred of legitimacy to this Army-dominated Japanese enterprise. Some in Japan had grand notions of what might be accomplished there on the continent, a model state perhaps, a paradigm of what the Army could do, given a free hand, even in the homeland.

The Soviet Union, a glowering presence on the northern frontier, was still too weak to challenge the Japanese. The Western powers, following the lead of the self-righteous American Secretary of State Henry L. Stimson, withheld recognition of Japan's act. But none of them was prepared to do anything of substance to forestall the Japanese in such a remote (to them) part of the world. Anyway, Westerners were annoyed not about the Japanese being in Manchuria but with the blatantly aggressive manner in which they got there. It shattered the comfortable fictions of collective security and the maintenance of integrity in China which the Washington Conference had attempted to sustain.

The imperial Army sought to prepare for war on the Asian mainland: a continuing struggle with China, a possible conflict with the U.S.S.R. The imperial Navy faced the other way. Its vital interest in secure access to petroleum, plus the nation's need for other resources and minerals, such as rubber, bauxite, and tin, to be had in Southeast Asia, propelled the Navy southward toward the European colonial world and conflict with the maritime powers.

The two strategic objectives, continental and maritime, led Japan in opposite directions and were entirely unrealistic for a nation of Japan's power to cope with successfully. Japan went to war with the United States in 1941 without resolving the dilemma.

After 1931, the Japanese had a valuable new continental sphere to protect. To do so, they felt obliged to master the politically soft and inert northern provinces of China so that they could erect a strategic buffer between the Yangtze Valley, where the strength of the Chinese Nationalists centered, and Manchukuo. This activity led Japan in 1937 to all-out war with the Chinese: both Nationalists and Communists.

Although Japan's entry into the anti-Comintern Pact (1936) and the Tripartite Pact (1940) made the nation a member of the Axis with Germany and Italy, that disparate partnership remained a "hollow alliance," an arrangement of small substance. Japan stood essentially alone in world affairs.

Japanese Foreign Minister Matsuoka Yosuke's walk out of the League of Nations in 1933 simply illustrated the solitary path which Japan had already chosen. Chest-thumping ultranationalism and Shinto fanaticism, the side of Japanese national behavior foreigners disliked and feared most, flourished in the newly closed Japanese environment, causing Japan's psychic distance from the outside world to grow even wider, handicapping the Japanese from obtaining a true picture of the world and their place in it.

Japanese and Americans both suffered from ignorance of each other. The Japanese reassured one another that the Americans were self-indulgent and flabby, with no stomach for war; and too many Americans had only contempt for the Japanese, seeing them as toothy bespectacled caricatures adept only at aping other people and other cultures.

In China, after 1937, cheaply won early victories drew the Japanese on, sucking them into a quagmire from which ultimately they could not extricate themselves. The Kuomintang government lost its seaports, its manufacturing and commercial centers, its capital cities; but it staged a successful epic retreat deep into the fastnesses of the interior, where the full onslaught of Japanese power could not penetrate, and whence Chiang, his supporters, and the growing Communist movement under Mao Tse-tung could continue the struggle. The Japanese still hoped, with increasing anxiety, to persuade the Chinese to see reason—at best to capitulate, at least to negotiate. But the Chinese were stubborn, and the morass in which the Japanese were mired simply worsened.

As the economic and psychological investment which Japan put into the continent swelled, the possibility of extrication shrank. Even those Japanese who might have been willing to contemplate the nation's cutting its losses, ending the war, and pulling out of China recognized that the prestige of the Army was so committed to Manchukuo and its defense that any major continental withdrawal would trigger extraordinary violence and upheaval at home.

How then did the unfinished "China Incident" (as the Japanese called it) mushroom into the Pacific war? America and Japan were unable to separate out their differences from the maelstrom of tensions, rivalries, and conflicts besetting Europe and its empires. Both America and Japan had, during the late 1930s, bound themselves increasingly to Europe: Japan through its alliance with Germany and Italy, America with its ever-deepening informal ties with Great Britain. The Tripartite Pact of September 1940 may have been intended by the Japanese to discourage American entry into the war, but it had the opposite effect. To Americans, Nazism seemed thoroughly evil. Great Britain, in desperate struggle after the fall of France, was the only major power fighting Hitler, and many Americans were convinced that they could not allow the British to collapse.

In the American eye, Japan's choice of alliance with the Nazis, coupled with its growing intransigence in East Asia, made it an inevitable enemy. The Japanese were persuaded that Americans were committed to maintaining Western supremacy over Asia, tolerating European colonies but objecting to Japanese ones.

The Japanese believed they could not break the deadlock of the China war without moving south, severing China from sources of help and gaining control of more resources for themselves. But if they plunged ahead against the virtually defenseless European colonies, the Japanese risked American intervention. Every preliminary step they took provoked response, in what became a vicious circle of advance by the Japanese and reprisal by the Americans.

American diplomacy appeared inflexible. Secretary of State Cordell Hull, a former United States Senator from Tennessee, never troubled to conceal his dislike of the Japanese, and he piously lectured their envoys on the pursuit of morality and justice in international affairs. On specific issues, he was laconic and unbending.

Hence, the Japanese military concluded, with the concurrence of civil leadership, the time would never be better for violent and quick resolution of the issues. In this narrow sense, they were quite right.

(12)

Americans and the Chinese Revolution

WHILE JAPANESE AND AMERICANS moved slowly onto a collision course, one central reality with which both nations had to cope in the late nineteenth and early twentieth century was recurrent turbulence in China. The country's massive size, huge population of perhaps 400 million, chronic disorder, demonstrable weakness and (as some saw it) bright future, all combined to make China a focus of great-power conflicts as well as occasional cooperation. To many observers on the scene, the China mess was incomprehensible and hopeless. Others, at times, perceived something more hopeful: a nation awakening, even prospects for transformation of a heathen and backward people into Christians and democrats. Yet none could forecast the ultimate outcome of the imperialist assault against China: the rise of Chinese nationalism in a very potent form.

We deal here with one of modern history's most notable phenomena: the Chinese revolution, a process deeply rooted in the nineteenth and early twentieth century—and one still at work in the Maoist and post-Mao People's Republic. On the basis of hindsight, one can identify such a process in Chinese ethnocentrism (or culturalism) as it met the Western incursion and tried to respond. One can also identify the roles played by some Americans as witting or—more frequently—unwitting participants in this revolutionary process.

When did this process begin? Who helped begin it? Or, on the other hand, why was it so late in coming, relative to many Western nations and Japan? Why did it take such particular forms, or follow such special channels? How did Americans affect its course through

162

action or inaction? And what might the United States have done to
change that course—and when? These are questions that have sometimes haunted the conscience of concerned Americans. To put the
matter in terms of our conventional mythology: Here was a sleeping
giant whom we gently helped come awake; we taught him, fed him,
and protected him, more or less; but then he up and bit us very hard—
and was still biting, rhetorically at least, until the Nixon-Kissinger turnabout of 1971–1972. It should be obvious that such questions and
speculations underlie that lethal query that once dominated American
politics, namely, "Who lost China?"

To understand the Chinese revolution, we must first look at early
manifestations of Chinese nationalism and nationalists. Such probing
is complicated, however, by the deep-rooted persistence of traditional
Chinese ethnocentrism from the early centuries of the Confucian
state—a quality of national self-awareness and superiority that allowed
foreigners to become "Sinicized" and even to participate in the Confucian order. Can, for instance, this characteristic be related to nationalism? The probing is further complicated in recent centuries by the
reality that China was in fact ruled by a dynasty of foreigners, the
Manchus, from the mid-seventeenth century until 1912.

How is one to classify the prolonged and massively destructive
Taiping Rebellion of the mid-nineteenth century? The aims and ideology of its leaders were certainly anti-Manchu; but they were not inherently anti-foreign, and the Taiping pseudo-Christian ideology was
deeply repellent to Chinese regional administrators who joined ranks
with the Manchus and helped put down the rebellion with foreign
assistance. Yet the Taiping rebels have been claimed by the Chinese
Communists as protoproletarian predecessors in the revolutionary process.

Or how, further, is one to classify the Boxer rebels at the turn of
the century? An outgrowth of traditional secret societies, the Boxers
were vehemently anti-Christian and anti-foreign. And although they
had originally been viewed as anti-Manchu as well, they served the
dynasty's anti-Western aims, joined forces with the Manchus, and were
supported by the court. Both Taipings and Boxers are difficult to label
as early expressions of "nationalism."

One faces much less of a problem in the boycott of 1905. Here
Americans can take rueful pride in the fact that China's first modern
boycott, an unambiguous explosion of nationalism, was directed against

the United States. What fueled that boycott was decades of discrimina-
tory treatment of Chinese immigrants, particularly in America's Western states. And its proximate cause was Congress's 1905 action in totally
excluding the entry of any more Chinese laborers.

In response to this news, an older tradition of merchant protest—
the cessation of business by local guilds—was expanded on a nationwide
basis to most of the treaty ports, but especially to Shanghai and Canton.
And new forces were added to the mix as students joined the merchants
in mass meetings and China's evolving modern press gave its support
to the agitation. For some months, American trade was damaged. But
the imperial government was cautious lest the movement become anti-
dynastic as well; and the boycott's effectiveness soon waned. Nonetheless, nationalism in a contemporary form had come to birth.

The year 1905 seems a watershed in other ways as well. With the
abolition that year of the Confucian examination system, Chinese students began to go abroad in larger numbers to obtain so-called Western
learning—first and foremost to Japan, but also soon to Europe and
the United States (particularly after Washington remitted the Boxer
indemnity funds and transformed them into scholarships).

For the next several years, Japan served as an example for young
Chinese who yearned for a strong and modern China, rid of the unequal
treaties; Japan also served as a hothouse for the growth of Chinese
nationalism and the nurturing of revolutionary nationalists. It was Japan
who had defeated China easily in 1894–1895, who had terminated
its own unequal treaties, and who had gone on to defeat imperial
Russia in 1904–1905. Japan, then, was both model and haven for a
wide range of Chinese, from late Ch'ing reformers to anti-Manchu
revolutionaries, between 1898 and 1914. And among the Chinese sojourners there was a rapid and heavy outcropping of student political
societies devoted to planning for the transformation of China.

Among the many figures of this era, two stand out as exemplars
of variant approaches to the building of a new China: Liang Ch'i-ch'ao
(Liang Qichao) and Sun Yat-sen. Both came from the Canton region
of south China, but here their similarities ceased.

Liang Ch'i-ch'ao (1873–1929) had been a disciple of K'ang Yu-wei
(Kang Yuwei), the father of the abortive reforms of the summer of
1898. Fleeing from the Empress Dowager's repression, he had gone
first to Japan, then to Honolulu and America, and then back to Japan.
Reared in the Confucian classics, he saw his role as that of reinterpret-

ing China within the context of world history. To Liang, K'ang Yu-wei was "the Martin Luther of Confucianism." But Liang had moved on to the discovery of Social Darwinism and a belief "that history consists essentially of races and nations competing for survival in the process of evolution."

Liang's hope for China lay in popular education for nationalism; as he put it, a "moral renovation of the people." From his reading and observation of Anglo-Saxon societies, he was attracted to self-respect, individualism, and public-spirited citizenship. Such qualities should be gradually instilled in his own people. Liang, in the end, was a gradualist and a constitutional monarchist.

Sun Yat-sen was cut from different cloth. He was one of the early professional revolutionaries of modern times, and in some ways he was ideally suited to the role. Still regarded in very disparate quarters as "the father of the Chinese Revolution," he was also one of the great non-successes of history. Yet both wings of the bifurcated revolution—Nationalists and Communists—have claimed him as a progenitor.

Sun was born into a peasant family in 1866 in that part of Kwangtung (Guangdong) neighboring Portuguese Macao—an area that produced generations of Chinese who sought their fortunes overseas. Tutored by an uncle who had fought for the Taipings (who were, as John Fairbank has put it, "modern China's romantic equivalent of the American Confederacy"), Sun found a boyhood hero in the Taiping rebel leader Hung Hsiu-ch'uan. As a thirteen-year-old, he was sent off to join an older brother in Honolulu; on his return three years later, he denounced the superstitions of his villagers, smashed the family idols, and was sent off to Hong Kong. Ever enterprising, Sun found a protector in the person of a Scottish medical missionary, earned himself a Hong Kong medical degree, and in 1892 started up his own practice in Macao. Soon thrown out by the authorities, he tried his hand as a reformer by sending a petition on China's future to Viceroy Li Hung-chang—to which he received no reply. Whereupon the now thoroughly frustrated young man turned to the path of revolution.

By 1894, Sun Yat-sen had formed his own secret society; and a year later he launched the first of a multitude of unsuccessful plots—this time to seize the Canton provincial government offices. Though his co-plotters were caught and executed, Sun escaped to the United States and then on to Britain, where, now a man wanted by the Peking authorities, he was kidnapped and held in China's London legation.

His luck once again won out. He was able to get word of his captivity to his old medical teacher, and the public outcry that the wily doctor arranged was sufficient to obtain Sun's release and also to make him an international figure of some note—all this by the age of thirty.

He next emerged in Japan in the thick of the Chinese exile movement—and countless abortive plottings—after the turn of the century. Sun's problem in such a setting was one of competition with his rival revolutionaries. By 1905, he had fashioned both a new organization of about a thousand members—the T'ung Meng Hui (Tongmenghui)—and also a three-pronged program.

The program of Sun's group, the so-called Three Principles of the People, was to be the rallying cry of the T'ung Meng Hui's successor, the Kuomintang, or Nationalist party. The first of these principles was "nationalism," which Sun defined as both anti-Manchu and anti-imperialist (although the second aspect was de-emphasized whenever help was sought from the Western powers). The second principle was "democracy," by which Sun intended an anti-Confucian egalitarian republicanism under a five-power constitution. As for the third principle, "the people's welfare," or "socialism," its definition proved more elusive or at least protean. Prior to 1923, Sun clearly had in mind an eclectic and non-Marxist version of socialism that was heavily influenced by the writings of the American populist Henry George. George had urged the use of a single tax to appropriate the future unearned increase of land value and thus check the enrichment of speculators and monopolists. But Sun also borrowed from a spate of others whose books he had happened upon—including an obscure Brooklyn dentist and amateur political philosopher, Maurice William, author of *The Social Interpretation of History*.

How, then, on the eve of the Ch'ing dynasty's collapse, can one appraise the revolution's most famous leader and the program he had designed? First of all, unlike Liang Ch'i-ch'ao and many others, Sun Yat-sen was a "foreignized Chinese," by no means a member of the traditional scholar elite. No gradualist, he wished for China a sudden transformation through revolution. His solution was—in an ancient Chinese phrase—for the nation to "make one all-out effort and be forever after at ease."

As many observers have noted, Sun's greatest asset was personal charisma. His eyes were especially arresting, his rhetoric spellbinding. His greatest liability, however, was a preoccupation with intricate plots and grand paper plans, neglecting the problem of implementation. He lacked administrative skill. The Three Principles themselves lacked simple practicality—they didn't tell people what to do or how to do it.

Such was the nature of Sun Yat-sen—and Sun Yat-senism—until a later event of critical importance: his decision in 1924, a year before his death, to reorganize the Kuomintang (KMT) along Leninist, or "democratic centralist," lines. This was a decision that brought the infant Chinese Communist party into a first united front with the KMT.

So much for a viewing of two variant streams in the nationalist forces that were moving toward flood tide on the eve of the collapse of the dynasty. When that collapse came, in October 1911, it was characteristic of the revolution's "father" that he read the news of this success (after years of failure) in a Denver newspaper on an American railroad train. He hurried back to China to be elected the republic's first President; and it is also characteristic of the man that he at once lost control to the former Ch'ing supporter General Yuan Shih-k'ai. Sun spent the rest of his life trying to rebuild his power base in southern China in order to oust Yuan and his warlord successors, and was never to see the triumph of his KMT successor, Chiang Kai-shek.

Yet Sun Yat-sen's brief success and multiple failures from 1911 until his death in 1925 tend to obscure a phase of the Chinese revolution that was to have vast and permanent consequences for the shape of China, Sino-Western relations, and the American role in East Asia. Here one confronts a most curious aspect of the history of modern China: the fact that the decade of chaos, warlordism, and appalling suffering that followed the death of Yuan Shih-k'ai in 1916 produced for the first time a continuous eruption of Chinese nationalism and, simultaneously, an intellectual revolution of far-reaching significance. In both of these developments Americans and America played a role— although the role was not always the one citizens and policymakers would ideally have chosen.

Central to the Chinese revolution is something called the May Fourth Movement; it is a term that applies narrowly to an "incident" and more broadly to a period of time.

The May Fourth "Incident" was, in brief, the Chinese reaction to Woodrow Wilson's vicissitudes at the Paris Peace Conference—specifically, Chinese reaction to the news that, as one of the victors in World War I, Japan would be awarded the territorial rights and concessions in Shantung Province that Germany had seized and secured from 1898 onward, and that the Peking government had acquiesced in this arrangement.

When word of the Shantung settlement reached China, on May 4, 1919, some three thousand students from thirteen of Peking's colleges massed in T'ien An Men (Tian An Men) Square to denounce the betrayal. Their manifesto concluded with the following appeal to their countrymen: "China's territory may be conquered, but it cannot be given away. The country is about to be annihilated. Up, brethren!"

What followed dramatized the new national spirit. The Chinese authorities used violence to suppress the demonstration and jailed over 1,100 participants. But the news quickly spread to other Chinese cities, triggering a nationwide outpouring of anti-government and anti-foreign demonstrations. Overnight the Shantung outrage gave birth to a movement that encompassed an extraordinarily diverse mix of groups—merchants, the press, Sun Yat-sen in Canton, and Peking's warlord rivals in other provinces. Although students took the lead through newly formed unions, the modern scholar class—teachers, writers, journalists—also joined in the marches, street rallies, and boycotts of Japanese goods. So, significantly, did the normally conservative Shanghai merchants; and workers went on strike in forty of the city's factories. By late May and during June, general strikes closed down schools in over two hundred cities throughout the nation.

The final result of the May Fourth Incident was victory for the protestors. Three pro-Japanese government officials were ousted; the Cabinet resigned; and China refused to sign the Versailles Treaty. Most significant of all, students had proved themselves a potent new force in Chinese politics, under the banner of anti-Japanese patriotism.

Now, clearly, such events do not occur in a vacuum. What had brought about this dramatic shift in the behavior of large sectors of Chinese society? Here we come to the significance of the May Fourth "Movement" as a period of time, roughly the years 1917 through 1921, which witnessed a major transformation of China's economic, social, and intellectual life.

A number of factors helped produce this transformation. World War I, for instance, had cut China off from Western imports and had thereby stimulated the growth of an indigenous economy, especially in the treaty ports sheltered from warlordism. With such growth came the rise of a new Chinese administrative and entrepreneurial class.

And with it, too, came a steady influx of workers from the rural hinterland to the cities. By 1919, it is estimated that the urban labor force was well over one million—a harbinger of change for an overwhelmingly peasant society. Also present—undoubtedly the catalytic agent—was the new class of Western- and Japan-educated students, a group acutely aware of the disintegration of Chinese society and political institutions after the collapse of the empire and the rise of the warlords. Students spread a sense of urgency and crisis; they also saw themselves as potential national saviors in a society in which the scholar class had traditionally played a leading political role.

It was not, however, in the treaty ports but in Peking itself that the intellectual result of the new national mood was most vivid. Certain institutions at critical junctures in history seem magically endowed with seminal roles and the leadership to play them. Such is certainly true of Peking National University (or "Peita [Beida]") under the chancellorship of the German-educated Ts'ai Yuan-p'ei (Cai Yuanpei) from 1917 onward. For it was here that the national sense of urgency met myriad possible solutions—ideas in conflict at a fever pitch of intensity. It was Ts'ai's strong advocacy of freedom of thought that produced this unprecedented ferment. Such freedom was also abetted by the weakness of the Peking government, especially after its 1919 capitulation to the student demands. For Ts'ai Yuan-p'ei, education had to be "above politics . . . beyond political control." And under such a rubric he presided over a rare generation of the intelligentsia, one that bridged the old world of Confucianism and the new world of Western ideas. It was also a generation of skeptics, caught in the turbulence of the West's own ideological search.

Two key figures are often cited to illustrate the polarities of the May Fourth Movement, and indeed their lives moved in opposite directions when the movement finally split apart. The first is Peita's Dean of Letters, Ch'en Tu-hsiu (Chen Duxiu), who had studied in Japan and France and was deeply attracted to themes within the French Revolution. Ch'en, who attributed China's decay to Confucianism, called on Chinese youth to be "independent, not servile . . . progressive, not conservative . . . dynamic, not passive . . . cosmopolitan, not isolationist . . . utilitarian, not emptily formalistic . . . scientific, not [merely] imaginative."

A second prototype within the May Fourth Movement was Hu Shih (Hu Shi), a scholar who had received a B.A. degree from Cornell and a Ph.D. from Columbia University between 1910 and 1917. At Columbia, Hu had been deeply influenced by the educational philosopher John Dewey. He had returned to China committed to an emancipation of the Chinese people from the tyranny of the stylized Confucian literary forms. Instead, he said, people should write the way they spoke—in the vernacular, the language of everyday life. In 1917, he launched, with Ch'en's strong support, a campaign for a national "literary renaissance." It was through literacy, education, and scientific precision, he said, that China would ease off its Confucian straitjacket.

By 1919, Peita had become the meeting ground of a proliferation of ideas, people, and journals. Virtually every possible "ism" of the West in that period was examined and debated on campus—realism, utilitarianism, pragmatism, liberalism, individualism, socialism, anarchism, Darwinism, materialism. For Ch'en Tu-hsiu, presiding over the ferment, the key guides for the debate should be "Mr. Democracy" and "Mr. Science." "Only these two gentlemen," he wrote, "can cure the dark maladies in Chinese politics, morality, learning, and thought."

It was against this background, then, that the May Fourth Incident took place. And the prime result of that incident was the fusion of the Peking intellectual revolution with the intense new nationalism, and the spreading of this fusion throughout the nation through journals, lecturers from abroad, and violent polemics about China's past, present, and future.

Despite the variety of ideas and passions in collision, two common themes seem to have dominated the May Fourth debates. The first was to bury Confucianism once and for all, or, as Hu Shih put it, "to overthrow Confucius and Sons." The second theme was to discover some viable alternative to Confucianism—some ideology that would adequately meet the needs of a chaotic and impotent nation. In addition to such themes, one can detect two phases of concern within the movement and its successors. From 1917 to 1921, central attention was given to the emancipation of the individual. But after 1921, another concern emerged as paramount: how to strengthen the nation, how to achieve national wealth and power, an old preoccupation now revived to save the state from disintegration.

Both concern with the individual and concern with the state clearly deal with the central problem of Chinese history in the twentieth century: what one might term the problem of the vacuum—the vacuum left by Confucianism as an ethic to order the life of the individual, and the vacuum left by Confucianism as a political mechanism for ordering the life of the state. Confucianism had been an all-embracing civic religion. What might possibly replace it?

Faced with such fundamental questions, it was inevitable that the May Fourth Movement would eventually split apart; and so it did, after 1921. On the one side stood the academic practitioners, the scholars who believed in reformism and gradualism as a cure for China's ills. And on the other side stood the political activists, those who increasingly believed that the nation's salvation could only be achieved through direct action, violence, and revolution. Hu Shih was the chief spokesman for the first group—a man committed to individualism, pragmatism, and gradual transformation through education. But to many Chinese, including his old colleague Ch'en Tu-hsiu, Hu Shih's solution was an inadequate answer to China's needs for power and unity and freedom from foreign oppression. By early 1921, Ch'en had ended his four-year collaboration with Hu Shih and had become a founder of the Chinese Communist party. And in due course the passions of nationalism unleashed in this period had their most violent consequences yet in the nationwide demonstrations that followed upon the May Thirtieth Incident, in 1925, when British police fired upon protesting workers in Shanghai. With that event the Chinese revolution took a dramatic new turn.

The May Fourth era poses, in retrospect, some interesting questions for Americans and the history of Sino-American relations, precisely because the movement and its 1921 split and aftermath unleashed the major intellectual and political forces that have shaped modern China since that time. Given the critical nature of that juncture, it is useful to ask about the American role at the time. What was the content and strength of United States influence in this period of creative ferment? Was there an American "opportunity" to help shape the outcome?

There was, of course, a political and diplomatic dimension to America's Asian role in this interval: the policies of the Wilson and Harding administrations, culminating in American leadership at the Washington Conference. But policies generally sympathetic to China and wary of Japan could build on very little, given the shaky existence of the Peking government and the proliferation of warlordism. Merely the protection of American lives and property was the usual preoccupation of the embassy and consulates in this period, and protection often meant actions to buffer against outbursts of nationalist violence.

There was, as well, the American economic stake in China. Trade and investment were almost entirely confined to the treaty ports; and their value continued to run well behind the totals for Great Britain and Japan. It should be added that American trade and investment were viewed by most May Fourth leaders as part and parcel of the imperialist stranglehold that the West and Japan had imposed on China through the unequal treaties.

It was in two other aspects of the American presence that the Chinese revolution might well have been affected: in the Protestant missionary movement, and in the efforts of secular intellectuals who had taught some of the May Fourth leaders during their study abroad. Yet the American missionary and secular offerings of the time carried built-in liabilities.

At first glance, the post–World War I missionaries were in a position of greater influence than ever before. They numbered over five thousand by the early 1920s; and unlike the businessmen and consuls, their work spread well beyond the treaty ports and deep into the hinterland. Furthermore, missionary educators and YMCA-YWCA officials had constant contact with large varieties of middle school and college students through much of the nation—the very group that was at the heart of the May Fourth ferment.

Missionaries had viewed post-1911 China with enormous hope. For a time it seemed to them that the "Christianizing" of a republican China was a feasible goal. A nation hungering for salvation through new ideas seemed ripe for conversion to both Christ and Thomas Jefferson. Nor were the hopes totally illusory. In no other twenty-year period did Christianity make so rapid an advance in China as it did from 1900 to 1920. Not only was there a tripling of the number of converts (though still only a tiny fraction of the population), but much more significantly these decades also saw the establishment of six new church-sponsored colleges—including the first college for women, Ginling in the city of Nanking. There was a similar expansion of medical missions, and the church was also making headway among the new urban work-force. These were years, as well, of China tours by prominent American evangelists—notably Sherwood Eddy and John R. Mott, who, in 1914–1915, visited fourteen Chinese cities, appealing especially to students. It is estimated that Eddy addressed some 120,000 people during his tour. China communicated a thrilling sense of "opportunity" to these visitors and their co-religionists.

Yet it is ironic to note that most of the Western writers whose ideas were permeating Chinese universities were antithetical to missionary orthodoxy—such men as Rousseau, Comte, Huxley, Spencer, Kropotkin, and Marx, proponents at the least of "agnostic materialism." At the very moment of the church's greatest sensed opportunity, Western secular thought was actually bypassing the message of Christian democratic individualism.

In addition to such intellectual obstacles, the missionary effort faced a more imminent threat: the fact that after 1919 Chinese nationalism began to focus sharply on the missionaries themselves as beneficiaries of the unequal treaties. Anti-Christian agitation had always been a problem; but now it was becoming fused with the newly powerful nationalism. Missionaries could not avoid their increasing identification with "imperialism"; they carried it in their white skins, their higher living standards, their immunity from Chinese law—in short, their inviolable upper-class status. Nor was the problem exclusively outside the Christian community. Simultaneously there was growing within the indigenous membership and hierarchy of the Chinese churches resentment of Western and external control, a surge of pressures for "devolution," or the transfer of control of mission parishes and institutions fully to the Chinese. Such pressures produced great tensions, since most missionaries seem to have favored only gradual transition in this regard; they emphasized the need for the achievement of self-support prior to devolution. But to many Chinese Christians, such gradualism was much too slow.

Missionary alienation from most of the intellectual forces at work within the May Fourth Movement was reciprocated—and therefore reinforced—by the views of the movement's leaders that Christianity offered no answer to China. Under Hu Shih's aegis, even the reformist wing of the movement saw the church as foreign, superstitious, and unscientific. And as for the radical wing—in due course joined by the Communists—it viewed Christianity as far worse: an opiate, and the servant of status-quo capitalism. To radicals, the missionaries were simply "running dogs of imperialism."

In 1922, two events brought fire to the smoldering resentment against Christianity and its agents. The World Student Christian Federation had chosen Peking as the site of its general assembly that year; in response to this well-advertised gathering, Chinese student groups organized a nationwide anti-religious and anti-Christian movement. Furthermore, a committee of that federation had the poor judgment to publish a book celebrating the mission enterprise's successes under a highly provocative title: *The Christian Occupation of China*. The result, of course, was a further outburst of nationwide protest.

For the missionary offering, then, the results of the May Fourth transformation were not merely unfulfilled hopes but also an intensification of anti-Christian agitation that culminated, after the May Fourth Incident, in the most serious challenge that the church had faced since the Boxer Rebellion: the convulsion that accompanied the Kuomintang–Chinese Communist Party Northern Expedition, the United Front under Chiang Kai-shek that overthrew the warlords in 1926–1928 but also expelled vast numbers of Americans from China's interior, many of them never to return.

What of that other aspect of the American presence during this phase of Chinese history—the American secular offering to the nation's intellectual and political development?

It is not surprising to note that the chief foreign spokesman for a secular gradualist alternative was none other than Hu Shih's old mentor from Columbia, Professor John Dewey. At Hu's invitation, Dewey came to China in May 1919 and stayed for two years, lecturing in eleven provinces, with Hu as his interpreter. Dewey succeeded in kindling wide interest in his views on education and on pragmatism in general, and he developed a number of disciples not only to his educational theories but also to democratic reformism on a patient step-by-step basis.

Yet the gradualist and evolutionary approach to China's development that John Dewey proposed seemed strangely unreal and pallid in China's condition of acute chaos within and exploitation from without. For at a time when many Chinese intellectuals had moved from concern with the individual to concern with the salvation of the nation—with national power and wealth—Dewey and his followers were offering only the long road and the far distant goal. What Hu Shih urged was a rational and dispassionate focus on problems, not isms. "There is no liberation in toto," he warned, "or reconstruction in toto. Liberation means liberation from this or that institution, from this or that belief, for this or that individual; it is liberation bit by bit, drop by drop. Reconstruction . . . is bit by bit, drop by drop."

In retrospect, it seems apparent that "bit by bit and drop by drop" was less than an effective rallying cry to Chinese intellectuals and politicians in the post–May Fourth ferment.

So, with both Christianity and secular reformism examined and found lacking, and with constitutionalism a plaything of warlords, the prospects for an American-sponsored alternative to Confucianism in China seemed somewhat bleak by the winter of 1926. The nation seemed instead ripe for more radical solutions.

Yet, as events would have it, a reprieve of sorts was on its way out of the south—a so-called Red Marshal named Chiang Kai-shek, who was shortly to reveal himself as not a red at all. With Chiang's arrival in Nanking, and his establishment of a Kuomintang government there, we move into the story of what might well be regarded as America's last chance—prior to the late 1970s—to shape the course of the Chinese revolution.

(13)

Americans and the Nanking Government

IN THE SPRING OF 1927, the Chinese revolution took an abrupt shift in course, or rather a violent split into two channels—a development that was to affect profoundly China's internal relations for at least the next fifty years.

What happened was this: The alliance of convenience, a "united front" against the warlords and imperialists—between Sun Yat-sen's Kuomintang (KMT) and the infant Chinese Communist party (CCP)— was terminated by the late Dr. Sun's soldier-successor, Chiang Kai-shek, through a bloody coup de main and purge. Having occupied the key cities of the lower Yangtze Valley—Nanking and Shanghai— Chiang's forces turned on the CCP and its supporters, killed them or drove them into hiding, and made successful overtures to the anxious treaty-port powers (and the Chinese business community), whose interests had heretofore seemed gravely threatened by the revolutionary armies. For the time being, the Chiang faction came as a reprieve to Shanghai entrepreneurs—though in due course Chiang's government would become more predatory than business-minded, a form of bureaucratic capitalism that "squeezed" and taxed the modern private sector.

Despite much subsequent jockeying among the victorious KMT leaders, by 1928 the Peking regime had vanished and China had been at least technically reunified, with Nanking as its new capital, for the first time since the overthrow of the empire in 1911. And for the next two decades this China was more open to Western, and especially American, ideas, influence, and assistance than ever before. Aid, of course, was the paramount Chinese desire—aid for rehabilitation and modernization in the first decade; but after the beginning of the all-out Sino-Japanese War in July 1937, aid for resistance and survival in the face of Tokyo's devastating armies and airplanes.

In response to this "new" China and its needs, Americans—both officials and private citizens—proceeded cautiously at the outset, with good reason, thanks to the violence done to American property and persons in the mid- and late 1920s. Yet Chiang Kai-shek, the "Red Marshal" of those years, was to become the Christian "Generalissimo" of the 1930s—a bulwark against anti-foreign radicals and the Japanese, and after Pearl Harbor and the outbreak of the Pacific war, America's often beleaguered but heroically staunch Asian ally—a role he would continue to play throughout the 1940s, after his government's eventual exile to the island of Taiwan, and well beyond.

The American relationship to Nationalist China constitutes a vivid and enduring chapter in both societies. In their state of weakness and siege, KMT leaders developed a gradual dependence on their American friend and (after 1941) formal ally, a dependence that was both damaging to Chinese pride and also a volatile factor in Chinese internal politics. American support for Chiang—at first tentative and unofficial and then fully official—deeply embittered Chiang's adversaries, especially, of course, the CCP.

As for the impact of the relationship on the United States, China policy—somewhat divisive in the 1930s—was to become a factor of extraordinary power in the poisoning of America's postwar domestic politics and even civic discourse. Out of the Chinese revolution—and its violent split of 1927—one can trace major roots of the Cold War and the McCarthyism of the 1950s.

Four contexts of Sino-American relations in the Nanking years are especially pertinent.

First, despite China's nominal reunification under the KMT and Dr. Sun's Three Principles, such unity was generally achieved (and sustained) by Nanking only through a system of alliances with regional and provincial military figures retaining armies whose first loyalty was to their generals and not the central government. Chiang Kai-shek's actual domain was therefore confined to the provinces of the lower Yangtze—until his dramatic detention and release by dissident troops in December 1936 turned him temporarily into the nation's paramount symbol of unity against Japan. So a first context in which these events should be viewed is the inherent fragility of the Nanking regime's claim to national governance.

A second context is the *official* American perception of the Nationalists and their government. During the Nanking years, Chiang was challenged by at least six military uprisings led by rivals (not to mention the continuing Communist insurrection) and as many more political conspiracies. American diplomats on the scene, whose own ranks had been reduced and frozen as a result of the Great Depression, were deeply skeptical of the new government and its leadership. They were in no position to be forthcoming on KMT requests for assistance, and they cautioned their bosses and fellow citizens against getting involved.

In Washington, after 1933, Treasury Secretary Henry Morgenthau, Jr., found ways to bolster Nanking's currency reforms; but Secretary of State Cordell Hull remained cautious and confined his support to rhetoric. Even in the spring of 1937, after Chiang's emergence from captivity as a hero, the American ambassador in Nanking gloomily reported that the generalissimo was a man with no friends, "who lives like an Oriental despot, isolated from his own people, who cooperate with him through fear and because they want the national unity for which he stands."

A third and related context was the existence and behavior of Japan. Although many Chinese Nationalists had been trained or given refuge in Japan prior to 1911, their increasingly successful revolution was occurring at a time when Japan was entering a new phase of economic anxiety, civil-military tensions, ultranationalism, and pressures for expansion onto the Asian continent. The victory of Bolshevism in Russia— and the efforts of its Marxist allies in China—had reawakened an older Japanese fear. China's chronic disorder seemed both a danger and an opportunity; China was "up for grabs." Later, China's gathering order and unity would also seem a threat.

Japan's opening strike came in September 1931, with the occupation of vast and rich Manchuria. From the end of 1932, North China was under constant pressure toward economic and political neutralization and gradual incorporation into Tokyo's expanding empire.

To the Japanese threat, Nanking responded mainly with appeasement, or at best an effort to play for time. To Chiang Kai-shek's supporters, the strategy made national unity the prerequisite to resistance.

To Chiang's critics, however, such a policy was a sellout dictated by his obsession with eradicating communism.

As for Washington's reaction to the continuing "Far Eastern crisis" from 1931 onward, American options were severely limited by the ravages of the Great Depression, by the enduring force of isolationism, and by the realities of America's military and naval weakness. In response to "Manchukuo"—a blatant violation of China's territorial integrity and the Washington Conference treaties—Secretary of State Henry L. Stimson could only disinter and decree "non-recognition" (Secretary Bryan's response to Japan's Twenty-One Demands in 1915). Economic sanctions were rejected by President Hoover as "sticking pins in tigers." His successor, Franklin Roosevelt, was no more bold for a while. So oil and scrap iron continued to be sold to the Japanese aggressors until late in the decade. Meanwhile pro-China "idealists" and more acquiescent "realists" feuded about how to respond.

A fourth context for Sino-American relations—much more important to Nanking than to Washington—was the continued existence, contrary to repeated obituaries, of the Communist wing of the Chinese revolution. Despite Chiang's Shanghai coup and several abortive efforts to launch countercoups under instructions from their mentors in Moscow, many CCP members survived underground in the treaty ports or took to mountain hideaways in the tradition of rebels against previous dynasties. One such rural fastness was in the rugged terrain on the Kiangsi-Fukien (Jiangxi-Fujian) border, where in 1931 the infant Kiangsi Soviet Republic, operating out of the town of Juichin (Ruijin), "declared war" on Japan.

The Nanking government's central military preoccupation, after the loss of Manchuria to Japan, was to destroy once and for all its former Communist allies. And it was during a fifth so-called campaign of encirclement and annihilation, personally directed by Chiang Kai-shek in 1934, that the Kiangsi Communists broke through the Nationalist lines and started on their famous Long March to China's northwest and a new refuge in the caves of Yenan (Yanan). For a while thereafter, Nanking announced the extermination of the Communists; and thanks to an effective KMT blockade, neither the Chinese nor the wider world much doubted the truth of Nanking's word. Meanwhile, in the midst of that Long March, a Hunanese named Mao Tse-tung (Mao Zedong) had risen to top leadership in the CCP.

Only hindsight tells us that of the several settings for Sino-American relations in the 1930s, the regrouped survival of the Chinese Communists and the success of Mao in *his* struggle with rivals are probably most significant. And yet the CCP might not have succeeded if the Nanking government had not been pressured, virtually from the moment of its birth, by Japan. Once again in Chinese history the attempt to rule China was severely constrained by both internal rebel and external aggressor. In this case the external aggressor would, eventually and ironically, help bring to power what it feared most: a truly unified China under Communist control in league with Japan's bitterly feared adversary, imperial and now Soviet Russia.

The enigma, the successes, the hopes, the wartime glory, the sharp decline and the disastrous failure of the Chinese Nationalists as rulers of the Chinese mainland are products not only of events but also of a person, and those few he let into his inner circle.

That person was, of course, Chiang Kai-shek, the son of a Chekiang (Zhejiang) gentry family, whose education had been entirely as a soldier, both in late imperial China and then in Japan. A recruit to the KMT cause, he had become head of the party's Whampoa (Huangpu) Military Academy (with a man named Chou En-lai [Zhou Enlai] as one of his political commissars), and from there he had succeeded—after Sun Yat-sen's death—to the leadership of the Northern Expedition to unify the nation. This new national guide was entirely a soldier (whose greatest heroes were legendary Confucian generals and whose values were those of the Japanese samurai). He had never traveled abroad, except to Japan—and briefly, to the U.S.S.R. in 1923—and never again did until the Cairo Conference of 1943 during World War II.

So Chiang was by training and experience a late-Confucian military man—ascetic, authoritarian, puritanical, and parochial.

Such a person would not have inspired confidence in most Americans, whether officials or private citizens, and he did not begin to until his anti-Communist coup of 1927. But then two further events occurred that made the former Red Marshal more trustworthy to some Americans. First, also in 1927, he married the younger sister of Madame Sun Yat-sen, Miss Soong Mei-ling (Song Meiling) a graduate of Wellesley College and a Methodist; and second, by 1931 he himself quietly converted to his wife's brand of Christianity.

Meanwhile, his American ties were extended through his Sino-

American in-laws—the children of Charles Jones Soong, a Christian convert and successful entrepreneur who had sent his progeny to the United States for higher education. These included, centrally, Mei-ling's oldest sister, her two brothers, and a brother-in-law. Most influential were the Harvard-trained T. V. Soong (Song Zewen), and the brother-in-law, H. H. Kung (Kong Xiangxi), a graduate of Oberlin. Through much of the 1930s, Soong and, especially, Kung exercised firm and personally profitable control of China's finances and banking system. Despite doubts about Chiang himself, increasing numbers of Americans were drawn toward these English-speaking Westernizers— and especially toward Chiang's beautiful and strong-willed wife. Among those admirers were businessmen, journalists, and an occasional official; also impressed were missionaries within the lower Yangtze River basin, where the Chiang family's Protestantism sent hopes soaring after the anti-Christian violence of the previous decade. Missionaries in this region took hope from the visible signs of reconstruction and modernization as the Manchurian crisis eased in 1933 and the KMT began to enforce a period of relative stability.

Yet Chiang Kai-shek's curious mix of adroitness, luck, and limitations made for a complicated interlude in the Chinese revolution, one filled with contradictions. This overlord of the Westernizers, the self-styled heir to Dr. Sun, was Confucian by values if Christian by private practice. Not only Confucian, but Neo-Confucian in the Japanese samurai sense of Bushido (the way of the warrior). So it is not surprising that some Confucian observances that were discredited in the empire's collapse and denounced in the May Fourth Movement were gradually resurrected under the Nanking government. Revolution began to give way to "restoration." And an open-ended stage of one-party "tutelage" was firmly decreed.

But other ingredients also spilled into the mix that Chiang and his partisans tried to blend in order to form some cohesive ideology for Nationalist China, to give content to Sun's Three Principles. Out of Mussolini's Italy came the alleged precision of fascism (also some airplanes and instructors to help in the bombardment of Communist enclaves); and the KMT's right wing would eventually develop a fascist Blue Shirt movement of strongarm anti-Left vigilantes. The Blue Shirts were a highly organized secret force keyed to perpetuating Chiang's rule—the exaltation of the Ruler.

Out of Germany, then moving into Nazism, came military advisers

for Chiang's armies. And out of America, at the same time, came—
of all things—the YMCA as a model for Chinese youth. Chiang's much-
touted creation in early 1934, the New Life Movement, was explicitly
patterned—at least according to the generalissimo's later words—on
character building as accomplished by the YMCA and by churches
in the United States. Campaigns against flies, rodents, spitting, and
shoddy personal hygiene were a hybrid of both Confucian asceticism
and the Protestant social gospel—to be enforced, when necessary, by
KMT guardians and even the police. Behind it, unknown to most Westerners, stood the ruthless Blue Shirts.

Thus was a mass movement for national regeneration to be built
on the toothbrush, the mousetrap, and the fly swatter—but with fascism
as its covert sponsor and enforcer.

History tends to deal harshly with losers and their causes, and such
has been the fate of Chiang Kai-shek and the Nanking government.
Assaulted by aggressors and rebels, exiled to West China and ultimately
to the island of Taiwan, the KMT regime went through periods of
intense glorification and then excoriation in the Western, and especially
American, press. In the long run, China was "lost" by Chiang to his
former allies and eventual archenemies, the Chinese Communists. And
yet by the late 1970s, with Taiwan still under KMT rule, the post-
Mao government in Peking was reaching out to the non-Communist
West in ways that were curiously reminiscent of the Nanking government's outreach.

For despite the hybrid and fragile nature of Nanking's governance
in the 1930s, its modernizers turned for assistance to all possible
sources, and their achievements were at least promising. Foreign advisers, for instance, were hired by the scores in all areas of development.
The League of Nations was especially responsive, once Japan had
walked out; and the lower Yangtze provinces showed the impact of
much urban and rural experimentation. Chief among the government's
early successes were the stabilization of the currency and the creation
of a modern banking system. Progress was made in flood control, on
the basis of earlier pioneering efforts by the China International Famine Relief Commission and its engineers. Substantial improvements
were made in road and rail transportation. Agricultural experiment
projects struggled with pest control and increased crop production.
Chekiang Province, just south of Shanghai, was designated a model

province for land and tax reform—and had met its goals by the time
of the renewed Sino-Japanese War in 1937. And the thrust toward
modernization had a strong impact on both education and social relations. More and more Chinese sought middle school and college degrees from Western-type institutions, especially in the sciences, and
many went abroad for graduate study when scholarships were available. And women fought for, and occasionally found, greater educational
opportunities and careers than ever before.

Yet all this was happening within a historical pincer: between the
relentless encroachment of Japan from the north out of Manchuria,
and the enticement of the Chinese revolution's other wing, the CCP,
which was active in the cities, underground, and notably in some universities, as well as in the Communists' various rural redoubts. Caught
within the pincer was the KMT regime, its first military priority the
eradication of the Communists, despite its commitment to modernization. And hovering over the entire scene—as Nanking looked outward
for assistance from virtually any quarter—was a worldwide depression.

Among the ironies of Sino-American relations since the enunciation
of the Open Door at the turn of the century is the fact that when a
semi-reunified Chinese republic was finally, and rather desperately,
turning outward, the United States was turned inward. Isolationism—
that often misused word—was not the central problem. Washington,
having convened the conference that sought to reorder East Asia in
1922, had rejected the League of Nations but was not at all isolationist
about its Philippine ward, its continual Chinese concern and headache,
and its touchy rivalry with a volatile Japan. Washington's problem
was not isolationism but rather the near-collapse of the American economy within a global economic debacle.

With American foreign policy paralyzed, or at least cautious, after
1931, and with business in a deep crisis, the response to China's needs
was left largely to that small, old, often-frustrated but intensely caring
constituency of Asia-oriented Americans: the Protestant missionaries
and their more recent secular allies, including journalists, writers, and
philanthropic foundations. Of course, the missionaries, and their supporters back home, were equally victims of the economic pinch; and
the violence of the 1920s had cut their numbers from a high point of
about five thousand in 1925 to roughly half that number in the mid-
1930s. Meanwhile, the very idea of Christian overseas evangelism had

become the target of intense scrutiny and criticism in America. "Cultural imperialism" had not yet been coined as a term; but it lurked behind the words that went into a lengthy interdenominational study entitled *Re-Thinking Missions,* released in 1930.

Yet the China missionaries were, for the most part, dauntless. Adversity was not a new thing; and signs of hope were constantly to be found—especially as the KMT brought a modicum of stability and Chiang's extended family began to seem welcoming.

What brought about a new Sino-American relationship under the Nanking government was, fundamentally, a shared sense between some Westerners—mostly Americans, but also Europeans—and some Chinese that the cure to China's crisis and the key to China's future lay in the villages, in the more than 80 percent of the people who lived in the countryside in a state of poverty, sickness, and illiteracy. Although many missionaries had come to China with the conventional aim of "converting the heathen," more and more were now involved in the "good works" of education, science, medicine, agriculture, technology—an effort to bring "Western learning" to Asians that went back to Peter Parker, M.D., and well before him to Roman Catholic priests from Europe.

American and KMT efforts to treat the needs of village China were preceded and anticipated by the rural mass mobilization efforts of Chinese Communists in the 1920s. As Communists sought to mobilize peasants for political action, the condition of village China became central to the nation's future: a problem to be coped with in one of two ways—through (a) reform or (b) revolution. Here was a familiar posing of options; from at least 1898 onward, reform and revolution had alternated in the battle for control of China's destiny. In the Nanking years, the missionaries chose the path of reform. Reform was, after all, part of America's experience and temperament. Revolution was not.

The short-lived magic of the Nanking experiment had its roots in America as well as China. While Hu Shih (of Cornell and Columbia) had presided over one vernacular-oriented faction of the May Fourth Movement, James Y. C. Yen (Yan Yangchu), of Yale, had left his job as a YMCA secretary and started—with American financial support— the Mass Education Movement based in the village of Tinghsien (Ding Xian), Hopei (Hebei), in the early 1920s. And by the end of the decade,

"Jimmy" Yen and his multifaceted rediscovery of rural China were creating responses among all sorts of Chinese and Americans.

To encapsulate history: Yen, his predecessors, and his emulators helped create throughout significant parts of China—with much help from Americans, and also as a stimulus to Americans—a rural reconstruction movement, probably KMT China's most potentially reforming force prior to the movement's uprooting by the Japanese. What James Yen discovered was that "mass education," i.e., literacy, was not enough, and that what the peasant world of China (and undoubtedly elsewhere) needed was something much broader. In the 1960s, the term would become "community development," a complex approach to all the conditions of rural life, from public health and agricultural innovation to more equitable land-use arrangements.

Among the obstacles to the transformation of village China, three were of paramount importance in most of the nation. First was the problem of land tenure. By 1937, it was estimated that almost two-thirds of China's farmers were tenants; and the conditions of their tenancy were notoriously oppressive. Although the Nanking government gave lip service to "land reform," it shrank from alienating its landlord supporters. A second obstacle to rural reconstruction was the existence of a universally oppressive land tax structure, enforced by corrupt local and provincial officials—a structure which Nanking chose to perpetuate in order to keep its provincial allies loyal. A third and related obstacle was the pathetic lack of rural credit; surveys in the mid-1930s reveal that at least one-half of the rural population was always in debt.

It should be added that "landlordism" as China's chief affliction has been challenged by observers who have argued that the generally undernourished condition of Chinese agriculture was actually the crux of the matter: lack of technology and capital.

Whatever the explanation, in such circumstances it is hardly surprising that neither the small church experiments inspired by James Yen nor the larger governmental undertakings in rural reform could come close to achieving their often grandly advertised goals.

Despite the depression, and American self-absorption, China was not solely the domain of Americans of the missionary vocation. At least one major secular foundation was also at work there, had been so for many years, and attempted in this decade an experiment—short-lived—that might have given a future to the gradualist alternative within China's development.

In 1934, the trustees of the Rockefeller Foundation, after three years of exploration, approved an ambitious new China program on the basis of proposals submitted by one of its vice presidents, Selskar M. Gunn. Rockefeller involvement in China dated from 1913 and had mainly focused on medical education, in particular Peking Union Medical College (PUMC)—an investment totaling $37 million by the early 1930s, the highest figure for any of the foundation's foreign recipients.

On the basis of a brief China tour in 1931, Gunn had reported that "China has become plastic after centuries of rigid conventionalism"—and had warned that "the Foundation cannot neglect this tremendously important part of the World." Gunn's findings persuaded the Rockefeller trustees to send him back for a longer and deeper analysis of China's affliction and possible cures, a 1932–1933 trip that produced a major report in January 1934.

Gunn gave his trustees both bad news and good. The bad news was that years of expenditures centrally on medicine, somewhat on public health, and latterly on agricultural improvement had made no lasting impact on China's problems. Those problems lay primarily in rural China, in the villages; and highly skilled medical specialists who disdained the rigors of peasant life were not the answer.

The good news was that the rural reconstruction movement, with Jimmy Yen as its sparkplug, along with Chinese universities and the best of the thirteen Christian colleges, could provide the Foundation with an indigenous and village-based route to the reshaping of China's hinterland. Gunn moved on to propose that the trustees shift their China focus and initiate an entirely new program to meet the nation's needs—and respond to (the word recurs) China's "plasticity."

It is a memorable commentary on America's enduring desire to help reshape China that the Rockefeller trustees, excited by the fact that China was now "bound by few hampering traditions, and the plastic condition of her life and institutions at the present moment is an inviting challenge to a positive kind of service," decided to embark upon a multi-year "plan aimed at raising the educational, social, and economic standards of rural China." All this despite the patent precariousness of conditions in East Asia and the world.

Some lingering poignant questions were raised by the Rockefeller trustees in December 1934, questions that touch upon the heart of what might be termed an American obsession with China. "Is the welfare of mankind best served by enlarging our investment in China?" they asked. "Is China the outstanding strategic point in which we ought to push our attack? Is there no other sector of the world where we can hope to obtain as large a return in human happiness and welfare as we can in China?"

The answers in each case—after brief consideration—were resoundingly in the affirmative. An initial appropriation of $1 million was approved. And thereby was launched America's largest peacetime commitment to the reshaping of rural China prior to the 1970s.

By the time of the outbreak of the all-out Sino-Japanese War in the summer of 1937, the Rockefeller-created North China Council for Rural Reconstruction, together with other grants, had helped bind and strengthen the multiple secular and religious efforts of the past. And in some pilot areas, progressive officials were even joining the reformers in efforts to solve the basic issues of tenancy, taxation, and rural credit. The prospects seemed bright for emulation and expansion of Western urban training applied to the afflictions of village China.

Furthermore, at Sian (Xian) in December 1936 Chiang Kai-shek— for months under pressure from a resuscitated student movement to resist Japan's encroachments—had been forced into a change of heart through "detention" by mutinous generals who believed his priorities to be wrong. And after his dramatic Christmas Day release, a second, rather tacit united front began to emerge between the KMT and the CCP.

Japan's fear of Bolshevism in China as it had moved in from Soviet Russia would in retrospect later resemble America's fear of Communism's potential control of Southeast Asia. By the summer of 1937, China's second united front caused the self-styled promoters of Japan's destiny on the Asian mainland to provoke an "incident" at Marco Polo Bridge, just north of Peking, a provocation that led to all-out prolonged war and rapid Japanese conquest of most of eastern China. In response to alleged *Chinese* provocation, Tokyo's nervous rulers embarked upon a military course designed to keep China non-Communist and non-hostile. They called it the "China Incident," rather than a declared war, and it would take four years to blend into America's Pacific front in World War II. By that time, Tokyo's leaders had announced their larger Pan-Asian vision: the creation of the Greater East Asia Co-Prosperity Sphere, into which China would be centrally incorporated.

What had triggered Japan's renewed assault was not merely the specter of Chinese Bolshevism but the new temporary reality of Chinese unity under Chiang Kai-shek. And among the first targets of Tokyo's air force were such symbols of Sino-American progress as Nankai University in Tientsin, and several other centers of the Rockefeller-funded rural reconstruction program. Smashed to bits by bombs and armies—or relocated gradually to West China under KMT rule out of inaccessible Chungking (Chongqing)—were the elements, including Tinghsien itself, of what might have been (however fragile and inadequately rooted) a gradualist alternative to violent revolution in the Chinese countryside.

The Sian kidnapping, the new united front, and the Sino-Japanese War had important results both among Americans in China and their supporters back home. In a seminal study of American images of Asia, published in 1958, the veteran journalist Harold Isaacs probed the sources of the intellectual baggage of his country's "opinion-makers" when thinking about China and the Chinese. Among the most central of influences—including such cinema characters as the evil Fu Manchu and the benevolent Charlie Chan—were the novels of China missionary daughter and wife Pearl S. Buck, especially *The Good Earth,* and the publications and films of Time-Life's co-founder, China missionary son Henry R. Luce. During the mid- and late 1930s, a natural pro-Chinese and anti-Japanese constituency was forming in America, still distracted by the depression at home and the rise of fascism and Nazism in Europe.

By the autumn of 1937, a natural and disparate group of China sympathizers had come together in an initial effort to bring humanitarian relief to the beleaguered Chinese. And through the adroit efforts of missionaries, philanthropists, and others, a "lobby" of sorts took shape, the American Committee for Non-Participation in Japanese Aggression. Here, in embryo, was something a portion of which would later become a more politically powerful collective loosely labeled the "China Lobby." Yet in their early years, these friends of China had only middling success. Oil and scrap iron continued to be sold to Japan.

What turned the tide for China's supporters was Japan's gradual marriage to the European Axis powers. In 1940, Tokyo signed the Tripartite Pact. And from then on, the China cause—the "Free China" cause, the KMT cause, the Christian generalissimo's cause—became slowly but powerfully allied to America's more passionate anti-Hitler cause. Anti-fascism in Europe and anti-Japan sentiments in Asia were finally fused. "Free China" was on its way to becoming a full partner in the Western world's struggle against fascist tyranny. And with the Japanese attack on Pearl Harbor in December 1941, Chiang Kai-shek's China slipped into a curious but barely examined role as one of the planet's "Big Four" powers.

Well before this, Nobel Laureate Pearl Buck had turned her most famous novel into a film, whose viewers at home and abroad broke all records in numbers. Publisher Henry Luce had made both Chiangs cover figures on *Time* magazine, and Chiang would eventually be one of the public figures who most often graced that cover over the next dozen years. Meanwhile, from the summer of 1937 onward, that influential audiovisual medium of the pretelevision age, Luce's *March of Time*—brief documentaries distributed to movie houses throughout the land—brought to Americans gripping scenes of Japanese brutality and Chinese suffering. And missionaries ousted from the Chinese hinterland were indefatigable on the national lecture circuit, raising funds for China relief and elevating the KMT leaders to new heights of heroism in the public eye.

Thus was the stage set for a great American illusion about China, and a great disillusionment to follow: a Sino-American bonding that was to become more intense than ever before—and whose bursting apart as the Japanese were vanquished and the Chinese revolution again unleashed would poison America's foreign policy and domestic politics for a generation to come.

(14)

War in the Pacific

WHY DID THE UNITED STATES and Japan go to war? The Japanese call the conflict the "Pacific War." For them it was part of the unresolved struggle with the Chinese, an East Asian land war which had been going on sporadically since 1931 and the seizure of Manchuria. For the United States, war in the Pacific was, of course, part of the global World War II waged also against the Germans and Italians.

The United States and Japan had slipped into a position of increasing incompatibility during the 1930s. The mood of compromise and harmony struck by the Washington Conference and lingering throughout the 1920s now evaporated; relations across the Pacific took on a sharp and competitive edge. In Japan, strong civilian leadership vanished; and the military, principally the Army, wrenched power from other competing elites. But the nation did not lie in the hands of a ruthless, conspiratorial, and irrational Nazi-like gang, although many Americans saw it that way.

For one thing, no such certainty or unity of purpose existed within Japanese leadership. The now freshly stated goal was national security, to be achieved through a self-sufficient economy. Was this so new or so irrational? Was it so different from that of the Meiji era? Was it so inconsonant with the world of the 1930s?

The Japanese argued that they were simply seeking those advantages enjoyed by the other powers. Japan, one of its statesmen remarked, "had to have a special position in China in order to have the same degree of economic freedom as Great Britain and the United States of America with their vast internal markets," the British with

190

their empire, the Americans with their huge continental spaces.

But China, a presumed solution to the constriction of Japan, remained a problem to the Japanese. As we know, the Japanese were riding a tiger there. All they could wrest from the obdurate Chinese was territory. No popular support welled up from those whom the Japanese "liberated," and the Japanese failed to grasp the intensity of Chinese revolutionary nationalism.

Americans, bound by sentiment to China, preached the principle of self-determination. Were China to be incorporated in a Japanese-led Pan-Asianist sphere, America's economic and cultural role there would be severely compromised, perhaps even ended. One of the premises of Pan-Asianism, in China as in Japan, was, after all, the elimination of the remnants of Western imperialism and the inroads of Western culture and values. As Secretary of State Cordell Hull put it, the United States was at the "Oriental crossroads of decision," in that there seemed no way both to accommodate Japan in China and to preserve an independent American presence and role in East Asia.

Even so, the evidence suggests that the China problem alone would not have provoked war between the United States and Japan. Too many Americans felt China wasn't worth it; too many Americans opposed war at all, in any form; too many Americans sensed that Chinese nationalists were themselves so anti-foreign that American interests in China would be endangered whoever should win. And people like Ambassador Joseph Grew in Tokyo thought that the Japanese would in the end wind down their involvement in China for reasons of their own, having to do with the expense and unpopularity of the war at home in Japan. Diplomat John V. A. MacMurray, in a prescient memorandum of 1935, perceived that China was the geopolitical meeting point of several contending forces, which held each other in balance to a certain degree. The elimination of one of these forces, Japan, would therefore open the way for another, such as Russia.

What eventually stirred the leaders and shapers of American diplomacy was not the fate of China, but rather the "European Connection"—the relationship they perceived between war in Asia and war in Europe. Both Secretary Hull and the President considered the war in China their line of defense against the spread of war to Europe. This was because they believed that peace depended upon the credibility of the international community's commitment to collective security, and the strength of its consensus that aggression was immoral and inadmissible in international relations.

Failure to respond effectively to aggression in Asia would encourage outbreaks of violence elsewhere, Hull and Roosevelt judged. They were encouraged in making this connection by the seemingly interlocking character of events on three continents—in close succession there came the Italo-Ethiopian war (1935), the Spanish civil war (1936), and the reopening of war in China (1937)—and by growing evidence of what appeared to be parallels between European fascism and what was emerging in Japan. Comparisons among Germany, Italy, and Japan were strengthened by the soundings for a German-Japanese alliance (1938) and the actual conclusion of the Tripartite Pact (September 1940). Although that alliance was to be of little real importance to the Japanese, to Americans it was compelling evidence that the Nazis and the Japanese were but birds of a feather.

After the outbreak of the European war in 1939, and particularly after the fall of France in 1940, there was a growing tendency in Washington to regard what was going on as "one war, in two theaters," to use the phrase of the State Department's Stanley K. Hornbeck; or, as Roosevelt himself put it, "a single world conflict," requiring in the United States "a global strategy of self-defense."

The linkage of American security interests in Asia and Europe was a somewhat paradoxical development. On the one hand, it greatly strengthened American resistance to Japan. With only one exception—namely, the decision in July 1939 to give notice of the ending of the American commercial treaty with Japan in order to open the way for economic sanctions—all the critical stages of escalation in United States containment of Japan occurred after the outbreak of the European war and were directly related to European considerations.

Thus the fall of France, in June 1940, was followed within a month by the American decision to place exports of aviation fuel and high-grade scrap iron and steel under license, and within three months by Ambassador Grew's famous "green light" message from Tokyo giving his assent to the use of economic sanctions against Japan. That same month, in September 1940, Japan invaded northern Indochina with the helpless acquiescence of French colonial officials there; and the United States responded by placing an embargo upon the export of scrap metals to Japan. So also, in July 1941, after the German invasion of Russia had freed Japan from the threat of Russian land power in northern China, Japan overran the remaining parts of French Indo-china, and the United States responded with its trump card, the freez-ing of Japanese assets, which automatically ended the export of all American oil to Japan.

Finally, to take another example, it was the urging of Winston Chur-chill at his Atlantic Conference meeting with Franklin Roosevelt that the United States do something to protect British Malaya and the Neth-erlands East Indies—with their tin, rubber, bauxite, and oil—that prompted Roosevelt to issue his very thinly veiled warning to the Japanese ambassador in August 1941 that any new military expansion that threatened American interests would bring active intervention.

On the other hand, and this is the paradoxical element, the same linkage that served to strengthen the American position against Japan served also to define it as peripheral: a function of America's much greater and more vital interest in the survival of the anti-fascist allies in Europe. China, and East Asia more generally, became the occasion and the immediate issue of a steadily deepening confrontation of the United States with Japan; but it was not the ultimate American concern.

If events in Europe had not raised the specter of a twofold world, divided between fascist aggressors and peace-loving democracies, and if the Japanese had not exacerbated the resulting tensions by striking southward to seize the oil and mineral resources of the European em-pires in Southeast Asia, it is most unlikely that the United States would have frozen Japanese assets and imposed an oil embargo. And had there been no oil embargo hanging over the Japanese Navy, it is not at all clear that Japan would have resigned itself to a war that many of its own officials knew in their inmost hearts was likely to end in defeat.

Out of this paradox grows one of the great ironies of Japanese-American relations during the late 1930s: namely, that while there was some fatalism, especially in the navies, about the inevitability of eventual war between the two potential hegemonic powers of the Pacific, prior to 1941 neither side really expected that a war would result from their current confrontation over China. In Japan, it seemed axiomatic to Premier Konoye and the Pan-Asianists that America, which had always confined itself to rhetoric in East Asia, would do so again and would eventually accept the logic and the profits of the Japanese redivision of the Asian world into a new set of spheres. This is one reason why they pressed ahead so hard and so recklessly.

In America, on the other hand, one of the strong arguments for the use of economic sanctions had always been that they would prevent war by breaking the momentum of Japanese expansion and making clear the risks involved—which is why the United States applied sanctions on the assumption that they might gain peace. It was the perception of global issues in the East Asian context that escalated the American response beyond anything Japan had thought probable, and placed the Japanese in the untenable position of having either to fight or to back down because of dwindling oil reserves. The matter was urgent; without oil the Navy could not put to sea. On September 6, the Konoye cabinet decided tentatively for war and set the wheels in motion.

Many Japanese conceded that the American war-making potential was quantitatively far greater than that of Japan; America was larger, richer, and more industrially developed. In fact, in 1941, Japan had only one-tenth the productive capacity of the United States. This meant, for example, that the United States could build two million trucks during the war, the Japanese only 155,000. In addition, Japan suffered from the disadvantage of having a large part of its military strength and air power already committed to the China theater.

What the Japanese counted on to offset this was the supposedly qualitative superiority of their war-making capacity, particularly the discipline and almost mystical spirit of many of the officers and men, and the priority that would predictably be given by Americans to the European theater of the war. If a flabby America, badly wounded at the beginning, fought with less than half its strength in the Pacific, then a smaller but highly disciplined and purposeful enemy might bleed it badly enough to destroy its spirit. And in that case, there was hope for a limited Japanese victory: a settlement of a rather eighteenth-century character involving a loss of wealth, prestige, and overseas territories, but leaving the home governments and territories intact. Thus Japan blundered into a twentieth-century total war, expecting a limited war like those of the past.

Like Hitler grappling with the British "nation of shopkeepers" whose spirit he proposed to break, the Japanese underestimated American will—underestimated, in fact, the degree to which their own surprise attack at Pearl Harbor was a factor in strengthening rather than weakening American will. But in other respects, their hopes were not entirely forlorn. Indeed, historian Samuel Eliot Morison goes so far as to say that their strategy *"nearly worked."*

The United States was committed from the outset to a Europe-first strategy. Even before America's own entry into the war, President Roosevelt had become convinced that the survival of Britain as a great power was essential to the security and well-being of the United States; and in the so-called ABC Conferences between members of the American and British military staffs, during the first three months of 1941, he allowed American strategists to define Germany as the enemy of highest priority, should America ever enter the war, and to base their contingency planning upon that premise. Until 1945, American war plans did indeed call for the bulk of American power to go to the European theater.

An American decision made early in the war seemed to give further credence to the notion that the United States was fighting a limited war against Japan. This was the giving of highest priority in the allocation of resources to the development and deployment of strategic air power for massive strikes in 1943 against the industrial heartland of Germany. This carried several implied advantages for the Japanese. Obviously, it meant that most American airplanes would be flying thousands of miles away from Japanese troops and ships. But more subtly, it meant that the United States had committed its primary emphasis to a weapon—the strategic bomber—that could not then, or in the foreseeable future, be used against Japanese cities and factories, because the distances from America's existing bases were too great. The maximum range for heavy bombers then was 1,500 miles.

Concomitantly, the emphasis upon air power led to a drastic reduction in the projected size of the American Army. In September 1941, the War Department had estimated that 215 divisions would be necessary to defeat the Axis powers. In fact, only eighty-nine American divisions were formed during the war. The decision for a small Army simply ruled out of the question any thought of committing major American ground forces in China or continental Southeast Asia. It left most of Japan's landholdings outside America's sphere of effective action. And this, in turn, is one reason why American planners became convinced by 1945 that they would need the assistance of the Russian Army in Manchuria at the end of the war: namely, that there just were not enough American troops available to invade and occupy both the Japanese home islands and Manchuria at the same time. If Japanese armies on the continent decided to fight on after those in the homeland were crushed, it would be useful to have Russian military power to help subdue them.

The United States assumed that the Chinese were incapable of defeating the Japanese Army in their country and would have to receive massive assistance from some outside source. The American strategy in China during the war was to promote Chinese unity and supply China with as many of its military needs as America could without disrupting major Allied efforts in Europe and in the Pacific islands— and to do this in the hope of draining off Japanese strength by making the Chinese land mass a great sponge for Japan: what Russia had been for Napoleon and was being for Hitler.

But the steady erosion of American confidence in the military and domestic policies of the Kuomintang discouraged realistic hopes that China could do much more than soak up an uncertain amount of Japanese military resources. And after Chiang intrigued successfully for the removal of General Joseph Stilwell, and ruled out the possibility of a Chinese offensive directed by American officers, Washington substantially gave up on China and let that front stagnate. So there was no real expectation that the Chinese by themselves could take on the remaining Japanese armies in Manchuria in 1945, even in their then debilitated state.

What the Japanese had not counted on was the pattern of events that led the United States to undertake a limited offensive in the Pacific only half a year after Pearl Harbor, beginning in the summer of 1942. The attack on Pearl Harbor had destroyed the American battleship fleet but missed the aircraft carriers, which were cruising at the time. This was an extraordinary piece of luck, because naval aviation was improving to such a degree that in the ensuing war carrier-borne airplanes, rather than battleships, decided the control of the seas.

As it happened, American naval aviation was considerably more refined than its Japanese counterpart. In May 1942, at the battle of the Coral Sea, American carriers broke the Japanese offensive in southern New Guinea and frustrated the Japanese fleet in its attempt to isolate Australia. It was, incidentally, the first battle in history in which no ship on either side sighted the enemy. At the battle of Midway, June 1942, American carriers won control of the central Pacific by sinking four large Japanese carriers and turning back the Japanese battleship fleet.

These early victories in the theater of the war in which many Americans were most interested, coming at a time when large-scale European operations had not yet even begun, persuaded American strategists to depart from their overall plan and authorize a limited offensive in the Pacific. Interservice rivalries led to the undertaking of a two-pronged offensive. The Navy thrust across the central Pacific through the Marshalls, the Carolines, and the Marianas, slicing through that Japanese spider web. The second prong was an Army thrust up from New Caledonia in the South Pacific, by way of the Solomons and New Guinea, to the Philippines, capitalizing on the use of Australia as a staging area. Although it was hard going, the Japanese resisting with stubborn determination, there were limited successes from both these drives. Admiral Chester Nimitz's commanders won Tarawa, and General Douglas MacArthur's troops dislodged the Japanese from the eastern tip of New Guinea, where the dark, dripping, lush jungle made fighting particularly difficult. MacArthur had been adamant that liberation of the Philippines be high on the list of Allied priorities.

Accordingly, the Pacific theater took on a momentum that had not originally been foreseen, either in Tokyo or in Washington. By the end of 1942, not only the Navy but the Army as well had more forces deployed in the Pacific against Japan than in the European theaters against Germany and Italy. And the next year, in 1943, when British opposition forced the postponement of major landings in France until 1944, American strategists decided to have both Nimitz and MacArthur undertake major Pacific offensives. By November 1944, when the Air Force began strategic bombing of the Japanese mainland from newly liberated Guam, the Navy had already cut off the home islands from access to the resources of Southeast Asia, the American submarine service was wreaking havoc with Japanese merchant shipping.

In the early phase of the war, within five months after Pearl Harbor, the Japanese had overrun a huge area; the entire northern Pacific west of the international date line lay in their hands, and more than 100 million people had fallen under their dominion. India on the west and Australia to the south trembled. Were they to be next? Some in India fervently hoped they were.

If one adds occupied China and Korea to Japan's new conquests, they now embraced nearly one-quarter the population of the globe.

Japan's success severed old ties between much of East and Southeast Asia and the Western world. It gave powerful impetus to local nationalisms, Japan's armies thus playing a role similar to that of the soldiers of Napoleon in Europe 150 years before as dissolvers of old allegiances. For the Westerner in Asia, things would never be the same again.

But, capricious, arbitrary, and often harsh, Japan's military leaders built a war-won empire of only negative importance. The victors failed to bind the far-flung territories into effective support for the demands of the Japanese war machine. Petroleum and all the other resources so desperately required did not flow to the north as had been anticipated. That all of Southeast Asia was brought under one rule for the first time in history would have no lasting significance. Japan failed even temporarily to win the allegiance of the peoples of Southeast Asia, and whatever cooperation developed between Southeast Asians and Japanese was purely from expedience. The marriage was unequal, short-lived, and strictly one of convenience. And it generated a legacy of hatred which, long after the war was over, would plague the Japanese trying to build economic linkages with that part of the world.

Americans were naturally most concerned with their own erstwhile colonial empire, the Philippine Islands. By the Tydings-McDuffie Act (1934), the United States had made the Philippines an internally self-governing commonwealth, with an elected president and a constitution of the Filipinos' own making. For a period of ten years, an American high commissioner, the successor to the governors general of former days, would continue to exercise a limited veto power; and the United States would retain control of defense, foreign relations, and tariff matters. At the end of the ten years, the islands were to become fully independent.

This act had been the result of a convergence of Filipino and American desires during the early years of the Great Depression. On the Philippine side, independence remained the most emotional and inclusive issue in the islands' politics. Elitist politicians ran on the issue and used it as a way of rallying popular support and winning sanction for their rule without having to undertake social and economic reforms of a sort that would endanger the power of their interests or the comfort of their status. They needed the independence issue.

On the other hand, most Filipinos of this stripe were psychologically binational; and by the end of the 1920s they could see real, tangible reasons for postponing independence in favor of a more moderate solution like the commonwealth. Specifically, they were reluctant in the middle of a depression to face the economic costs of losing either free access to the American market for their exports or infusions of American capital for internal improvements; and they were afraid of Japan and of fledgling revolutionary movements inside the islands that were at least as much anti-elite as they were anti-American.

So in the late 1920s and the very early 1930s, a number of the most powerful Filipino politicians, including Manuel Quezon, let it be known to American friends that if the job could be done quickly and deftly, they were prepared to accept the political risks of agreeing to dominion or commonwealth status on the Australian model instead of immediate independence.

In the meantime, while Filipinos were evolving toward the American position, Americans were coming more than halfway to meet them. The high economic hopes that many Americans had held for the Philippines in the early 1920s proved within a few years to be grossly inflated. And by 1931 there was a solid phalanx of American interests that wanted to be rid of the Philippines: idealists who feared retention would sully American honor; isolationists who feared the islands' location would involve the United States in an Asian war; nativists, racists, and labor unions that opposed Filipino immigration; farmers and their allies afraid of competition in the midst of a depression from Filipino raw materials. Even bankers wanted to cut the islands loose. Some, among them the National City Bank of New York, had overinvested in Cuban sugar. They now felt they needed a tariff against competitive Philippine sugar imports to save their Cuban investment.

The advocates of independence stimulated a larger public, comprising new constituencies that had never before taken an active interest in Philippine freedom; and their combined force simply rolled over what was left of the old retentionist alliance. But in America, as in the Philippines, there were counterforces and restraints at work inside the country. Neither the Hoover nor the Roosevelt administration wanted to give the impression of simply ditching the Philippines when the going got rough. And so, for Americans as for Filipinos, gradual independence, achieved by way of a commonwealth, came to seem a desirable middle ground.

The Commonwealth of the Philippines, then, was a political compromise: a step toward independence, but not the thing itself. It was meant in part to provide time and an American protective shield behind which Filipinos could find shelter while they developed the ability to defend themselves; but, in fact, continuing links to the United States probably made the war worse for Filipinos than it would have been if they had been independent.

The presence of American forces in the archipelago at the outbreak of the war, instead of protecting the islands, undoubtedly made the Japanese conquest more cruel and bloody than it otherwise would have been; and the obligation of honor General MacArthur felt to liberate the islands in 1944, when he could perfectly well have leapfrogged around them, left the Philippines one of the most war-devastated areas in the world.

The Japanese occupation divided Filipinos from each other. Some Filipinos had admired the discipline and purpose they perceived in Japanese society, and responded enthusiastically to Pan-Asianist ideas; naturally these people cooperated with the Japanese and staffed the civilian Filipino government that Japan was eager to establish in place of military rule. But the overwhelming majority of people either actively or passively withheld their allegiance. Filipino personal and social ethics center upon a strong and supple sense of reciprocity. And these people figured that they owed the Americans something because, after the violence and duplicity of the turn-of-the-century encounter had passed, Americans had treated them well. After all, America was the only imperial power that had voluntarily conceded independence to an Asian people.

For one group in the society, however, the question of collaboration with Japan was agonizingly difficult. This was the elite. They needed to control politics in order to secure their social and economic eminence. They needed access to the police power of the state; they needed to control the definition and discussion of public issues; and they needed the leverage upon mass emotions that they got from political leadership. It was obvious that the Japanese as part of their pacification program would entrust political authority over domestic matters to Filipinos who would cooperate; and since the best guess at the time seemed to be that the Japanese occupation would last for as long as five or ten years, there were powerful arguments from class and self-interest for collaborating with the occupiers.

Precedent encouraged such a course. The Americans, forty years before, had also been occupiers who had seized the islands from an alien master. Furthermore, there was the rationale—sometimes ingenuous and sometimes not—that by taking a role in the government, members of the elite might be able to soften Japanese rule and protect the people. And there was the expedient awareness that, unlike the common folk, the professional and landowning elite were highly visible and could not easily escape Japanese pressure to collaborate.

So, as a group (and with some exceptions), the elite did collaborate; and when they did, the sense of betrayal that their collaboration provoked created for the first time a nationalist sanction for class hostility, legitimizing violence against the elite and permanently compromising their authority.

When the Americans and the Filipino officials of the commonwealth returned to the islands in 1944, they faced an acute problem in restoring the authority of the state in a polarized society. They had to choose, in re-establishing the commonwealth on Philippine soil, between the established corps of leaders, who were safe and conservative known quantities but badly tainted in American eyes as well as in those of the Filipinos by their collaboration—and the leaders of the guerrilla resistance, who had real popular roots but had alienated many people by the extent of their violence against Filipinos as well as Japanese during the war, and who clearly had a proto-Marxist class orientation. When the old elite scored a controversial electoral success over the former resistance leaders in the presidential elections of 1946, the surviving guerrilla units gave up on the political process, went underground, and became the core of the HMB, or Huk, movement of the late 1940s and early 1950s.

Bombing supplemented blockade and gave the coup de grace to Japan's emaciated economy. The machinery virtually ground to a stop; the people were brought to the brink of starvation. Bomb tonnage dropped on Japan was far smaller than what the Germans received from the Allies, but the vulnerability of Japan's cities—most of their buildings were wooden—made the impact very great. Incendiary raids were particularly destructive, and they were cheap for the attacker: 1.4 American bombers were lost for every square mile of Japanese city destroyed. In the great raid of March 10, 1945, fifty square miles of Tokyo burned, in a greater disaster than the cataclysmic earthquake of 1923.

For most Japanese, the atomic bombs, when they fell in August, were simply one more agony in a lengthy catalogue of disaster, their genetic effects not clearly understood. After the war, Americans in large numbers read with sickening horror John Hersey's vivid report, *Hiroshima,* and came to realize what the new age of nuclear warfare meant to humankind. And in the years since, Americans and Japanese both have pondered the dropping of the two bombs—their necessity at the time, and the moral implications of their use.

The bombs speeded the concluding of the war but until the very end, responsible officers in the Imperial Japanese Army were still talking of a last-ditch stand, defending the precious homeland with sharpened bamboo spears wielded by every man, woman, and child. Those Japanese who wanted peace steadily gathered adherents, but the need to achieve a consensus among the governing elites made the process agonizingly slow.

The guns were stilled on August 14. And what had the great conflict accomplished? Millions of lives had been lost or maimed, countless treasure expended, immeasurable suffering endured. For Americans, the human costs were far less than for the Japanese. The destruction of Japan solved only the problem of Japanese militarism. Inexorably, Americans were sucked into the resulting power vacuum in northeastern Asia—and with incalculable results.

(15)

Supine Japan

FLAME AND STEEL relentlessly seared and pounded the cities of Japan and the hapless people inhabiting them in the dreadful weeks of spring and summer 1945. The Japanese government delayed accepting the surrender terms laid down by the Allies in the Potsdam Declaration. Hiroshima, then Nagasaki, suffered nuclear attack. The Soviet Union entered the war and quickly began to overrun Japanese-held northeastern Asia. Thousands of Japanese troops, members of the erstwhile crack Kwantung Army, by now an empty shell, abjectly surrendered on the plains of Manchuria.

Frantically, Tokyo sought to determine what the Allies proposed to do about the Emperor in the peace settlement. Finally, the Japanese accepted the Potsdam terms with the stipulation, ignored by the Allies, that the imperial prerogatives be unaltered. Each side, Allied and Japanese, chose to put its own interpretation on the terms of agreement. The Emperor himself, breaking all precedent, spoke to his people in a noontime radio broadcast on August 15, and in words echoing those used by his imperial grandfather, the Meiji Emperor, when he announced the acceptance of the humiliating Triple Intervention of 1895, Hirohito said the Japanese must again "endure the unendurable."

Japan was not only defeated in war, but for the first time in the nation's recorded history it was to be garrisoned by enemy troops. Japan had in the past engaged in large-scale cultural borrowing from overseas. Never before had the process been compulsory. Never had there been so many resident tutors.

203

Military occupations were a common enough phenomenon and there were several going on in the world at that time. The Soviet Union in Eastern Europe was occupying countries which were territorially contiguous and culturally similar. Germany was split into zones and governed directly by the occupying powers.

The American occupation of Japan was unique. In world history it was the only cross-cultural instance of one advanced nation occupying another advanced nation and attempting to change its politics, economy, and society in some rather basic ways, using the government of the occupied state to effect the changes. Since the two nations were on a rough parity in technology, the encounter was not in the classic imperialist mode of cultural confrontation. It was for East Asia a new kind of Western presence.

Considering the colossal scale of the attempt, the success of this great American undertaking in Japan is a tribute not only to the American teachers but to their Japanese students. Not surprisingly, those aspects of occupation policy enjoying the most success were the ones with roots in what had already been evolving in Japanese society (liberation of women, the growth of the labor movement, land reform), issues about which people on both sides could be enthusiastic.

The Americans carried along to Japan ideas and emotions which would both consciously and unconsciously form and direct their evolving policies. The occupiers were, for one thing, convinced of the universality of American culture and its values. Crèvecoeur and Whitman, the themes of the city on a hill and westward the course of empire had nourished these beliefs. The Declaration of Indpendence had given them first formal statement.

Many of the occupiers had a strong missionary urge: to proselytize democracy, Christianity, and industrial technology, to bring these attributes of America to the benighted. To someone like Douglas MacArthur these qualities of American civilization appeared inextricably linked. That missionary impulse had, of course, peculiar reference to East Asia, since Americans had felt for more than a century that it was their destiny to revitalize the decadent civilizations of East Asia. China had, as we know, been the paramount target, but now Japan was wide open. For Christianity, as more than one churchman exulted, it was the greatest challenge and opportunity since the days of the Roman empire. In American eyes, the feudal and militarist values so prominent in Japan during the prewar period now had to go. The time was ripe for what General MacArthur would call a "spiritual revolution."

Ancillary to the missionary urge was American optimism and self-confidence. Americans never doubted they would win the war, even in the disastrous weeks and months following Pearl Harbor. Now they had saved the world from Hitler. They were leaders in establishing a new world organization to maintain the peace. Americans were sure of their power to change others as well as to improve themselves. One might say they were captives of the planning myth: that they could totally subject complex social change to rationality. Such was the continuing influence of the New Deal, faltering at home, still vigorous overseas.

Finally Americans brought to their task in Japan a shallowly implanted attitude of dislike, even hatred, toward the Japanese. Pearl Harbor, "the sneak attack," and reports about Japanese treatment of American prisoners of war created a sense of outrage and provided a basis upon which the American public could construct a fantasy of the Japanese: subhuman, simian, squat, fan-toothed, myopic and barbarous people, addicted to cruelty, indifferent to human life, gifted with guile and cunning that bordered on the magical. Even American leaders were infected with this virulence, which appeared to dim the prospects for a happy and successful occupation of Japan.

Americans arrived in a devastated and exhausted nation. The trains still ran; the farmers still worked their fields; but in the cities the smoke of fires from air raids had replaced that of factory chimneys; the industrial life of Japan had virtually come to a halt. What factories were not destroyed or heavily damaged were obliged to shut down because they had no raw materials. Nothing could be brought in from overseas; Japan's merchant marine for the most part lay at the bottom of the sea. Because fertilizer was scarce, crop yields dropped. Land, machinery, and people throughout the country were run down. Tired out, undernourished, and half sick, most Japanese were concerned foremost with survival: food, shelter, and how to get through the coming winter.

The American occupiers brought all their own food. The Japanese had expected them to live off the local economy as the Japanese themselves had done in their vicious and exploitative occupation of China. That the Americans brought their own supplies provoked an immediate and powerful wave of sentiment in their favor. And both sides were agreeably surprised that the other was so different from what they had expected. The Americans did not behave like rampaging beasts, beating up the men and raping the women; Japanese fanatics did not attack the occupiers, screaming *banzai* and brandishing sharpened bamboo spears.

Both sides learned they had been the victims of wartime propaganda. An American Marine, landing in an advanced party at Sasebo with the vow on his lips to "kill a goddamn Jap," was soon handing out chewing gum and chocolate bars to swarms of curious, hungry children. Lonely GIs were dating Japanese girls within weeks after the first apprehensive Americans landed in Japan—despite the Army's initial discouragement of "fraternization."

There were not the same deep residues of anger, grief, and hatred for Americans to overcome in Japan as there were in Germany. The Bataan death march, bad as it may have been, was not to be compared to Buchenwald. And the Japanese appeared to bear little overt resentment over the bombing, even the nuclear attacks, by the Americans. They were ready to defer in every way to the conqueror, even stepping off the sidewalk to let him pass. What anger the Japanese people showed was focused on their own military leadership, whose ineptitude, they judged, was responsible for the debacle. Lieutenant General Robert Eichelberger, commander of the occupying Eighth Army, confided to his diary that the Japanese gave him the impression of liking the American military much more than they did their own.

The punitive feelings of the American occupiers rather quickly softened, in official policy as well as in the realm of personal relationships. The "purge," as it was unfortunately called, of those leaders Americans judged by category to have been responsible for Japan's march into war was soon softened, and the war crimes trials, although carried to their grim denouement, became something of an embarrassment. Occasionally the desire for vengeance would flare up, but it never became a dominant theme in the occupation. Working harmony rapidly developed; no acts of violence of any significance occurred. From the first weeks it was clear that America and Japan would not have an adversary relationship.

Not long after the occupation began, the Supreme Commander recommended to Washington that food be imported for the Japanese lest starvation occur. He could advance practical, not simply humanitarian, reasons for this: a disease-ridden Japanese people risked the health of the occupying troops; a Japanese people driven to disorder by shortages of food would make the task of governing them far more difficult. In that first winter, almost every Japanese lost weight, malnutrition was widespread, and many were gnawed by hunger. But few starved. Japanese society was not convulsed, its fabric did not unravel, and the occupiers could undertake their mission with relative equanimity.

General Douglas MacArthur was named Supreme Commander* in August 1945. He was then and later widely regarded as a good choice by temperament and ability for this high responsibility, which he clearly relished exercising. Of MacArthur, it can be said that never has an American been given such great power over so many people for so long a time.

In personality, MacArthur bore striking resemblance to that earlier American military statesman Commodore Matthew Perry: senior officer and war hero, proud, forceful, and self-assured, with the skill and the taste for self-dramatization. Neither MacArthur nor Perry was a cultural relativist. Each carried to Japan a sense of mission; each was firmly convinced of the rectitude of American purpose, and fully persuaded of the universal applicability of the American ideal. Each, in short, personified the desires of a large number of his compatriots at a particular time.

Although the late 1940s may have been a pinnacle of American power in the world, Americans, uneasy with their new crown, were possessed by a sense of menace. The nuclear bomb thrust a new uncertainty into warfare, worrisome even when the United States enjoyed a monopoly on nuclear weapons. Relations with the Soviet Union rapidly worsened and the possibility of another major war loomed darkly on the horizon. Europe struggled desperately to revive.

The era was one of profound unease. But Japan was one area of American activity where the American public saw things as going right. MacArthur was a man of outward serenity and strength. His grandiloquence, anachronistic though it may have been, and his moral certainty reassured, even captivated, many Americans and Japanese. MacArthur could in his person embody and articulate that spirit of confidence

---

* Known as SCAP—Supreme Commander, Allied Powers. The acronym was also freely applied to MacArthur's staff and to the Tokyo headquarters of the occupation.

and idealism with which the United States undertook the occupation.

Erik Erikson and other psychohistorians would find rich fare in a study of "Young Man MacArthur," probing, for instance, his relationship with his mother. Mrs. MacArthur was ambitious for her boy, and constantly lobbied on his behalf with her friends and acquaintances in high places. When Douglas entered West Point, she came along, taking a room in a nearby hotel so that she might see him every day. One of his classmates later said that "Doug was the first cadet whose mother went through the Academy with him."

Whether or not his mother's presence helped him, Cadet Mac-Arthur made an outstanding record at the Point, a superb beginning to a brilliant career. A "boy wonder" in World War I when he became the Army's youngest general, he was the nation's most decorated soldier when he arrived, at the sunset of his career, to take up in Japan the most important assignment of his life. For this great task MacArthur had an appropriately lofty attitude. On arrival, he told a group of journalists that he had only two advisers: George Washington and Abraham Lincoln.

The "Blue-Eyed Shogun," some Japanese called him, living and working as he did within a narrow Tokyo orbit. In contrast to the Emperor's new routine, which carried him into public view, the Supreme Commander was rarely seen, except arriving and departing his office at the Dai Ichi Insurance Building in downtown Tokyo. The general hardly ever traveled; he went nowhere else in Japan except out to the airport; he saw those whom he wished to see, not many Japanese among them, but invariably all important visiting Americans. He evinced no interest in Japanese culture, unlike a number of those working for him who began to cultivate such pursuits.

The occupation was an American enterprise. In theory and in name it was "Allied"; in practice the United States had virtually absolute authority. Back in Washington, the Far Eastern Commission, an Allied group, was charged with the responsibility of forming policy, and it maintained eyes and ears in Tokyo by means of the Allied Council for Japan on which the four leading powers (the U.S.S.R., the U.S.A., Great Britain in the form of the commonwealth, and Nationalist China) were represented. The FEC was slow to get under way, its first session coming six months after the occupation had begun. As a result the major lines of policy had already been set, principally by the Supreme

Commander himself, and the Allies could only go along with them.

The American government seemed glad to have General Mac-Arthur seize the initiative and keep it. As long as no crises erupted in Japan, Washington was glad to let MacArthur alone. The general was too prickly a personality to be easily dealt with. Even presidents handled him with care. Furthermore, Japan was only one of a large number of postwar problems compelling the attention of statesmen in Washington. It was most comfortable for them to leave MacArthur to handle Japan as he saw fit.

So, one of FEC's members ruefully remarked, "We were supposed to tell General MacArthur what to do and of course couldn't." The Allied Council in Tokyo proved to be simply a forum for staging public arguments among the great powers. The British commonwealth, or at least its Australian spokesman, resented its small role in the occupation, and displayed that irritation in protracted nagging criticisms. Commonwealth troops joined the garrison forces but had no role in governing the Japanese.

But the chief acrimony broke out between the Soviet Union and the United States. The Russians, excluded completely from the occupation, were quick to fault American policies; and the Americans were quick to take offense. Cold War rivalries soon embittered and increased the debates. Yet there was little these other nations could do to affect what the Americans sought to accomplish in Japan. Only the Japanese themselves could do that.

Below MacArthur was his circle—his "court," as the critics would have it—jockeying for favor, taking positions sometimes on grounds of personal rivalry rather than policy or ideology, although sharp differences of philosophy did exist. Fierce loyalty to the Supreme Commander was the common bond of these men; many of them had served with him for a long time. Among these people were men of real ability, but MacArthur was not a man to share headlines or to encourage highly ambitious associates.

Below the exalted first circle within Tokyo GHQ and beyond, scattered throughout Japan, were the rest of the "occupationnaires," men and a few women of wide-ranging talents and viewpoints. Opportunities being good at the time back in the United States, it was not always easy to lure first-rate people to the service of the occupation. The opportunity for authority and responsibility beyond what one might otherwise attain attracted some. Other people came to Japan because the pay was generous and the living standards high. Perhaps the plumbing and heating were not of "Stateside" quality; but servants were abundant and food, liquor, and entertainment cheap. As the occupation progressed, observers complained that the quality of those recruited to serve in it appeared to decline.

Roughly two million Americans passed through Japan during the eighty months of the occupation. Some of them were there for the entire period. Few knew anything about Japan when they arrived, and most of them did not learn much while they were there. Exceptions, of course, existed. But the Old Japan Hands—missionaries, diplomats, and merchants who had spent a long time in Japan before the war and knew the language and culture well (there were a *few* such Americans)—were not used by MacArthur. None had a prominent policymaking post in Japan during the crucial early stage of the occupation. Thus, if the occupiers had a common denominator, it was ignorance of Japan.

Since few Americans in Japan spoke enough Japanese to get along comfortably in that language, they were obliged to rely upon interpreters or upon those Japanese who spoke some English. Some of the former, like Otis Cary and Donald Keene, were outstanding. Nisei played a big role. Second-generation Americans, they had learned Japanese in order to communicate with their immigrant grandparents. Often they did not read the language. Nor did they necessarily have any understanding of, or sympathy for, Japanese culture. Many of them were not particularly well educated. Like many ethnic groups in America at that time, they were trying to be as "American" as possible. In Japan, because they spoke Japanese, other Americans tended to defer to them as authorities on everything Japanese.

The average GI was given little inducement to learn much about Japan. The PX-commissary world which was created inside the large fenced space of every American base in Japan provided a comfortable and cheap life, much like that on any American military base anywhere in the world. Food, housing, entertainment, and, of course, work were all there; one never needed to leave.

The Army did encourage travel within Japan. At first, in fact, the trains were free to the occupiers; and they were never expensive, even for the lowliest GI. He could vacation at luxurious seaside or mountain resorts, the best Japan could offer, at very little cost. Commandeered from their Japanese owners, these hotels were Army-run extensions of the military-base world, but at least the visitor was obliged to move through Japan in order to get there.

And, of course, many Americans did venture out of the cocoon. Some even learned the language, some developed an interest in Japanese culture, in theater, the martial arts, the fine arts and folk arts. People shopped and collected. But it was within the milieu of popular culture, the world of the bar and the brothel, where the intercultural exchange took place for the largest number. Every base entrance was ringed by a cluster of tawdry shops, often catering or pandering to the lowest tastes but offering the average GI the easiest opportunity to meet Japanese girls.

Out of this unpromising milieu came many of the interracial marriages of the occupation. Others of them had more respectable roots; although both sides, the American and the Japanese, had to fight against the racial and cultural prejudice which discouraged such unions. For many Americans, being in Japan was the first experience of living among another race and as a minority, albeit a highly privileged one.

In Germany, Americans found that invasion and desperate large-scale fighting at the end of the war brought not only the ravaging of much of the material culture but also the collapse and disappearance of most of the apparatus of government. In Japan, Americans arrived to find the civil government completely intact and smoothly functioning. American authority could be relatively easily superimposed on top of Japanese structure. The American decision to insert themselves in this fashion, like that of squeezing out the Allies, was made before the occupation began.

The question of the future of the Emperor remained unclear until the drafting of the new constitution early in 1947 in which he was declared to be simply a symbol of the state. At war's end public opinion in the United States had strongly favored doing away with the imperial institution. But the Emperor's name was absent from the list of war criminals drawn up by the occupation authorities in the spring of 1946, and to the Japanese, American policy implied that the Emperor could be retained. This proved a powerful incentive to them to cooperate with the Americans.

The American decision to use the Emperor, along with the rest of the Japanese civil government, happened to be entirely consonant with customary Japanese patterns of governance. The only change was that the orders now came from an alien source, from outsiders. For in Japan real power was traditionally concealed behind a facade of those—like the Emperor—nominally exercising power. So when SCAP issued orders or informally made suggestions, the Japanese carried them out and found the process reasonably comfortable.

MacArthur's mandate was sufficiently vague as to allow considerable opportunity for creativity. Like the Meiji reformers three-quarters of a century earlier, MacArthur and his men were pragmatists when it came to specific programs. The Meiji leaders were concerned primarily with building military strength; the MacArthur group were concerned primarily with wiping out such strength. The Americans began, acutely aware of past failures in other military occupations. The general himself had been in the Rhineland after Germany's defeat in 1918. That had not been a success, a fact he well knew.

Uncertainty as to how long the occupation should last and conflicting views of what Japan ought to be in the future were among the dynamic elements keeping the situation in a state of flux, and preventing those in charge from developing and executing an overall detailed plan. Among the disparate individuals working at GHQ were former businessmen, Wall Street lawyers, ex–New Deal bureaucrats, Midwestern agricultural experts, teachers, and career Army officers. One has the feeling that each had his own private vision of what Japan ought to be.

Furthermore, the changing world political climate had a powerful impact on the evolving occupation: growing hostility toward the U.S.S.R., with whom the American relationship had always been ambiguous; and, with the triumph of the Chinese Communist revolution in 1949, the collapse of American hopes there. These tensions obviously caused Americans to reflect on the inadvisability of a continuing hostility toward Japan. Perhaps Japan could replace China as America's Far Eastern ally. In 1948, Thomas E. Dewey nearly became the first Republican President since Herbert Hoover. The climate of opinion in the United States had grown more conservative. This too had its impact on the evolution of American thinking about Japan. Critics of the occupation—Americans and Japanese, then and later—charged that the American authorities, aided in unspoken alliance with Japanese conservatives, backed away from significant democratic reform. In fact no political reforms were changed, or even social ones, though there was a decided scaling down of economic reforms.

Japanese responses to the occupation were not, of course, simply passive. Prime Minister Yoshida Shigeru, longtime professional diplomat, who, with his cigars, his wing collars, and his Rolls-Royce, liked to play the part of the English aristocrat (nothing pleased him more than to be likened to Winston Churchill), proved a wily manipulator of the Americans—who did not perceive the degree to which the Japanese guided their conquerors. Americans, although keenly aware of Japan's economic borrowing, were largely ignorant of the long Japanese tradition of conscious cultural borrowing, of adaptation, of preserving the essence of their own ways while taking on the appearance and manner of another.

The first order of business for the occupiers was to disarm the Japanese, to destroy their ability to make war. Getting the soldiers and sailors out of uniform was accomplished entirely by the Japanese themselves, rapidly and efficiently. With equal speed and competence, the Japanese moved six million of their people, on everything from aircraft carriers to sailing ships—soldiers, officials, teachers, technicians, clerks, engineers, wives and children—back home from the far-flung former empire. These individuals had to begin life all over again in a homeland which some of them had never seen before.

Much of the imperial Navy had been sunk or severely damaged in the fighting. What ships survived, their ferrying duties successfully completed, were now either distributed as spoils to the Allies or scrapped. Although the imperial Army on the home island, unbloodied by conflict, had been largely intact, by December 1945 it too had ceased to exist.

Vast quantities of war materiel remained from both services, and much of it—like guns, tanks, airplanes, and ammunition—had to be ferreted out and destroyed. This time-consuming and dangerous task was accomplished under American supervision but largely by Japanese hands.

All of this was perfectly straightforward; the Japanese were cooperative. The unexpected ease with which the breaking up of the great war machine was accomplished swelled American expectations of what could be done in Japan and how fast they could do it. But more complicated than destroying the means to make war was the question of how the victors should cope with Japan's will to make war. Disposing of the instruments was insufficient; the Japanese had to be convinced of the foolishness of using war as a means of solving national problems.

This meant altering Japan's political culture. Democracy, the Americans thought, would be the best form of government for the Japanese, the kind most likely to insure peace. It was "good for us, therefore it should be good for them too," the theory being that social justice and civil liberties ought to lead to rational political behavior. The idea is certainly plausible but is not one about which there was much speculating. It was taken as a given, and plans sprang from the assumption.

Although the reformers could build upon Japan's experience of the 1920s with a British type of political system, the Japanese required new institutions to root the sources of authority firmly in the people. All the people should choose the Diet, a parliament to which a cabinet and prime minister would be responsible, with a place made in political life for those hitherto politically inert, inarticulate, or voteless: labor, women, and youth. The old leadership, blamed for bringing about the war as well as for inhibiting popular government, had to be excised and cast aside. The Japanese anticipated that Americans might concern themselves with a wide array of Japanese affairs. One military government officer, stationed out in the provinces, was startled to be asked by a middle-aged Japanese woman, "Does military government have a plan whereby the Japanese people can get sexual satisfaction?"

Americans judged that Japan required sweeping changes, and they were ready to see them carried out in legal codes and local government, through the police, in land-holding patterns, and in the organization of big business. Many believed the large combines, *zaibatsu*, to have been powerful anti-democratic forces which had promoted war.

Since a continuing successful democracy could not be established by fiat, particularly one issued by a foreign occupying army, reform had to begin with the Japanese educational system so that the youth of the nation would grow up to demand democracy, to support it, to fight for it. Teachers, curricula, ways of teaching and learning, all required change. Americans laid out the pattern of what they wanted done with Japan's schools; the Japanese carried it out. Nearly a million teachers and education officials were, for a starter, screened for suitability to the new spirit of democracy.

The Japanese were constantly exhorted to follow the American model. But few Americans seem to have thought very much about whether that model was appropriate to Japan. New teachers and new courses eliminated the ultranationalism and militarism to which the

Americans so vigorously objected. Coeducation became prevalent. The initial enthusiasm of Japanese boys for having girls in their classes was somewhat dampened by the realization that the girls were not going to clean the classrooms for them. New methods of teaching were attractive to many Japanese, particularly the students. But the large number of schools and colleges suddenly elevated to university status, the reorganizing of the school years so that the Japanese could have junior high schools like the Americans—all this put severe demands on the limited amount of money postwar Japan had to spend on education. And that budget was already strained to the utmost by the need to repair and to replace the damage of war: burned-out school buildings, smashed laboratory equipment, and lost books. Yet in this specific field of reform, as in others, the Americans conspicuously failed to engage the sympathies of the Japanese intellectual community. These people—scholars and critics, writers and journalists—were much more drawn to Marxism. They became the hottest and most persistent critics of American policies and the American presence in Japan.

Land reform was one of the two most important specific changes carried out at the prodding of the occupiers. Here was an area in which the reformers could be virtually as radical as they liked, for the sturdy Jeffersonian farmer tilling his own soil was an image pleasing to almost all Americans. Unlike the breakup of big business in Japan, land reform did not strike uncomfortable parallels with what might want doing in the United States. But the Americans were not merely agrarian reformers, they were more revolutionary than that.

The occupation authorities recalled that the Meiji constitution had served the needs of both parliamentary democracy and military oligarchy. Freedom requires highly specific guarantees; and although a constitution may be less important for what it says than how people choose to interpret it, the law is nonetheless of great importance for spelling out human rights.

Therefore, the Americans instigated a new constitution, the second of their two most important reform measures for Japan. This constitution of 1947 provides, among other civil rights for citizens, specific legal equality for Japanese women, something that Americans had yet to secure more than 30 years later. Douglas MacArthur thus goes down in Japanese history as, among other things, a radical feminist.

Article Nine, the most controversial and most radical clause of the constitution, renounces war and pledges that Japan will not maintain armed forces. The clause has inhibited armament; it has not prevented it. For both the American and Japanese governments have chosen to interpret the law as allowing the Japanese to maintain armed forces for self-defense. After more than three decades, the constitution remains unchanged.

Japan emerged from the occupation with a working democratic system and a high degree of social stability; the nation was poised for the brilliant economic success which would flower in the 1960s. No one, even the Japanese, anticipated such a triumph. Americans perceived Japan as a weak client state long after reality was quite different. Only from a purely military point of view did Japan remain weak. The misperception was serious, because it inhibited Americans from responding to Japan's economic power. The occupation mentality lingered; Americans were not ready to learn anything from the Japanese. The burst of study and learning about Japan in America inspired by the demands of war was not sustained; and the Japanese continued to exhibit more interest in and to learn more about the United States than Americans about Japan.

Looking back at the occupation, for the United States the experience was a high point of national self-confidence. "We knew what was best for the Japanese," said one of the occupiers. Many would have agreed with him, including a lot of Japanese. The paradox is that despite profound American ethnocentrism and despite profound American ignorance of Japan, the occupation went well. Japan has a much greater aversion to armaments and their use than any other power; Japan remains friendly to the United States. Sir George Sansom, the great British scholar-diplomat, musing about the occupation, said, "Although I could criticize, I could write a long book showing all the mistakes the American government made, I think the thing was a great success."

For the Japanese, naturally, it was a profound relief to have it over. The signing of the San Francisco peace treaty and a mutual security agreement brought the formal end of the occupation on March 28, 1952, and the Emperor could greet the arrival of spring with a poem:

> Winter with bitter cold wind
>   has gone
> And much awaited spring comes round with double
>   cherry blossoms

(16)

Americans and the "Loss of China"

HISTORY GIVES, and history takes away. America's much touted "success" in Japan found its simultaneous antithesis across the Yellow and East China seas in what was widely described as the "failure" of American policy in China.

"Failure" was actually among the gentler terms applied to the triumph of the Chinese Communists and the collapse of the Chinese Nationalists between 1945 and 1949. Instead, the so-called "loss" of China was denounced by many as a "sellout" or "betrayal," the result not merely of incompetence but of conspiracy and even treason among covert American Communists and their liberal "fellow travelers."

The intensity of American reaction to the victory of Mao Tse-tung is difficult to recreate for those of a later generation. Even those who experienced it are sometimes baffled in retrospect.

Yet if you had described to an informed observer, on the eve of Pearl Harbor in late 1941, the shape and condition of Sino-American relations a decade later, in 1951, he would undoubtedly have judged you demented. Recalling the world of 1941—heroic China struggling for survival against the mighty Japanese empire allied to Hitler's juggernaut—consider the American–East Asian scene ten years later.

In Asia, a strong, reunified China under Communist rule was fighting the United States to a stalemate in Korea. Nationalist China's leaders, their supporters, and some troops—about two million in all—had fled to exile on the island of Taiwan, a hundred miles off the coast. Communist-led insurrections were smoldering in many other parts of Asia, most notably in Malaya and Indochina. And with Japan de-

217

feated, occupied, and disarmed, the United States was playing as never before the role of gendarme of the Pacific.

Meanwhile, at home in America, a process of recrimination over China's "loss" and the Cold War—a major Communist scare—was well under way. This was a process that would eventually destroy or maim scores of careers, in and out of government. It would oust the Democratic party from power after twenty years in highest office; and it would make many Americans distrustful of their neighbors and colleagues, "security"-conscious as never before. It was also a process that would lead the American government into an unaccustomed stance of formal Pacific and East Asian militancy in an effort to "contain and isolate Red China."

The question is fairly obvious: How can one explain such a total transformation and the trauma it produced?

The answers lie in the complex tangle of wartime China. Out of that tangle, three general developments seem overriding: the disintegration of the Chinese Nationalists; the simultaneous strengthening of the Chinese Communists; and the new reality of American intervention in Chinese politics, from Pearl Harbor onward.

The Kuomintang's failure is the easiest to diagnose. The central government had been unable in its Nanking years to cope with the dual problem of internal rebels and external aggressors. It had also failed, moreover, in its hybrid and halfhearted efforts to fill the vacuum left by the collapse of Confucianism as an ideology and social cement. During the years of its first united front with the Communists in the 1920s, the KMT had been for a while infused with Marxism-Leninism— which meant democratic centralism to increase the party's effectiveness, and a commitment to both social revolution and anti-imperialism. But when Chiang Kai-shek broke with the Communists in 1927, and indeed tried to restore a facade of Confucianism in the 1930s, his regime lost touch with large numbers of the nation's intellectuals and students. It lost further touch with such catalytic groups during its efforts to appease Japan prior to 1937, since major objectives of Chinese *nationalism,* in all its forms and superheated fervor, were the attainment of national power and the ouster of all foreign imperialists.

Simultaneous with the early and continuing defection of the students and intellectuals was—as we have seen—the KMT government's failure to treat the fundamental causes of acute rural distress, and therefore the eventual defection of vast numbers of peasants once a more promising alternative was available to them. It must be stressed further that this KMT government was initially sustained by its ties with treaty port bankers, merchants, and industrialists on the seacoast—the modern sector of the economy, including a goodly number of American-trained "returned students" who helped staff its bureaucracy. But after the Japanese invasion, Chiang and his colleagues were severed from that more modern, and sometimes progressive, sector as a source of support. And with the retreat to Szechwan (Sichuan) in 1938, the KMT had to rely increasingly on its two other internal sources of support: the landlord class, and several leftover warlords with semi-private armies. In this transition, the Chinese Nationalists became both weaker and much more conservative.

To weakness and conservatism one must add the malaise of creeping demoralization. Although "Free China" rejoiced in the aftermath of Pearl Harbor, now allied to strong friends abroad in a worldwide struggle, its leaders soon discovered that China's role would be largely a holding operation—pinning down Japanese armies of occupation while the "real war" was fought elsewhere. While America's Pacific strategy became a process of island-hopping for the aerial bombardment of Japan, Free China became "the end of the line," with a central minimal purpose of being "kept in the war." Such a role, in the shrouded dankness of Chungking, could only breed corruption, laziness, inflation, and sinking morale.

A simultaneous major development out of the tangle of wartime China was the growth of the Chinese Communists in strength, population, and territory. Survivors of the CCP's several rural redoubts, regrouped after the costly Long March of 1934–1935, had settled in a rugged three-province area of Shensi (Shenxi), Kansu (Gansu), and Ninghsia (Ningxia), with headquarters eventually in Yenan. Chiang's kidnapping and Japan's renewed assault had brought about a new united front in 1937. But this time the partnership was built on intense mutual distrust; and from early 1941 onward, the front was essentially replaced by the renewal of sporadic civil war in the midst of Sino-Japanese stalemate. During these years the Communist troops practiced with considerable success their hard-learned guerrilla tactics. They infiltrated the countryside behind Japanese lines, capturing arms, recruiting troops, and organizing the peasantry. In the regions they held or liberated, they established local regimes, redistributed land, and instituted tax reforms.

Wartime conditions gave the Communists opportunities to expand into territory they had never previously held, and such expansion had major consequences. First, they were able to create "border region" governments, consisting of a pyramid of "people's councils" to administer CCP programs. Second, party membership expanded from about 40,000 in 1937 to 1.2 million in 1945. And finally, party members were given rigorous ideological indoctrination, especially in the writings of Mao Tse-tung, who was already emerging as an independent reinterpreter of Marxism-Leninism. By the time of Japan's surrender, the Communists had put together a tightly disciplined party and an army of more than half a million; and they could claim control over an area of nearly 100 million people. All this was accomplished, it should be noted, despite the KMT's relentless efforts to enforce a "blockade" of the Communist territories.

The third key ingredient in the Sino-American transformation, between 1941 and 1951, was American involvement in Chinese politics on a scale heretofore unmatched. Such involvement had a series of phased consequences: initially, extraordinary glorification and glamorization of Nationalist China and its leaders among Americans back home; then, increasing frustration with the realities of Free China, as reported by resident American journalists and officials; and finally, the total collapse of American interventionist efforts to bring about a peaceful compromise resolution of the civil war that erupted in the wake of Japan's defeat.

Before and especially after the shock of Pearl Harbor, glorification came first. It was a welling-up of national sentiment, in the midst of a new world war, sentiment that built upon several decades of sympathies and hopes for the Chinese, but suspicion and competition with Japan. Chiang Kai-shek and his wife had become, through influential media, living symbols of a Christian, anti-Communist, anti-fascist, and pro-American China. The KMT government's impact on the American public reached its zenith during Madame Chiang's triumphal American speech-making tour early in 1943. Her address to a joint session of Congress—her command of English, her passionate rhetoric, her imperious beauty and charisma—produced an extraordinary ovation and ringing pledges of support for Free China. Later she evoked similar adulation from a live audience of 17,000 in Madison Square Garden and a radio audience of millions more.

As A. T. Steele, veteran China reporter for the New York *Herald Tribune* has written of that zenith year, "There was a saying among the cynical that Mme. Chiang was worth ten divisions to the Generalissimo. In terms of her influence on American public opinion this was no exaggeration. It can probably be said, in all truth, that Mme. Chiang at that time commanded more popularity in the U.S. than in her homeland." Steele nicely summarizes America's love affair with Nationalist China in the early and mid-1940s: "This was a fantastic period in Sino-American relations—a period of dreamy unreality, in which the American public seemed prepared to accept and believe anything and everything good and wonderful that was said about the Chinese, their Generalissimo, the Generalissimo's wife, and the heroic Chinese people."

Glorification and glamorization at home in the United States were not, however, paralleled by similar euphoria among American observers in China itself. There something quite different was happening.

For the Chungking government, and for its new American allies in World War II, that partnership was a long and mutual immersion in frustration and ill-concealed anger. First, in the military sphere, Chiang tried but failed to get agreement to a coordinated Allied strategy centered on China. General Joseph W. Stilwell ("Vinegar Joe"), as Chiang's American Chief of Staff, was given the hopeless task of defending Burma, and then, when Burma fell to the Japanese, the grueling three-year task of reopening a land route to China through northern Burma. Stilwell's arch-rival, General Claire Chennault of "Flying Tigers" fame, eventually got five big airfields constructed in unoccupied China; but almost at once the main base for the bombing of Japan was shifted to the Mariana Islands, supplied by sea and closer to Tokyo. And Chennault's bases would trigger a deeper Japanese invasion.

So, entering the Pacific war as a prospective Allied base for defeating Japan, Nationalist China found that the job was being done by sea—with China cut off, a low-priority sideshow. The result was the deepening demoralization of Chiang's supporters. As for the generalissimo, he artfully fended off his American advisers, forced the recall of Stilwell, and clung, in haughty isolation, to declining power. The Stilwell-Chennault controversy prefigured a protracted debate about military tactics in Asia, one that would linger into the 1970s.

Frustration and anger on the scene had other sources as well as the exigencies of Allied global military planning. Free China, and especially Chungking as its refugee capital, was a not so happy haven for American diplomats, military officials, journalists, and also private citizens who did not like what they saw. In its state of weakness, corruption, fear of Communism, and psychological depression, KMT China up close was increasingly unattractive to American observers. Economic deterioration and political suppression of KMT critics were compounded by heavy-handed efforts at censorship of negative reporting.

The Chungking regime's unattractiveness was sharply intensified for those Americans who were eventually permitted by Chiang to visit Yenan and the Communist territories. Here the contrasts were astonishing. Morale was extraordinarily high; there was no evidence of any gulf between rich and poor, landowners and the landless; corruption seemed nonexistent; a form of participatory democracy was widely practiced, not just preached (albeit under careful CCP control); the leaders lived simply, mingled easily with the people, and were bluntly and warmly forthcoming in extended conversations with the foreign visitors. Little wonder, then, that the Yenan experience was in almost every case a "persuading encounter" for Americans who had known the other China of Chungking. Indeed, the Chinese Communists tended to remind American visitors of their own idealized selves.

It was against the backdrop of such divergent views of conditions in wartime China—the outlook from the United States, and the observed realities on the scene—that the American government attempted a major intervention in the Chinese revolution, one destined to failure. That intervention was based on an increasingly strong perception among American officials, from late 1943 onward, that the ongoing struggle between the KMT and the CCP might well result in all-out civil war once Japan had been defeated. To avert such an outcome, American policymakers developed a twofold aim: first, to encourage some form of political settlement between the bitter rivals— a political settlement which even Chiang Kai-shek himself advocated as early as September 1943; and second, to strengthen the Nationalist government's position for such negotiations, partly by building up Chungking's armies, partly by pressing for some basic governmental reforms. In pursuit of these aims, it can be said in retrospect that the KMT's armed forces were in fact much improved in training and equipment, but that all efforts at broadening the government's political base and reducing its multiple abuses (notably, corruption, economic exploitation, and political oppression) were a failure. Chiang and his colleagues remained adroitly resistant.

As for efforts to achieve some form of viable political settlement, talks between the KMT and the CCP were resumed, at American urging, in 1943. Meanwhile, American policymakers sought to move on several levels: internationally, to try to make China a great power in form if not in substance; in Nationalist China, to create a modern army and air force—an effort in which, under Generals Stilwell and Albert C. Wedemeyer, a thousand American instructors and advisers helped train and equip some thirty-nine divisions; and in the Chinese political arena, to resolve the Chungking-Yenan split. In the last of these efforts, high-level American missions came and went, achieving no real results, most notably Vice President Henry Wallace and General Patrick J. Hurley.

Hurley, an Oklahoma Republican and Secretary of War under President Hoover, was dispatched by President Roosevelt as a special emissary and then became U.S. Ambassador to China in 1944–1945. A man of mustachioed military handsomeness, much bravado, no knowledge of China, and not a touch of subtlety, Hurley visited Yenan, thought he had negotiated a Chiang-Mao agreement, but was soon undone by the distrust the two leaders had for each other. Chiang especially could not bring himself to cooperate. In the end, Hurley felt betrayed not by the Chinese but rather by the foreign service officers in his Chungking embassy who had deeply doubted—and had reported to Washington their doubts about—his simplistic perception of the KMT-CCP struggle (a struggle much like ones between Republicans and Democrats, he had said more than once). Hurley vented his spleen in two ways. He insisted on the transfer out of his embassy of all who had signed a long and dissenting February 1945 cable to the State Department while he was temporarily in Washington; and, on his resignation in December 1945, he fired a scatter-shot salvo at those American diplomats both in China and in Washington who had allegedly undermined—even sabotaged—his China mission by sympathizing with the Chinese Communists and pushing their cause.

Here, in Hurley's fiery valedictory charges, was the central seedbed of what would eventually become the McCarthy-McCarran investigations five years later, and the hunt for China scapegoats that would follow.

Despite wartime American efforts to avert civil war, Japan's submission in August 1945 triggered a China race for territorial control. While the United States used its major air- and sea-lift capacity to move half a million Nationalist forces back to the coastal centers, Communist troops sped overland to expand their domain by accepting Japanese surrenders in northern China. And even as Americans back home began to relax and demobilize, the long foreseen civil war began to erupt. "This was a moment"—in the words of John K. Fairbank—"when the American people were least prepared, emotionally and intellectually, to face a Chinese crisis. We had no intention in the winter of 1945–46 of fighting another war in East Asia."

How, then, to cope with this renewed China upheaval? One response, by President Truman, was the appointment of victory's chief architect, the revered General George C. Marshall, to go on a special mission to negotiate peace between the two civil war contestants. But the mutual distrust ran too deep, and Marshall's heroic efforts, in 1946–1947, came to naught. Meanwhile, Washington veered between intervals of attempted neutrality (and brief aid "freezes") and increasing military assistance to the Nationalists—a course pressed upon a very skeptical Democratic administration by a newly elected Republican-controlled Congress in January 1947. But the civil war burgeoned, with initially some three million KMT troops battling Communist forces totalling one million—and with American aid to the Nationalists eventually running to over two million dollars in all, between 1945 and 1948.

While the KMT retained control of all the significant cities—including, soon, Yenan—the Communists were highly successful in seizing control of the countryside, especially in Manchuria and northern China. In due course, Mao's armies would skillfully surround and choke off Chiang's urban fortresses one by one. To American military advisers on the scene, KMT military strategy seemed largely "medieval" and grotesquely self-defeating; but American generals, from Stilwell onward, had had a record of non-success in influencing the stubborn generalissimo. Afterward, the last of those advisers, General William Barr, would testify that the Nationalists had never lost a battle through lack of arms or equipment.

The end for the KMT on the mainland, now headquartered back

in Nanking, came in massive pitched battles on the North China plain, after the loss of all Manchuria and the peaceful surrender of Peking by its commanding general, in the autumn of 1948—battles in which the outnumbered Communists regularly prevailed, and the surviving Nationalist troops surrendered, fled southward, or defected in increasing numbers. In the big coastal cities, KMT and "third force" efforts were unavailing; and a final indicator, from September 1948 onward, had been the astronomical inflation rate for Nationalist currency: four *new* Chinese dollars to U.S. $1 that month, but 60 million to one by the following February. By early 1949, the Chinese civil war was basically all over—except for slow-motion mopping up by the victors, a process that would take all year, up to the "liberation" of Szechwan late that autumn.

On October 1, 1949, with the KMT remnants removed to Taiwan, and most of China under CCP control, Mao Tse-tung triumphantly proclaimed in Peking's T'ien-an Men square the establishment of the People's Republic of China. To the world he announced, "China has stood up!"

Back in Washington, a newly re-elected but distracted Democratic administration, facing a hostile Congress and also mounting problems in other parts of the world, had nonetheless seen clearly the Nationalist debacle—and had tried to cushion the public's learning of the bad news, a Communist victory in China, by preparing a "White Paper" on United States–China relations, a document issued in August 1949. It was a large document that printed selected classified dispatches relating to America's intervention in the Chinese civil war. Its basic message, conveyed by Secretary of State Dean Acheson, was that despite all that the United States could do, China had been lost to the Communist faction by the multiple flaws and errors of the nation's Nationalist leadership. As for the future, Acheson added orally, Washington would "wait for the dust to settle."

Rather than mute or calm the China debate that autumn, that White Paper would enflame it for years to come.

What next happened raises a familiar question: How can one explain the recurrent American obsession with China and the Chinese people? More specifically: How can one explain the effect of China's "loss" to "Communism" on large sectors of American public opinion—and especially the electorate's representatives?

In seeking to understand the American reaction to the Nationalist debacle, one deals with many intangibles. Answers largely lie in the mystery of subterranean forces that shaped the mood of the American people. Yet there is obviously one central ingredient: the very high hopes, building upon deep-rooted sympathy, that Americans had harbored for postimperial China, and, simultaneously, the dashing of those high hopes by a hostile new regime, soon firmly allied to the Soviet menace—a regime that charged Washington with supporting Chiang Kai-shek (while American Republicans, ironically, were charging quite the opposite). To put the matter simply: Here was our ward and tutee and, most recently, ally—and it had been turned against us, had up and bit our helping hand. The key feeling was betrayal; but the key question was, Who had accomplished it, and how?

Beyond China and Asia, however, other factors—a series of alarming events—contributed to the convulsion that China's "loss" caused within the United States. Here are some of them:

In general, Americans knew that fascism had been defeated; but now the nation had an uneasy sense that it had been cheated out of its victory by the sudden new threat of communism. Specifically, the Soviet ally had been sensed increasingly as an adversary in the process of several postwar negotiations, especially regarding Eastern Europe. In 1947, the Democratic administration perceived the danger of a Soviet threat to both Europe and the Middle East; the results were the Truman Doctrine for Greece and Turkey and the Marshall Plan for Europe. But then in 1948 came the Czechoslovakia coup d'etat and the Berlin Blockade—and the Cold War, already begun out of mutual distrust, was a vast glacial reality.

That summer in America came the case of Alger Hiss—the epitome of the Eastern intellectual, a Harvard man, law clerk to Justice Holmes, a lawyer-diplomat who had hovered at the right hand of Franklin Roosevelt at the Yalta great-power conference in early 1945, and then had been a chief functionary at the founding conference of the United Nations in San Francisco later that year. Hiss had been accused of being a Communist agent by Whittaker Chambers, a confessed former Communist and later a *Time* magazine editor. The Hiss case went through two trials that tore the nation apart. The first produced a hung jury, but the second found him guilty of perjury, in January 1950. The question that many were forced to ponder, both friends and foes, was, If such a paragon of integrity and achievement as Alger

Hiss *might* be a Communist plant, how many others—everywhere—might there be?

Such rising anxieties were compounded by dangerous frustrations within the two-party system. Republicans, repeatedly denied the White House since 1933, were astounded and embittered by their candidate's loss to President Truman in 1948, a "sure-thing" Republican year. From then on, the Democratic administration was the central target for newly angry and often irresponsible assaults by members of the opposition party.

And potential ammunition kept becoming available to Truman's opponents. The State Department's White Paper on China, in August 1949, was immediately seized upon by Chiang's American admirers as a "whitewash" of the "sellout" of Free China, a biased selection of documents designed to cover up the policymakers' incompetence, or worse. Denunciation of the White Paper became Republican rhetorical habit. In 1949, as well, the Soviet Union broke the heretofore reassuring American nuclear monopoly and tested its own atom bomb. And to confirm suspicions of treason as the instrument for breaking that monopoly, there erupted a series of cases of alleged Soviet espionage: not only the Hiss trials, but the case of atomic scientist Klaus Fuchs in Britain and alleged courier Judith Coplon in America.

In June 1950 came the most alarming development of all: the totally unexpected outbreak of the Korean War. While the administration responded with extraordinary speed—pulling the United Nations along in its wake—Republicans were quick to note that Secretary Acheson, in a major foreign-policy address in January, had not included either South Korea or Taiwan within America's Pacific defense perimeter. Although Acheson's speech had had the unanimous endorsement of the Joint Chiefs of Staff at the time, his critics would argue for years to come that it had been an "open invitation" to Communist aggression. And in that same January, Acheson, a mentor of Alger Hiss, had said at the time of the Hiss conviction—quoting the New Testament—that he would not turn his back on his friend. Such times would eventually drive even the cold and usually non-demagogic Republican leader Senator Robert A. Taft to assert that "The blood of our boys in Korea is on Dean Acheson's hands."

All these alarming events at home and abroad were contributors—along with the loss of China—to the ensuing convulsion. To sum up their impact: They helped create a nation deeply shaken, even traumatized, by yet another crisis after a global "war to end all wars." They helped create a nation sown with the seeds of mutual suspicion and multiple recriminations, a nation of people unsure of whom to trust anymore. By 1952, it would become a nation with one of its two major political parties out of highest office for nearly twenty years. The left-out Republican party was one which had practiced bipartisanship in the European policy sector, but had felt both bypassed in administration planning for the Far East and also acutely in need of a foreign-policy issue in order to win the next election. Specifically, some frustrated Republicans—watching American aims thwarted abroad—were willing to run on a very shrill indictment of the Democrats: "Twenty Years of Treason." Others, the "moderates," would settle for "Korea, Communism, Confusion, and Corruption."

Most specifically, the unfolding of the Cold War abroad and the frustrations of the "out-party" at home produced a large group of activists, and their millions of supporters, who were ready to find out once and for all an answer to the cosmic question "Who lost China?" For what had been lost was not merely a valiant wartime ally, not merely 400 to 600 million potential Christians and customers and tutees, but also a very, very big country, the most populous on earth. And it had been lost to communism and, it seemed, to permanent enslavement by Moscow.

What ensued was an extended and relentless search for The Culprits—those responsible for China's alleged loss, the network of conspiracy at home and abroad that had produced this outcome. It was a search heavily fueled by a variegated group of Nationalist China's admirers among Americans, out of both the Nanking and Chungking years. That group—a loose coalition of politicians, businessmen, journalists, missionaries, diplomats, military men, and others—would soon be labeled the "China Lobby," and there would be allegations of covert KMT funding during and after the retreat to Taiwan. But if it was a "lobby," it was more probably held together by shared fears, hopes, and wrath about the China situation than by any secret Nationalist expenditures. No such bribery was needed by a collectivity of true believers in the iniquity of communism and the virtues of Chiang's Nationalists—a collectivity that included, to name a few, publisher Henry R. Luce; China textile importer Alfred Kohlberg; and former medical missionary and by then Minnesota Congressman Walter Judd.

Such longtime China advocates developed powerful allies in the Congress and particularly in the Senate—Republicans looking for an effective issue with which to capture the White House, and also men of both parties (though mainly Republican) who were sincere in their alarm over communism's successes. Among the leaders of a "China Lobby" on Capitol Hill were Senators William Knowland (Republican, California), Styles Bridges (Republican, New Hampshire), Bourke Hickenlooper (Republican, Iowa), Owen Brewster (Republican, Maine), William Jenner (Republican, Indiana), and Pat McCarran (Democrat, Nevada). The men who would shortly rise to most astonishing prominence and power in the search for culprits were first, a rather obscure junior Senator from Wisconsin, Republican Joseph R. McCarthy, and second, the veteran Democratic chairman of the Subcommittee on Internal Security of the Senate Judiciary Committee, Pat McCarran.

That search for culprits seems in retrospect to have gone through three phases. The first was dominated by Senator McCarthy, and lasted for four years, until his censure by his colleagues in 1954 on matters unrelated to China and his subsequent death. The second was dominated by Senator McCarran in 1951–1952, and it had consequences for some years to come. And the third was dominated by Secretary of State John Foster Dulles and his colleagues, once the Republicans took over the White House in 1953. Meanwhile, in the second Truman administration, the embattled Democrats contributed to the search— in a desperate effort to ward off their critics—by setting up a complex new program for the review and enforcement of "loyalty" and "security," a program that ironically helped legitimize the phenomenon called "McCarthyism."

McCarthyism—phase one: What was it all about? Basically, it was about an obscure, persuasive, shallow, and sometimes charming Air Force veteran who hit upon the right issue at the right time, in terms of the national mood. By the time he was well launched on "communism in government" and the "loss of China," enthralling the media and their audiences, many of the most undemagogic conservatives and moderates would admit that, although they might disapprove of his methods, they shared his aims. Or, as others would put it, in the midst of the Senator's wide-ranging charges, "Where there's smoke, there must be fire." (It was one of McCarthy's prime targets, Secretary

Acheson, who acidly responded that one of the things his service in the Navy had taught him was that where there was smoke, there was usually a smoke machine.)

McCarthy's charges were centrally about the existence of Communists in government, and eventually—when party membership or even Communist sympathies could not be proved—about what became known as "guilt by association." The Senator concentrated initially on the State Department; and his charges first achieved national prominence in a speech he gave in Wheeling, West Virginia, in February 1950. His sensational claim that the State Department contained over two hundred Communists produced demands that he name names. In due course, in a dramatic revelation on the floor of the Senate, he announced the name of only one, allegedly Moscow's "number one agent" in the United States: Professor Owen Lattimore of Johns Hopkins University, a longtime China specialist, occasional federal government consultant, and briefly a wartime adviser to Chiang Kai-shek. Lattimore was also at the center, as an editor, of the major and respected international conglomeration of serious Asian specialists, the Institute of Pacific Relations (IPR).

It is not difficult to fathom how McCarthy—a man of no previous China background—when pressed to name names, finally came up with Professor Lattimore. From 1943 onward, one of the IPR's members from the business community, Alfred Kohlberg, had been bombarding first the institute's board and then its membership with accusations of anti-Kuomintang and pro-Communist bias in its publications. The indefatigable Kohlberg—who lost out in his efforts with his fellow members—had continued his campaign with broadsides to a much wider audience, and Lattimore was his chief target. An accomplished publicist, his voluminous "documentation" was known to many.

In Kohlberg's accusations, McCarthy had found what he needed. And in McCarthy—and soon McCarran—Kohlberg had finally found a forum as well as spokesmen of high visibility.

The outcome of this first phase of what some would call the "China witch-hunt" was slow motion and generally unspectacular, though destructive to all involved. One Senate investigative committee, under Millard Tydings (Democrat, Maryland), cleared Owen Lattimore of all charges. But McCarthy's response was to orchestrate the defeat of Senator Tydings at the next election on the grounds of "softness on Communism." Lattimore meanwhile became a prime target for the second phase and was eventually indicted on grounds of perjury (a matter to which we will return), but all indictments were years later dismissed. Lattimore, financially broken and psychologically wounded in the process, moved from Johns Hopkins to the University of Leeds, in Britain. Meanwhile, McCarthy had shifted, scattershot, to other targets—alleged Communists in government—but literally *never caught one*. In the end, when he had broadened his focus to the United States Army itself, under a Republican President (and retired general), his heretofore cowed but now embarrassed Senate colleagues cut him off through a vote of censure. His influence abruptly ended, thanks in part to more careful media analysis of his charges, especially the efforts of Edward R. Murrow on television.

The second phase of the search for culprits was clearly stimulated by McCarthy. Senator McCarran, the fiercely anti-Communist silver-haired Democrat from Nevada, took up where the more volatile McCarthy had left off with Owen Lattimore. Between July 1951 and July 1952, McCarran's subcommittee conducted an intensive investigation of Lattimore's extended professional club of academics, journalists, businessmen, officials, and many others who shared an interest in Asia: the Institute of Pacific Relations (IPR). In the course of that year of hearings (with the volumes of testimony and documents it produced, and the committee's ultimate report) the informal fraternity of East Asianists—and particularly China specialists—was temporarily split, out of fear and malice, suspicions and recriminations. Meanwhile, it must be added, President Truman's "loyalty-security" program was reviewing and rereviewing accumulated and recurrent charges, old and new, against foreign service officers who had had any China experience—now that China was definitively "lost." Confessed former Communists and "informers" were overworked throughout the nation, producing ever new lists of remembered suspects for Senate committee staffs, loyalty-security boards, the FBI, and virtually anyone who would listen.

The IPR had been created in earnest innocence by, largely, a group of Asia-oriented YMCA secretaries meeting in Honolulu in 1926. As noted, the institute eventually included in its membership most of those with a serious professional interest in the Pacific region, both in the United States and abroad. The organization sponsored conferences, issued newsletters, and published a scholarly journal, *Pacific Affairs*. For twenty-five years, it was the foremost international academic and research organization concerned with contemporary East Asian studies.

What fueled McCarran's year-long foray into the IPR was not merely McCarthy's assault against Lattimore or Kohlberg's long campaign, but also testimony by several former Communists against leading China academic experts who were also IPR members. The central and repeated charge, of course, was that these professionals had done all within their scholarly and consultative powers to advance the cause of the Chinese Communists and to bring about the defeat of the Chinese Nationalists. What McCarran and the committee staff sought to prove was secret Communist party membership, or agency on behalf of the Communists, or adherence to "the Communist line," or association with known Communists, or at least "sympathy" for the Communist cause.

The McCarran hearings resulted in the unearthing of not one single hitherto unknown Communist. They did result, however, in the vilification of major Asia and especially China specialists, both inside and outside government, some of whom lost their careers entirely. As a few terrified academics testified (to save their skins) about their own colleagues' alleged views back in the 1930s, the senior China academics were rent asunder, their profession badly jarred for some years to come. Meanwhile, the committee, unable to come up with real culprits, found a formula for the entrapment of its victims: committee expropriation of all IPR documents, the witness's failure of memory when questioned about the documents' contents (the date and place of a lunch many years before, for instance), and then the formal charge of perjury. And meanwhile, too, witnesses were regularly libeled on the floor of the Congress and in committee reports—where the libel laws could not be applied.

The McCarran investigation produced at least one suicide (of a gifted Canadian diplomat, a major Japan scholar), the eventually quashed indictments of Professor Lattimore, a number of destroyed careers, and heightened public and media paranoia about China experts. It also caused, by 1955, the virtual collapse of the IPR through the removal of its tax-exempt status (its now skeleton staff moved to Vancouver, Canada).

Some China specialists whose major sin was simply prediction of communism's China success (also guilt by association with Chinese Communists) were luckier than others. To cite one case only: the ac-

knowledged dean of modern-China historians, Harvard's John K. Fairbank, survived fairly well. He was maintained on his university's payroll
despite charges against him, his history of long and close association
with Lattimore, and intensive committee interrogation; but in the process, General MacArthur's headquarters denied him a permit to spend
a scholarly sabbatical year in Japan. In the end, the McCarran final
report judged him to be "a witting or unwitting agent of the Stalinist
conspiracy." For a decade thereafter, Fairbank was no longer consulted
by any government agency; and in that same period, he was no longer
invited to review books for the New York *Times*. The Fairbank case
was widely duplicated in various ways. The central outcome was the
denial to the American government and to the general public of the
views of the nation's most seasoned China specialists.

The third and perhaps most poisonous phase of the search for culprits came with the installment of the Eisenhower administration in
January 1953—the first Republican President in twenty years. General
Eisenhower had seemed a moderate in the preceding months of parti-
san fury; and in office he would often be so. But on the subject of
China, his internationalist but fiercely dogmatic (and very Presbyterian)
Secretary of State, John Foster Dulles, felt and shared the pent-up
heat of the congressional witch-hunters. By now, Truman's loyalty-
security apparatus had gone to work on scores of China-related diplomats, most notably John Carter Vincent, John Stewart Service, and
John Paton Davies ("the three Johns"), plus John K. Emmerson and
O. Edmund Clubb—all nearly household words after many months
of congressional and executive hearings. Most had been "cleared" repeatedly under the Democrats, with the ironic exception of Mr. Service, who, dismissed by Secretary Acheson, fought for and won
reinstatement by the Supreme Court in 1958 (a Pyrrhic victory; he
ended his career, under a fearful Kennedy administration, as consul
in Liverpool, England).

What Dulles faced, and too easily succumbed to, was the right-
wing Republican desire to settle scores finally on the matter of China's
"loss." The result was, in simple terms, a wide-ranging purge of all
China experts in the bureaucracy (and especially in the State Department) who had shown any signs of sympathy for the Chinese Communist cause. One after another, the most visible ones were dismissed
or forced out (Vincent, Davies, and Clubb), despite their proven innocence of all charges. The less visible ones, facing new harassments,

departed. And those in between, whose names had been on some interrogator's list but against whom nothing could be proven, were simply sent "to pasture" in places like Latin America, Belgium or the Netherlands. Dulles largely delegated the administering of this housecleaning to his Assistant Secretary of State for the Far East, an archconservative Virginia Democrat named Walter Robertson, and especially to his Director of Security and Consular Affairs, Scott McLeod.

By the end of the Dulles-Robertson-McLeod housecleaning, everyone who had signed the famous cable from Chungking in February 1945 that had so infuriated Ambassador Patrick Hurley (or had supported the contents of that cable) had been removed by one means or another. And in that removal, between 1953 and 1957, an entire generation of America's most carefully developed, and rare, China expertise had been thrown out or banished. With that achievement, and also the severing of ties with the China academic community, America's China policymaking was placed entirely in the hands of people who had little or no experience or understanding of the Chinese revolution, its bifurcation, and the extraordinary complexities of the Chinese civil war.

It would be difficult to overestimate the costs of China's "loss" and the trauma it produced among Americans, from presidents and secretaries of state all the way down to young people looking for vocations and millions of grassroots voters. For nearly a quarter of a century, America's policies in Asia would be skewed by these things. So would American politics, education, and society. Out of that skewing came two perhaps entirely avoidable wars—in Korea and Indochina—at the least, collisions that might have been muted and resolved without massive bloodlettings.

But it was not to be so. Benevolence and sentimentalism toward postimperial China had been transformed into fear and hatred of Communist China, part and parcel of American fear of China's new mentor, Stalin's Soviet Union. Some fear of Stalinist Russia was undoubtedly appropriate. But the extended China trauma exceeded all bounds of reason. Benevolence turned into paranoia, at home and abroad, idealism into grandiosity, a grandiosity newly equipped with the most potent arsenal of weaponry history had ever known. And America's East Asian relations became engulfed by years of blind and lethal zealotry.

(17)

The Korean War

HUDDLED CLOSE TO CHINA was Korea, the most important of its tributary states in the imperial age and the last nation in the Confucian world to be opened to the West. French (1866) and American (1871) warships bombarded the Koreans in an attempt to correct their unfriendly behavior toward visiting Westerners, but these explosive encounters were not followed by successful negotiations. Rather it was the Japanese in 1876—using naval diplomacy like that of Commodore Perry—who first brought the Koreans into the realm of modern Western practices of international relations. Korea remained shielded from a major Western presence and an all-out onslaught of Western culture.

Yet by the end of the nineteenth century, the "Hermit Kingdom," as Westerners called it, had become a vortex for northeastern Asia, a battleground for wars fought by other people: first the Sino-Japanese War of 1894–1895, and then, a decade later, Japan's war with Russia. In 1910, after five years as a protectorate and without foreign protest, Korea slipped entirely into Japan's orbit, becoming Japan's most important colony. The culture of the outside world could then enter Korea only through a Japanese filter. Curiously, a millenium earlier, Korea had been the filter for Japan, when the Japanese were struggling to absorb much of Chinese civilization.

Korea's tragedy has been that the nation is alone, precariously situated between the major cultures of China and Japan, with no neighbors comparably small or weak. Korea is a place where the interests of the great powers have met and conflicted for reasons that may have little or nothing to do with Koreans. Today Korea is the only country in the world which is enveloped entirely by the power of the four most important nations on the globe—China, the USSR, Japan, and America—"a shrimp among whales," as the old Korean saying has it.

More than a century before Charlemagne's short-lived attempt to fashion a state unifying much of Western Europe, the Koreans had achieved political unity. With one language, one ethnic group, and one society, Korea is one of the world's oldest and most homogeneous nation-states, stubbornly retaining its distinct cultural identity despite periodic invasions and recurring waves of foreign influence. Perhaps this cultural tenacity is in part due to the challenge posed by the outside world.

Certainly geography was little help to internal unity. Korea is mountainous; iron it flat, and it would cover the earth, they say. Although rivers and seas separate the peninsula from the rest of Asia, primitive roads and modes of communication made it challenging to knit together the society with the early and continuing success the Koreans achieved.

Until 1945, most Americans had barely heard of Korea. Hundreds of American missionaries and teachers had gone there; but the United States maintained a tiny diplomatic colony, and Americans had few commercial interests in Korea. By 1910, the United States had quietly accepted Japan's dominance of the peninsula. Choson, "Land of the Morning Calm," was a traditional Korean name for the country, taken up by American missionaries, perpetuated by the Japanese as Chosen.

Christian missionaries enjoyed a huge success in Korea, rivaled in Asia only in the Philippines. Christianity, an alternative to Japanese cultural values (which the conqueror pushed hard), probably owed some of its success in Korea to its role as partner rather than competitor to nationalism.

At the Cairo summit conference in 1943, the Allies present promised that Korea should have its independence "in due course" after the war. Franklin Roosevelt and others assumed the Koreans were not ready for self-government. In 1945, the Koreans translated the promise to mean immediate independence. But first the Japanese had to be sent home. In August, the Russians moved in to accept the Japanese surrender; the Americans then hastily sent troops originally intended to garrison Japan. The Soviet Union graciously accepted the quick American proposal of the thirty-eighth parallel as the line of demarcation for dealing with the Japanese. Two young lieutenant colonels in the Pentagon (one of them named Dean Rusk) chose the line. They had no map at hand showing the provinces of Korea; they had to act fast; they felt that a parallel was a line which each side could know and recognize right away. But the line was, of course, topographically and in every other way irrational. Splitting Korea at any point made no sense in terms of the history and culture of the peninsula.

The Moscow Conference of Foreign Ministers in December 1945 considered various proposals for trusteeship of Korea, all of which were opposed by the Korean people. And, in any event, the Soviet Union and the United States were unable to agree. Korea remained divided.

What division meant would extend far beyond surrender arrangements. Separate nations emerged, with differing political philosophies and differing cultural orientations, increasingly hostile to each other. Power coalesced around two strong personalities: in the north the young Kim Il Sung, in the south the old Syngman Rhee. The one had been a major in the Soviet Army, the other was a Princeton man. Each wanted to unify the country, through war if necessary. And these domestic rivalries served to inflame international tensions. Thus, when war came it was more than a civil conflict.

Two-thirds of Korea's people lived in the agricultural South, the remaining nine million in the mineral-rich North. Economically the two had been mutually dependent. And the wrench caused by bisecting the nation was compounded by the abrupt departure of 700,000 Japanese colonialists—engineers, technicians, teachers, and officials—who, by running the nation exclusively themselves, had kept the Koreans innocent of the complexities of modern economic life and political administration. Small wonder, then, that life in postwar Korea was turbulent.

American GI's moving in as occupiers were bewildered, even repelled, by the effervescence of the Korean personality and the strangeness of their culture. Its smells, for example: *kimchi,* the Korean pickle, ubiquitous, spicy, even offensive to the foreign palate; and night soil, the human excrement commonly spread as fertilizer on the farmers' paddies. The GI's modified the traditional phrase to "Korea, Land of the Morning Calm, the Afternoon Demonstration, and the Night Soil."

Unfortunately, these superficial negative impressions dominated the Americans' exposure to Korean life. The visitors were not prepared in the least to occupy Korea. The U.S. 24th Corps on Okinawa was expecting to participate in the Japanese occupation but was directed at the last minute to take charge in Korea. No wonder Korea and its culture seemed odd to them.

The Soviet Union had a major interest in Korea because of proximity—a short shared frontier along the Tumen River—and because of a large Korean minority living in the Maritime Provinces of the U.S.S.R. From these people many cadres had earlier been chosen and trained for political and military duties, providing all the apparatus for the People's Republic which would be centered at Pyongyang after 1945, although partisans of the Chinese model of Communism vied with the pro-Russians among North Koreans.

For the United States, Korea certainly did not have the same strategic importance that it had for the U.S.S.R. Only as a buffer for Japan did it matter at all. The Joint Chiefs of Staff wanted no American commitment there, and Douglas MacArthur as well as Dean Acheson said publicly that Korea lay outside America's defense perimeter.

The Americans failed to negotiate a successful agreement over Korea with the Soviet Union and therefore referred the problem to the United Nations in September 1947. The Russians had proposed the simultaneous withdrawal of American and Soviet occupying forces. The North Koreans objected to the proposed visit of a United Nations commission and refused to send delegates to a national constituent assembly in Seoul. The result, in August and September 1948, was the establishment of two separate Korean governments, North and South. The one enjoying Russian blessing, the other American. The United Nations recognized the South as the legitimate government of all Korea, a fact of great importance later.

At dawn, Sunday, June 25, 1950, the North Korean People's Army (NKPA) struck south with full force—more than seven divisions, with 150 Russian-built tanks—across the length of a 150-mile front at the thirty-eighth parallel. Earlier, Syngman Rhee had rattled the saber— "We could take Pyongyang in three days," he boasted in October 1949—and the North claimed that Rhee had attacked first. The claim was plausible, but there is no proof. Indeed, evidence provided by neutral observers is all the other way. And certainly the wretched performance of the Republic of Korea (Southern) Army in the early days of the war indicated little preparation for conflict. But the Southerners had only four divisions to face the foe, and they lacked tanks or heavy weapons. The ROK Army was little more than a police force.

Such was the stormy nature of Korean politics and the truculence of President Rhee that the United States had been unwilling to furnish the ROK Army with heavy weapons.

At President Truman's direction, soon after the invasion began, General Douglas MacArthur flew from Japan to Korea to inspect the unfolding chaos there. Immediately he saw that the ROK Army was on the verge of collapse. American ground troops—as well as planes and weapons—were needed, and fast. "Give me two American divisions and I can hold Korea," the general asserted. He underestimated the enemy, but he was not alone in doing so.

Within five days of the invasion (June 30), the United States was totally committed to fight the North Korean People's Army with whatever force could be spared, excepting only nuclear weapons; and Harry Truman had made what he later would call the toughest decision of his presidency.

The electrifying words of the President that the United States would come to the aid of the South Koreans, and the resolution of the United Nations to join in the effort to repel aggression, won approval from the overwhelming majority of the American nation. Voters of every stripe were persuaded that the President had acted rightly. The issue, people judged, was a moral one, not something of strategic or any other kind of significance. Memories of the 1930s and the rise of Hitlerism were still strong. Korea, people felt, could well be another Rhineland or Czechoslovakia. The alternative to intervention would have been appeasement, and everyone knew where that led. Almost no one in America thought of what was happening in Korea as being merely a civil war. Rather it was intimately linked to what Americans and many others then perceived as the restless aggressive swell of the world Communist movement which, if unchecked, would flow over and inundate the "Free World."

But Americans were unprepared physically or psychologically to fight the kind of war Korea demanded. The nation had virtually disarmed, the burden of national defense now falling almost entirely upon the Air Force, particularly the Strategic Air Command with its fleet of heavy bombers ready to carry nuclear bombs to devastate an aggressor. The Navy had shrunk dramatically after the glorious days of 1945, and the huge armada which could be gathered to overwhelm the Japanese at the end of the Pacific war was for the most part either in mothballs or scrapped. Of ground troops, a mere one and a half divisions remained within the United States as a strategic reserve. To Korea, MacArthur brought troops from his attenuated occupation garrison in Japan. But it was a while before these men were fully ready for combat; the pleasures of occupation duty had been poor preparation for that.

In the first days of the war, the NKPA not only had more and better trained soldiers but better weapons, it seemed. "You can't get a tank with a carbine," one GI pointed out to a reporter. Until the Americans got rocket launchers in, NKPA tanks rolled freely southward. Speedy American jets may have had the skies to themselves, but it was some time before their punch could have much relevance to what was happening on the ground. Dreadful instances of strafing their own side happened more than once. Men on the ground were confused by the tactics of the advancing NKPA, who could pass themselves off as Allies or take off their uniforms and pose as civilians. They easily infiltrated what were, at best, fluid lines.

Just as important as the material shortcomings were the psychological ones. Americans at the beginning had little sense of why they were in Korea, and they found it hard to stomach defeat. A holding operation, an organized retreat, which was what the first American arrivals were committed to, always saps morale. Those men who had been abruptly called back to active duty were particularly unhappy to have been uprooted from civilian life and sent to Korea. Some of them had just gotten settled after World War II. And as the war continued, those fighting it chafed at the notion that the war was a limited one. The fact that the enemy could enjoy sanctuary across the northern frontiers seemed well nigh intolerable.

The United Nations command enjoyed no successes during the first weeks of the war, and the North Koreans hoped they would sweep the peninsula clean within two months. Numerically, the sides were soon about even as the Americans, British, and others began to arrive. Amid the brilliant green of the rice paddies shimmering in the bright sun with extraordinary temperatures of more than 100 degrees slowing down foreigners unaccustomed to such heat, by the last of July the defenders had been pushed, gasping, into a space of some eighty by fifty miles in the southeastern part of the peninsula. There the port city of Pusan afforded close access to the Allied sanctuary and staging ground of Japan.

The NKPA pushed within thirty miles of Pusan. But the vital perimeter held. Lieutenant General Walton Walker, a short energetic Texan, took shrewd advantage of his interior lines to shuttle his reserves rapidly from point to point covering those parts of the line in greatest peril of rupture by enemy attack.

Back home, on maps torn from newspapers, Americans apprehensively studied the shrinkage. College students anxiously wondered whether they would be allowed to return to campus in the fall. Some of them volunteered for the service in order to end the uncertainty and to ensure themselves a better place in the armed forces. Others waited nervously.

From his Taiwan redoubt, Chiang Kai-shek offered to lend the UN command 33,000 of his troops. The offer was declined; Americans did not want a Chinese war on the Taiwan Strait. The United States lacked the ability to fight on two fronts simultaneously. President Truman had, soon after the war's outbreak, ordered the Seventh Fleet to take up station in the waters between Taiwan and the China coast, denying Chiang the opportunity to invade and try to recapture the mainland. More important was that the Seventh Fleet kept Taiwan secure from invasion and prevented the Chinese People's Liberation Army from attempting to destroy the last bastion of the Kuomintang.

Mr. Truman had decided in early August that the Nationalists should again receive American aid, a sharp reversal of the policy established in Secretary Acheson's White Paper. Again America was in the Chinese civil war. The British were unhappy with this unilateral action. Nor were all Americans satisfied with the Truman-Acheson policy toward Nationalist China. Republicans like Senator William Knowland (nicknamed the "Senator from Formosa") were ready to accept the generalissimo's claim that he could recapture the mainland, and they were also ready to provide help for him to do so. Douglas MacArthur's open sympathy for this point of view would ultimately lead him into deep trouble.

The defense of South Korea was a United Nations effort. Forty countries offered aid of one kind or another. Sixteen, in addition to South Korea and the United States, provided combat troops. Five thousand Turks and twenty thousand men from the British commonwealth, fought alongside Ethiopians, Hollanders, and Frenchmen. Blacks and whites, Europeans and Asians, fought side by side. The effort was multiracial as well as multinational. But American material and money were preponderant, and there were more American men by far than those of any other nation, except the South Koreans.

Deference had constantly to be given to Syngman Rhee, the dominant figure in the Republic of Korea. Old (75), stubborn, single-minded in his desire to unify Korea and his refusal to negotiate or to compromise, revered by many Koreans because he was a senior leader in a Confucian culture, Rhee was a difficult ally. His dictatorial manner and the bad political habits he had fostered in his government—arbitrary police behavior, disregard of civil liberties—gave it an unsavory character. Only by comparison with the Communist regime of the North did Rhee's government come off with a measure of respectability. But that comparison was important.

From a hilltop, binoculars held to his eyes, Douglas MacArthur watched ROK troops fleeing in disorder to the south, where ultimately they would form the Pusan perimeter. At this discouraging moment, the general conceived the brilliant stroke which he thought could destroy the NKPA and end the war. The likely alternative, he believed—a slow build-up at Pusan and a gradual rolling back of the Northerners—would be immensely costly. MacArthur resolved to use sea and air power to launch an amphibious attack which could penetrate hard and deep into the vitals of the North Korean war machine. And he was eager to do this before the cruel Korean winter set in.

Inchon, twenty-five miles west of Seoul, was his target. This area was not only of enormous psychological value as the capital district of the ROK but it was also the nerve center of communications between north and south. And now the bulk of the NKPA lay to the south, vulnerable to being severed in this fashion from its homeland.

Everyone was opposed to MacArthur's choice—the Joint Chiefs of Staff, the Marines, the Navy, and even many of MacArthur's Army associates. On all the Korean coast it would be difficult to find a more challenging place for a landing than Inchon. The harbor was guarded by a formidable fortified island which could menace the life of an approaching fleet of transports. The entrance channel was narrow and twisting.

Worse was the problem of the tide, thirty feet, one of the greatest ranges anywhere in the world. This meant that only two days during the selected month of September (typhoon season) were possible times for a landing, with, during those days, only two periods of scarcely three hours or so in which the tide would be sufficiently high to permit ships to bring in their troops and their equipment. A short time for the initial landing, and a long time before a wave of reinforcements could be brought in! The planners had nightmares of their landing ships grounded at low tide on the wide expanse of mud flats where they could be pounded to pieces by North Korean guns.

MacArthur, operating by intuition rather than by logic, admitted that his chances of success were five thousand to one, long odds even for MacArthur. In a grand historical analogy of the sort he so liked to make, he compared himself to Wolfe scaling the heights at Quebec in 1759 and routing Montcalm on the Plains of Abraham. MacArthur's point was that the choice of battlefield was so unlikely that the enemy would least expect an attack there.

Two hundred and sixty ships brought seventy thousand men, who began landing on September 15, scaling the sea walls with twelve-foot ladders, quickly subduing all resistance. The audacity of the Supreme Commander was justified. Although North Korean intelligence surely knew what was about to happen, nothing had been prepared for the invaders. The waters were not mined, the city and its approaches were but lightly defended. At the cost of very few lives, the Allies rapidly consolidated their landing, recaptured Kimpo Airfield, Korea's major airport, and moved toward Seoul.

In the meantime, the Eighth Army at Pusan, which had been barely holding on against the enemy onslaught, broke out of the southern perimeter. The NKPA faltered, began to withdraw, then virtually dissolved as, *sauve qui peut,* its men fled for the North and home. In Seoul, they staged a bitter fight, street by street, house by house, which continued even after MacArthur had declared the city liberated. In a ceremony in which MacArthur could give rich play to his theatrical talents, the general handed over the city to a grateful President Rhee.

The North Korean military machine was not only defeated, it was broken, crushed between the two UN armies. By the end of September, South Korea was free of enemy troops, and the UN was claiming 335,000 North Korean casualties: dead, wounded, and captured. The North Korean Army was reduced to a few thousand disorganized and dispirited men, but refused to surrender.

Now what? The great error following the Inchon invasion was the lack of hard plans for exploiting it. MacArthur had no specific plans;

neither did Washington. The military part was simple: Seek out and destroy what was left of the enemy. But the political issues were complex.

Should the United Nations be satisfied with repelling the attacker? Or should they seek something more? What would the Russians and the Chinese do? After some deliberation and with the implicit approval of the UN General Assembly, the Joint Chiefs of Staff authorized MacArthur to move north of the border unless the Chinese or Russians should intervene in force. The Chinese were daily threatening to do so.

Syngman Rhee knew what he wanted: unity of North and South, under his leadership. The United States, with British concurrence, declared its goal was free elections and unity for Korea, under UN supervision and protection. MacArthur pushed ahead, across the thirty-eighth parallel, to deliver the coup de grace. On October 19, his forces took Pyongyang.

MacArthur's troops continued to race northward, plunging toward the distant Yalu River, the Chinese border, and getting farther and farther from their sources of supplies and from each other. Some of them tossed away pieces of their equipment as they advanced, convinced that the war was all but over. Unreasoned optimism was their attitude and that of the Supreme Commander also, who urged his commanders to move even faster. Some around him were apprehensive about the increasingly uncoordinated sprawl of the UN troops.

In the general euphoria of October 1950, MacArthur was widely believed to have promised his men that they would be "home for Christmas." Critics later taunted him with it. But even at the time there were skeptics who could not believe the war was really over. As one cynic said, "Our boys will be back for Christmas all right, in wooden boxes!"

The brilliance and unexpectedness of the Inchon victory swelled both MacArthur's own confidence and that of others in his judgment. As General Matthew Ridgway dryly put it, If MacArthur had ordered a battalion to walk on water, someone would have suggested they try. Having been proved wrong about Inchon, MacArthur's critics hesitated to challenge him again.

And so the United Nations forces were abruptly swept from triumph into near catastrophe. Frigid weather and awesome terrain magnified the impact when 300,000 Chinese entered Korea to snatch the fruit of victory from the erstwhile triumphant United Nations forces in late November. Seldom has victory so quickly become defeat.

Chinese entry into the Korean War was the nadir of Sino-American relations. Chinese and Americans had by then very different perceptions of American policy in Korea. The Chinese saw it as vicious and predatory imperialism. Americans saw themselves as not threatening China, despite the oratory of their China Lobby and other Nationalist sympathizers, and despite American readiness to lump the Chinese with the Russians as co-conspirators in the world Communist movement. "Imperialist Mongoloid pan-Slavism" is what Major General Charles Willoughby, MacArthur's intelligence chief, called it.

Until the autumn of 1950, Dean Acheson and others still hoped the United States could recognize the new Chinese government and build good relations with it. Naively, many Americans expected the Chinese to believe their protestations of no hostile intent in Manchuria. And the American government attempted, through Soviet Russian channels, to reassure Peking of its intentions. For this reason, Washington wanted MacArthur to keep his troops (the non-Korean ones) away from the border with China.

Hindsight gives ample evidence of Chinese intentions. The Chief of Staff of the Chinese Army told the Indian ambassador to Peking that the Chinese would not permit the Americans to cross the thirty-eighth parallel. The ambassador had this confirmed by Chou En-lai. But private conversations and public statements alike were taken as a bluff by the Americans. General MacArthur had assured President Truman at their Wake Island meeting of October 15, 1950 that his intelligence informed him that China would not enter the war.

Indeed it was an implausible event. Had Peking and Washington been able to talk directly, avoiding intermediaries whom they distrusted, events might have been quite different. The Americans recognized Chinese capability, not Chinese intention. Were the Chinese to enter, why choose a time of UN strength rather than UN weakness? Moreover the Chinese were still consolidating their newly united revolutionary state, absorbing Tibet (Xizang), carefully watching the Nationalists on Taiwan. The nation had enormous economic problems: desperate poverty, few resources, too many people, the devastation of civil war, and an old-fashioned army.

A war of aggression would seem to be the last thing the Chinese would want. And Americans interpreted Chinese entry into Korea as aggressive rather than defensive. In short, it was as implausible as Inchon had been implausible. The results were similar. Inchon saved South Korea from being incorporated into a Communist North. The Chinese "volunteers" saved the Korean People's Republic from being absorbed into Syngman Rhee's Republic of Korea.

The Chinese moved in silently, "a phantom which cast no shadow." Their men were sturdily self-sufficient, carrying modest rations and enough ammunition to sustain them for four- or five-day stretches. For some weeks they assembled; on November 25 they attacked in full force. The UN troops, reeling under the onslaught, fell back as best they could to avoid being outflanked. Both sides suffered severely from the cold of the northern mountains, where night temperatures could plummet to forty below zero. Frostbite was common; the Chinese sickened from an outbreak of typhus. UN troop morale fell with the temperature; they were the ones in retreat.

As far south as Taegu, the UN forces were plagued by guerrilla activity. But their lines stiffened and held well to the north of that town. This time there would be no retreat to the edge of the sea. Matthew Ridgway's appointment as commanding general of the Eighth Army, after the sudden death of Walton Walker, breathed new fire and life into that force.

Ridgway successfully strengthened the resolve of his men to push the enemy to the thirty-eighth parallel and beyond. The process was slow; the emphasis was on tactics, the improvement of lines, rather than upon strategy. Battered Seoul was recaptured, changing hands for the fourth time during the war. Newspaper readers became familiar with names like Pork Chop Hill, the Hook, and Jane Russell Hill.

American air power, which the Communists could not challenge successfully, was helpful although not decisive, despite American hopes. A simple manpower economy like that of North Korea proved relatively impervious to bombs; so the NKPA, and later the Chinese, were seemingly unhampered. American sea power, unchallenged, kept American troops nourished, gave them mobility, and provided extra firepower upon occasion.

General MacArthur, impatient for victory, proposed to Washington that twenty or thirty nuclear bombs be used against Chinese targets in Manchuria, and that a radioactive zone be created along the Yalu frontier by dropping cobalt from American planes. Furthermore, he suggested that 50,000 Chinese Nationalist troops be brought from Taiwan to fight in Korea.

By early spring, President Truman was thoroughly incensed by General MacArthur's refusal to keep quiet on matters of international politics. Between the two men there was fundamental disagreement, complicated by the fact that MacArthur had little respect for Truman. The President saw Europe as most essential to the United States, and his chief worry was the Soviet Union. MacArthur was an "Asia Firster." The President dismissed the general on April 11, and a storm broke, for neither the President nor the war was by this time very popular with the American public.

MacArthur returned to a hero's welcome. He was a glorious symbol both of victory in the Pacific war and civic accomplishment in Japan. His dictum that there was "no substitute for victory" fell on the ready ears of those who craved total victory such as that achieved by the nation in World War II. For many, MacArthur's less happy experiences in Korea were not so much his fault as of those in Washington and elsewhere who did not understand the "Oriental mind" as he did.

The nation bent over its radios to listen to the general's speech before both houses of Congress ending with the words of a ballad: "Old soldiers never die, they just fade away." Which is just what MacArthur did. His words were more prophetic than he might have wished. His political career never got off the ground, and he retired to nurse his memories at New York's Waldorf Towers.

The foes of the Korean War at home were, for the most part, flag wavers rather than flag burners, right-wing Republicans, not left-wing Democrats. College students were not conspicuous among their numbers. In those days, they were staging "panty raids" rather than antiwar demonstrations. "We want silk!" the boys shouted to the co-eds, not "End the War Now!" Kim Il Sung, the North Korean leader, had no American partisans. The draft summoned many young Americans, but few of them were called upon to fight. Stalemate at the front reduced the need for more combat troops.

The American public, and especially the military, found it hard to accept the notion of limited war. The Americans had chosen to limit both the ends and the means in Korea. That there could be no total victory was a new and frustrating experience for Americans, who found it difficult to regard Korea as anything but a defeat. Like Lyndon Johnson later, Harry S Truman, in part because of this, would end his political career earlier than might otherwise have been the case.

Atomic weapons were not used. The Americans did not attack any targets on Chinese soil. The Chinese civil war was not reopened, and Syngman Rhee did not want Chinese troops of any persuasion in Korea, even if the American government had been prepared to bring them. The Soviet Union did not enter the conflict, except to send in some pilots. The Russians supplied their Chinese and Korean allies with jet aircraft, armored vehicles, guns, and trucks in quantity but not the best quality they had. And they exacted payment for what they gave.

On June 23, 1951, Jacob Malik, Soviet delegate to the UN, called for an armistice. Peace talks in Korea began shortly thereafter, although hostilities continued. By this time, the Communists were fielding an army which the Americans guessed was close to half a million men. General Ridgway described the negotiations as "tedious, exasperating, dreary, repetitious, and frustrating." Conditions along the lines came to resemble those of the Western Front in World War I, a world of trenches and barbed wire, blood and mud.

The United Nations forces held more than 140,000 Communist prisoners, the Communists considerably fewer. Many of the prisoners held in the South did not want to go home, either to China or to North Korea, a matter of some embarrassment to the Communist world. The UN side refused to consider repatriating these people by force, and until the Communists accepted these terms, the peace settlement was delayed for many months. The shooting finally stopped on July 27, 1953, with an uneasy armistice thereafter.

Charles Bohlen once remarked that the Korean War rather than World War II made the United States a world military and political power. After 1945, the United States had disarmed, as it had after 1918 and after wars previous. But the Korean War was not followed by American disarmament. For the first time in history, the nation maintained a large standing army. A big share of the national budget would go to support the military establishment. The military emerged as a powerful force in American public life. General MacArthur may have failed to use his military reputation as effective leverage to attain the presidency, but General Eisenhower did not. And, unexpectedly, he warned in his famous valedictory address of the danger to American society of "the military-industrial complex."

The Korean War created great fear in the United States, apprehension lest the war explode into global conflict, but also fear of a worldwide Communist conspiracy fusing all the Communist states and parties into a monolithic force infiltrating and subverting the top circles of power in the "free world" countries. Many Americans were moved by this fear into readiness to accept conspiratorial interpretations of complex historical events. Fear exacerbated tension with the Soviet Union; and with the American tendency to separate the world into "communist" and "free" nations, revolutionary nationalism most often fell into the first category.

The Korean War diverted American attention and resources from domestic reform, interrupting the programs of the New Deal and the Fair Deal, postponing their continuance until the 1960s. War served as a powerful stimulus to an already healthy economy, superbly managed by the Truman administration, which succeeded in keeping both inflation and unemployment low. Few Americans suffered very much from the war. It was not a national trauma; it was not to be compared with World War II. Some 33,000 Americans died, but that was less than one-fourth the number of highway and traffic deaths for the same period.

The power of the President in foreign affairs was greatly increased by the initiative which he had exercised in taking the nation into war. Likewise the prestige of the United Nations and the principle of collective security were greatly enhanced. But the post-Korea search for security carried the United States toward bilateral agreements and regional groupings. The United States furnished massive military aid to Western Europe: weapons, equipment, the building of air bases, ports, and pipelines; and the United States undertook to keep its own troops stationed on European soil. NATO was no longer simply a pious understanding but became a hard and specific alliance, to which the U.S.S.R. replied with a similar regional grouping, the Warsaw Pact nations.

In Asia, America again became entangled with the Chinese revolution by providing support, military and financial, to the Chinese Nationalist government. Between America and the Chinese People's Republic there now seemed no possibility of conciliation. The two nations were firm foes. To Americans for twenty years, China was "lost," until Richard Nixon "found" it in 1972.

Americans had new interests but uncertain goals on the Asian mainland: Korea, where American troops remained, and Vietnam, where, as the French let go, the Americans came in.

Japan, interested bystander in the war, profited mightily from it.

Sanctuary for the United Nations command, purveyor of goods and services of all description, Japan was able to move up from the economic uncertainties of postwar recovery into a firm pattern of growth. And Japan's nascent alliance with the United States was bolstered by America's need for an Asian ally.

For Korea, war brought death, suffering, and devastation which left no part of the divided nation untouched. At war's end, the two rival Koreas bound up their wounds. But unremitting hostility still divides the peninsula; the two states, armed to the teeth, are glowering at each other.

Since the time of the 1953 armistice, relations between the United States and the Republic of Korea have remained closely woven, if acutely asymmetrical. Historical accident threw the two nations together in an unequal embrace. Continuing international tension binds them still. And the resulting flow of ideas and influence has been overwhelmingly one-way. Even the Reverend Moon, probably the Korean best known to America, preaches a form of Christianity, not of Confucianism, to his American followers.

Two major bilateral problems are discernible: questions of military security and questions of political attitudes and policies. The cornerstone of security relations between the United States and the Republic of Korea has been the Mutual Defense Treaty, signed in 1953, which committed the United States to defend Korea against external armed aggression. The United States has sold and given arms to the Koreans and consistently deployed American troops on the peninsula. Americans have wanted to keep non-Communist states non-Communist. Moreover, American bases in South Korea, like those in Japan, have been viewed as essential to maintaining American military capability in East Asia.

But changing American definitions of security have not always coincided with Korean judgments. The result has been confusion and misunderstanding between the two nations, with the Koreans feeling that they are viewed simply as a means to an end (whether this be the defense of Japan, the containment of the Soviet Union, or whatever) rather than valued intrinsically.

A second continuing problem in American-Korean relations concerns Korean political practices. Harry Truman in 1949 declared the Republic of Korea a "testing ground for democracy," and the American military government favored, at least in theory, a Korean development of democratic institutions. Since that time, the Americans—with an intensity depending upon the degree of attachment to ideals of human rights of the administration in office—have more or less consistently pushed the Koreans in the direction of democratic practice.

Yet nominal democracy has yielded to actual authoritarianism, and it quickly became apparent that a vast gap yawned between what Americans—and many Koreans—hoped for and what the Koreans, inexperienced in governing themselves, could accomplish. Syngman Rhee's autocratic behavior has been mirrored by that of his successors, Park Chung Hee and Chun Doo Hwan, military men who have seized power through coups d'etat.

A 1960 State Department warning has been an American threnody: ". . . this Government believes that the demonstrations in Korea are a reflection of public dissatisfaction over the conduct of the recent elections and repressive measures unsuited to a free democracy."

The black shadow of the North, the ever live possibility of rekindled battle, provides the ROK authorities with an excuse for suppression of dissent. For its size, Korea is probably the world's most heavily armed area. Together, the two Koreas, in a land about the size of Minnesota, maintain the world's fifth largest armed force. Despite the financial drain, the South, at least, has been able simultaneously to increase standards of living.

The Republic of Korea has built one of the fastest-growing industrial and trading economies in the world, growth matched only in the developing world (aside from the petroleum-rich nations) by Taiwan, Hong Kong, and Singapore.

In 1959, South Korea was a war-ravaged backward rural economy. Foreign aid covered a large continuing balance-of-payments deficit, and the nation became one of the world's largest recipients of such aid, mostly supplied by the United States. For the period 1946–1976, the sum was $15 billion, of which slightly less than half went for direct military purposes. Only South Vietnam and Israel have received a higher level of per capita foreign assistance.

Out of this unpromising economic scene sprang vigorous and skillful entrepreneurship, encouraged and nurtured by the government, acting as a "senior partner" in the overall enterprise. In his eighteen-year rule, President Park Chung Hee led South Koreans to a per capita income of $1,550 (from a 1953 figure of $134, at 1970 constant prices). A look at rural infant mortality statistics indicates that life in the Korean countryside has improved. But income distribution in contemporary Korea compares unfavorably with Japan. And some of the Korean political tensions may relate to economic grievances.

The industry of both Koreas surpasses that of China in efficiency and quality and greatly exceeds it in quantity, relative to the sizes of the populations involved. Nothing has proven more wrong than Syngman Rhee's assertion to an American magazine that "without unification, economic viability would be impossible for Korea." South Korea is already a major industrial power in non-Communist Asia, and is likely in the future to be exceeded only by Japan and India. South Korea's emergence will add new complexities to the relationship with the United States.

Meanwhile, the peninsula's continuing division between two mutually hostile regimes, each allied to competing superpowers, remains a dangerous potential source of international conflict.

(18)

The Indochina Tragedy

IN FEBRUARY 1950, four months after the victorious Mao Tse-tung decreed the founding of the People's Republic of China and four months prior to the Korean War, the United States government granted diplomatic recognition to a regime far to the south of Peking, to the French puppet ruler of Vietnam, Bao Dai, the former Emperor of Annam, and proceeded to provide political, economic, and military support to his Saigon-based anti-Communist government and its French sponsors. In so doing, the United States became the enemy of Bao Dai's Vietnamese opponents, the Democratic Republic of Vietnam, led by the longtime nationalist and Communist anti-French rebel, Ho Chi Minh, who had established a regime in northern Vietnam in September 1945, right after the Japanese surrender.

A few weeks later, a veteran journalist and observer of Asian affairs, Harold Isaacs of *Newsweek*, wrote some extraordinarily far-sighted words in *The Reporter* magazine—words that should have haunted American policymakers over the next twenty-five years, had they read or remembered them.

With "this act of policy," Isaacs wrote, "the United States embarked upon another ill-conceived adventure doomed to end in another self-inflicted defeat. It will not help the United States in its struggle against Communism. It will help the Communists in their struggle against the United States. It has already driven a new wedge between the United States and the other countries of South Asia. If the United States now involves itself in the Vietnamese civil war, that gulf will widen. The real problem is not how to implement this policy but how to extricate ourselves from it."

"One may well ask," Isaacs added, "how the United States could let itself in for this disastrous prospect. The answers are bleak. The policy is the result of simple anti-Communist panic."

In retrospect, it seems that no journalist, scholar, or statesman was ever more prescient, or more entirely on the mark. The cause was, in fact, anti-Communist panic; the problem was, too, not implementation but extrication; and the process of extrication involved not only twenty-five years but also a massive waste of Asian and American lives and treasure, the devastation of much of Indochina, and the traumatizing of American society and its values.

Indochina's searing role in American–East Asian relations was one for which preceding decades offered minimal forewarning. For, with the notable exception of the Philippine Islands, Southeast Asia itself had long been peripheral to America's Pacific outreach.

The region was peripheral in a geographic sense in that it lay at the southern tip of the Asian land mass. It was also politically hard to reach—a region which had undergone various forms of colonization and absorption by other powers prior to America's arrival on the scene. Traditionally the repository of a mix of Chinese and Indian cultures, Southeast Asia had become the focus of successive European rivalries— first the Portuguese, then the Dutch, the British, and the French. By the late nineteenth century, the Dutch had consolidated their gradual control of what is now Indonesia; the British in Burma, the Malay States, Singapore, and the Borneo territories; and the French in the Indochina states—Tonkin, Annam, Cochin China, Laos, and Cambodia. Only Siam (Thailand) preserved a fragile independence, situated as a buffer between British and French spheres.

So, in most of Southeast Asia, access for Americans was subject to the whims of the European powers. Trade was possible, and, in fact, rose substantially between the two World Wars; but investment, missionaries, and the interventionist urge remained largely focused elsewhere, especially on East and Northeast Asia.

There is no equivalent, then, to the China "Open Door" stake in America's relations with Southeast Asia prior to 1945. And yet there were at least two glimpses of what would later become a central theme: the theme of *denial* to others of control of portions of the region. In 1898, for instance, one factor in the decision to annex the Philippines

had been Washington's fear that some other power might seize them—
a desire to deny them to others. And in the summer of 1941, Japan's
move into southern Indochina aroused fear that Tokyo might acquire
the resources of Southeast Asia—and again, a desire to deny those
resources to Japan. It was, of course, Washington's retaliatory freezing
of Japanese assets that summer that helped trigger Tokyo's decision
to go to war.

The theme of denial inevitably raises an ancillary question: Denial
to what end, for what purpose, where stakes do not previously exist?
And that question dominates the history of America's Indochina involvement from 1950 onward.

There was a further important, but seldom recognized, context
for American intervention in the Indochina peninsula from World
War II onward: the historical dynamics of conflicts within the peninsula.
Long before the arrival of the French colonialists in the later nineteenth century, a pattern of struggle had been played and replayed
involving Thais on the west, Vietnamese on the east, and Cambodians—
once the great Khmer empire—caught in the middle. And to the north,
throughout, sat the Confucian giant, China—sometimes expansionist,
usually not.

So the region which the foreigners sought to tame in modern
times—first the French, then the Japanese, then the French again,
and finally the Americans (with China often an anxiously brooding
onlooker)—was one whose dynamics of strife antedated both colonial-
ism and communism, and would assuredly outlast both. Indeed, the
hundred years of external intervention, however tragic, from the 1870s
through the 1970s can be seen as merely an interlude in an ancient
and ongoing struggle, one to which the peninsula apparently reverted
after the American defeat and withdrawal in 1975.

In March 1943, President Roosevelt suggested to the British Foreign
Minister, Anthony Eden, that postwar Indochina should be placed under international trusteeship as a way station to independence instead
of returning the territories to French colonial rule. "France," he wrote,
"has had the country—thirty million inhabitants—for nearly one hundred years, and the people are worse off than they were at the beginning. . . . France has milked it for one hundred years. The people
of Indochina are entitled to something better than that."

Despite Roosevelt's rather amorphous hopes, his trusteeship

scheme did not survive his death in April 1945. Instead, in the immediate postwar scramble by the colonial powers to regain their territories, France and Britain won support from a divided American government for assistance in French reoccupation of portions of Indochina. Meanwhile, however, an anti-Japanese fusion of Vietnamese nationalists and Communists, under the leadership of the veteran Communist Ho Chi Minh, had created a strong Vietminh party structure and an effective guerrilla army (under General Vo Nguyen Giap); and on September 2, 1945, Ho proclaimed the establishment of the Democratic Republic of Vietnam in words borrowed wholesale from the American Declaration of Independence.

What ensued was, in brief, a doomed but highly destructive nine-year effort by the French to retake all of Indochina, with heavy logistical and financial assistance from the United States—despite previously good cooperation between the American OSS (Office of Strategic Services) and Ho's guerrillas in the war against the Japanese. That assistance was much increased in early 1950, when Washington recognized the Bao Dai regime in Saigon. But by 1954, the forces of Ho and Giap had brought the French to their knees at Dien Bien Phu. And the outcome that summer of a Geneva multination peace conference, already in process, was international accords that accepted the reality of French defeat in a war that had grown acutely unpopular at home. Beyond a cease-fire, the central stipulation of those accords was that Vietnam would be temporarily divided, at the seventeenth parallel, between Ho's regime in the North and Bao Dai's regime in the South, pending elections by 1956 to achieve unification of the nation.

Although the other major relevant powers, both Communist and non-Communist, signed the Geneva Accords, the United States refused to do so, signing instead a statement of intent not to violate the accords. One must recall that the painful "loss" of China and the bitter Korean War stalemate were still fresh in the minds of Washington policymakers. Secretary Dulles had found the Geneva Conference and its outcome deeply distasteful. It had apparently angered him even to be in the same room with Communist China's Foreign Minister, Chou En-lai. And at a moment Chou was never to forget, Dulles refused to shake the outstretched Chinese hand.

The die, then, was cast. The French had had enough in Vietnam and would let the Vietminh take it over, slow-motion, through elections by 1956. But not so the Americans, who bridled at such a prospect and waited for better future fortunes in the battle to "contain" communism, worldwide but especially in Asia.

One seemingly promising prospect was soon on the scene: Bao Dai's anti-Communist Prime Minister, Ngo Dinh Diem, an aristocrat and a Roman Catholic, already well connected in American religious and political circles. Before long, Diem had achieved full power in Saigon, and Bao Dai had retired to the south of France. American assistance was flowing to the South, on the basis of an Eisenhower-Diem letter; and, with strong American concurrence, the 1956 elections were cancelled by Diem. Meanwhile, a flood of refugees from Ho's revolutionized society had poured southward, intensifying Vietnam's polarities. Out of a civil war, two mutually irreconcilable states were emerging, firmly tied to the two chief Cold War antagonists.

In the history of America's involvement in Indochina, people look for turning points. Certainly 1954 was one such point—American refusal to participate in the Geneva Accords. The virtually inevitable consequence, occurring finally in 1975, was North Vietnam's victory. And that result, long delayed by French and American intervention, happened more inhumanely, through so many years of foreign destructive power and the bitterness kindled among Vietnamese.

In any event, the American commitment was to South Vietnam and, in particular, to Diem and his extensive and often Western-trained entourage, bureaucracy, and military establishment. And this commitment, still writ small, was what President John F. Kennedy inherited in January 1961. Kennedy somewhat increased that commitment while he was alive. It was a commitment that President Lyndon B. Johnson felt he had inherited once both Kennedy and Diem had been assassinated in the autumn of 1963; and in 1965 Johnson vastly escalated America's response. It was also a commitment that Presidents Richard M. Nixon and even Gerald Ford felt some compulsion to keep—or at least to terminate on comfortable, slow-motion terms, thanks to the tutelage of Secretary of State Henry Kissinger.

But before one attempts to analyze and explain America's Indochina involvement since 1961 more closely, one should note a further theme out of history that is more recent than "denial" but equally potent: Southeast Asia as a *given* in terms of its allegedly vital significance to American national security.

Consider, for instance, a paragraph from an early 1952 National

Security Council statement on "U.S. Objectives and Courses of Action with Respect to Southeast Asia":

> 2. Communist domination, by whatever means, of all Southeast Asia would seriously endanger in the short term, and critically endanger in the longer term, United States security interests.

The reader might pause there to ask, What *are* those security interests? But no answer is offered. Instead, the supporting paragraphs career onward to declare that "the loss of any single country" in Southeast Asia would lead to communism in all Southeast Asia, then in India, then the Middle East, and finally, of course, "would endanger the stability and security of Europe." Here, well before President Eisenhower strongly publicized the concept, was an early statement of the famous "domino theory"—a most enthralling fallacy.

The domino idea was that all Asian states would act alike: if one fell down, all the rest would tumble. The concept required a combination of maps and rhetoric and ignorance. It was useful to all who needed to avoid complexity. But its gross oversimplification of history, politics, and geography was misleading to a generation of Americans.

Such "givens," and the accompanying official explications, helped shape American policies toward Indochina, and especially Vietnam, under six presidents of both political parties between 1945 and 1975.

Historians, students, and inquiring citizens in future decades will nonetheless be baffled by a central question that might be phrased, "How could the Vietnam War have happened?" To expand on the question: How did people of superior ability, sound training, and high ideals—American policymakers of the 1960s and early 1970s—create such costly and hugely unsuccessful policy?

In recent years, former officials and outside observers have offered a number of theories in striving to answer such questions. They range from assertions of presidential "inadvertence" (the "quagmire" concept), to its antithesis, presidential advertence; from a conclusion that the decision-making apparatus failed, to its antithesis, that "the system worked"; from a rigidly leftist explanation (based on economic imperialism), to a rigidly rightist explanation that America's military leaders were wrongly prevented from using the full arsenal at their disposal (bombing North Vietnam "back to the Stone Age").

How could Vietnam have happened? Answers must take into account a number of factors that shaped American decision-making in the critical decade of the 1960s. But first some chronology:

After the Eisenhower-Diem arrangement and the cancellation of the 1956 elections, American aid helped build and defend a South Vietnamese state. By the time John Kennedy became President and settled for a neutralized Laos, his advisers urged an increase in the American presence in Vietnam; and by the time of his assassination in late 1963, some 15,000 American military personnel were assisting the South Vietnamese regime, whose chief—Diem—was himself killed in the same month, with American acquiescence. Although Kennedy and Diem were at loggerheads over Diem's autocratic rule, it is difficult to predict what Kennedy would have done about the Vietnam commitment. Those closest to him say that he would have terminated it.

Lyndon Johnson inherited a South Vietnam that was soon plagued by military coups. During 1964, as he adjusted to the presidency and sought election, Vietnam was relegated to the post-election planners. In the summer of 1964, the Congress reacted to alleged North Vietnamese provocations by passing the Tonkin Gulf Resolution, giving the President a relatively free hand. And in early 1965, Johnson, elected by the largest majority in history, decided not to use that mandate to withdraw or negotiate, but rather to escalate: first, through systematic aerial bombing of North Vietnam (both to strengthen South Vietnam's wobbly spine and to punish Hanoi), and second, by the late spring and early summer, through the dispatch of American ground forces, to keep South Vietnam alive and well. The war, thereby, was soon an American war.

America's Vietnam War, once fully launched, had many aspects: extraordinary aerial tonnages of bombs dropped not only on North Vietnam but also on suspected Communist sectors of the South (and secretly in Laos and Cambodia); heavy military engagements on the ground, many of them very costly and unsuccessful; chemical warfare—"defoliants"—that made territories uninhabitable; and efforts to use counterterror tactics that matched the cruelty of the terrorists on "the other side." This war brought up to half a million American troops to Indochina between 1965 and 1968. It brought many advertisements in the United States of impending victory. It produced a major Vietnamese Communist counteroffensive in early 1968—the "Tet Offensive." And once that Tet event had happened, America's already volatile politics back home had been transformed. Democrat

Johnson, abdicating under pressures from the peace movement, gave way to Republican Nixon; and a slow but ultimately successful negotiatory process was at long last under way.

That process would take a long time—under Johnson, Nixon, and Ford. And the names of America's South Vietnamese clients—some of them more notable than others for their obstructiveness of the peacemaking process—would include Nguyen Cao Ky and Nguyen Van Thieu. In the meantime, the real father of Vietnamese independence, Ho Chi Minh, died in 1969. And Saigon—now renamed for him—finally fell to his followers in April 1975.

But back to the question: How could the American involvement in Vietnam have come about?

A first and central ingredient was the legacy of the 1950s—the so-called loss of China, the Korean War, and the East Asian policy of Secretary of State Dulles.

This legacy had an institutional result for the Kennedy and Johnson administrations: In 1961, the American government's East Asian establishment was undoubtedly the most rigid and doctrinaire of Washington's regional divisions in foreign affairs. This was especially true at the Department of State, whose Bureau of Far Eastern Affairs had been purged of its best senior China expertise and of farsighted dispassionate men as a result of McCarthyism.

Another aspect of the legacy was the special vulnerability and sensitivity of Democratic administrations on East Asian policy issues. In 1961, the memory of the McCarthy era was still very sharp, and Kennedy's margin of victory was very thin. The 1960 Offshore Islands TV debate between Kennedy and Nixon (the issue was whether the U.S. should defend Nationalist China's last toehold) had shown the President-elect the perils of "fresh thinking." The administration was inherently leery of moving too fast on Asia, and there was virtually no effort to bring back the purged or exiled East Asia experts.

There were other important by-products of this "legacy of the 1950s."

The Kennedy and Johnson administrations inherited and somewhat shared a general perception of China-on-the-march—a sense of China's vastness, its numbers, its belligerence; a revived sense, perhaps, of the Golden Horde. These administrations inherited and for too long accepted a monolithic conception of the Communist bloc. Despite much earlier predictions and reports by outside analysts, policymakers did not begin to accept the reality and possible finality of the Sino-Soviet split until the first weeks of 1962. Even thereafter, the inevitably corrosive impact on communism of competing nationalisms was largely ignored.

Further, these administrations inherited and to some extent shared the "domino theory" about Asia. This theory resulted from profound ignorance of Asian history and hence ignorance of the radical differences among Asian nations and societies. It resulted from a blindness to the power and resilience of Asian nationalisms. (It may also have resulted from a subconscious sense that, since "all Asians look alike," all Asian nations will act alike.) As a theory, the domino fallacy was not merely inaccurate but also insulting to Asian nations; yet it has continued to this day to beguile people who should know better.

Finally, the legacy of the 1950s was apparently compounded by an uneasy sense of a worldwide Communist challenge to the Kennedy administration after the Bay of Pigs fiasco in April 1961. A first manifestation was the President's traumatic Vienna meeting with Khrushchev in June 1961; then came the Berlin crisis of the summer. All this created an atmosphere in which Kenendy undoubtedly felt under special pressure to show his nation's mettle in Vietnam—if the Vietnamese, unlike the people of Laos, were willing to fight. It should be added that the increased commitment to Vietnam was also fueled by a new breed of military strategists and academic social scientists—both in Washington and in Saigon—who had developed theories of counterguerrilla warfare and were eager to see them put to the test. To some, "counterinsurgency" seemed a new panacea for coping with the world's instability.

So much for the legacy and the history. Any new administration inherits both complicated problems and simplistic views of the world. But surely among the policymakers of the Kennedy and Johnson administrations there were men who would warn of the dangers of an open-ended commitment to the Vietnam quagmire.

This raises a central question at the heart of the policy process: Where were the experts, the doubters, and the dissenters? Were they there at all, and if so, what happened to them?

The answer is complex but instructive.

In the first place, the American government was sorely lacking in real Vietnam or Indochina expertise. Originally treated as an adjunct of Embassy Paris, the Saigon Embassy and the Vietnam Desk at State

were largely staffed from 1954 onward by French-speaking foreign
service personnel of narrowly European experience. Such diplomats
were even more closely restricted than the normal embassy officer—
by cast of mind as well as language—to contacts with Vietnam's French-
speaking urban elites.

In addition, the shadow of the "loss of China" distorted Vietnam
reporting. Career officers in the department, and especially those in
the field, had not forgotten the fate of their World War II colleagues
who wrote in frankness from China and were later pilloried by Congressional committees for critical comments on the Chinese Nationalists.
Candid reporting on the strengths of the Viet Cong and the weaknesses
of the Diem government was inhibited by the memory. It was also
inhibited by some higher officials who refused to endorse and approve
such cables.

In due course, to be sure, some Vietnam talent was discovered
or developed. But a recurrent and increasingly important factor in
the decision-making process was the banishment of real expertise. Here
the underlying cause was the "closed politics" of policymaking as issues
became hot. The more sensitive the issue, and the higher it rose in
the bureaucracy, the more completely the experts were excluded while
the harassed senior generalists took over (that is, the secretaries, under-
secretaries, and presidential assistants). Another underlying cause of
this banishment, as Vietnam became more critical, was the replace-
ment of the experts, who were generally and increasingly pessimistic,
by men described as "can-do guys," loyal and energetic fixers unsoured
by expertise.

Despite the banishment of the experts, internal doubters and dissenters did indeed appear and persist. Yet such men were effectively
neutralized by a subtle dynamic: the domestication of dissenters. Such
"domestication" arose out of a twofold clubbish need: on the one hand,
the dissenter's desire to stay aboard; and on the other hand, the nondis-
senter's conscience. Simply stated, dissent, when recognized, was made
to feel at home.

A related point—and crucial, undoubtedly, to government at all
times—was the "effectiveness" trap, the trap that kept men from speaking out as clearly or often as they might have within the government.
And it was the trap that kept men from resigning in protest and airing
their dissent outside the government. The most important asset that
a man brings to bureaucratic life is his "effectiveness," a mysterious

combination of training, style, and connections. The most ominous complaint that can be whispered of a bureaucrat is "I'm afraid Charlie's beginning to lose his effectiveness." The inclination to remain silent or to acquiesce in the presence of the great men—to live to fight another day, to give on this issue so that you can be "effective" on later issues—is overwhelming. As for the disinclination to resign in protest, while not necessarily a Washington or even American special-ity, it seems more true of a government in which ministers have no parliamentary back bench to which to retreat. In the absence of such a refuge, it is easy to rationalize the decision to stay aboard. By doing so, one may be able to prevent a few bad things from happening and perhaps even make a few good things happen. To exit is to lose even those marginal chances for "effectiveness."

Through a variety of procedures, both institutional and personal, doubt, dissent, and expertise were effectively neutralized in the making of policy. But what can be said of the men "in charge"? It is patently absurd to suggest that they produced such tragedy by intention and calculation. But it is neither absurd nor difficult to discern certain forces at work that caused decent and honorable men to do great harm.

Here one must stress the paramount problem of executive fatigue. What was most seriously eroded in the deadening process of Vietnam policymaking was freshness of thought, imagination, a sense of possibil-ity, a sense of priorities and perspective—those rare assets of a new administration in its first year or two in office. The tired policymaker becomes a prisoner of his own narrowed view of the world and his own clichéd rhetoric. He becomes irritable and defensive—short on sleep, short on family ties, short on patience. Such men make bad policy and then compound it. They have neither the time nor the temperament for new ideas or preventive diplomacy.

Below the level of the fatigued executive in the making of Vietnam policy was a widespread phenomenon: the curator mentality in the post–World War II bureaucracy. By this one means the collective iner-tia produced by the bureaucrat's view of his or her job. At State, the average "desk officer" inherits from his predecessor the policy toward Country X; he regards it as his function to keep that policy intact— under glass, untampered with, and dusted—so that he may pass it on in two to four years to his successor. And such curatorial service generally merits promotion within the system. (Maintain the status quo, and you will stay out of trouble.) In some circumstances, the

inertia bred by such an outlook can act as a brake against rash innovation. But on many issues, this inertia sustains the momentum of bad
policy and unwise commitments, momentum that might otherwise
have been resisted within the ranks. Clearly, Vietnam was such an
issue.

To fatigue and inertia must be added the factor of internal confusion. Even among the "architects" of America's Vietnam commitment,
there was persistent confusion as to what type of war the nation was
fighting and, as a direct consequence, confusion as to how to end that
war. Was it, for instance, a civil war, in which case counterinsurgency
might suffice? Or was it a war of international aggression? (This might
invoke SEATO or UN commitment.) Who was the aggressor—and the
"real enemy"? The Viet Cong? Hanoi? Peking? Moscow? International
communism? Or maybe "Asian Communism"? Differing enemies dictated differing strategies and tactics. And confused throughout, in like
fashion, was the question of American objectives. Your objectives depended on whom you were fighting and why.

Similar confusion beset the concept of "negotiations" regarding
Vietnam—anathema to much of official Washington and Saigon from
1954 to 1965. Not until April 1965 did "unconditional discussions"
become respectable, via a presidential speech. Even then, the Secretary of State stressed privately to journalists that nothing had changed,
since "discussions" were by no means the same as "negotiations."
Months later, that issue was resolved. But it took even longer to obtain
a fragile internal agreement that negotiations might include the Viet
Cong as something other than an appendage to Hanoi's delegation.
And it took years, of course, to arrive at real negotiations.

As a further influence on policymakers, one must cite the factor
of bureaucratic detachment: what at best might be termed the professional callousness of the surgeon (and indeed, medical lingo—the "surgical strike" for instance—seemed to crop up in the euphemisms of
the times). In Washington, and also Saigon, the semantics of the military
muted the reality of war for the civilian policymakers. In quiet air-
conditioned thick-carpeted rooms, such terms as "systematic pressure,"
"armed reconnaisance," "targets of opportunity," and even "body
count" seemed to breed a sort of games-theory detachment.

There is an unprovable factor that relates to bureaucratic detachment: the ingredient of cryptoracism. Detachment seems to have been
compounded by a traditional Western sense that there are so many

Asians, after all; that Asians have a fatalism about life and a disregard for its loss; that they are cruel and barbaric to their own people; and that they are very different from "us." The upshot of such subliminal views is a subliminal question whether Asians, and particularly Asian peasants, and most particularly Asian Communists, are really people "like you and me." To put the matter another way: Would America have pursued quite such policies—and quite such military tactics—if the Vietnamese were white?

It is impossible to write of Vietnam decision-making without writing about language. Throughout the conflict, words were of paramount importance. Words had impact through rhetorical escalation; and they created the problem of "oversell." In an important sense, Vietnam became of crucial significance to the United States because American leaders so often *said* that it was of crucial significance.

The key here was domestic politics: the need to sell the American people, press, and Congress on support for an unpopular and costly war in which the objectives themselves were in flux. To sell means to persuade, and to persuade means rhetoric. As the difficulties and costs mounted, so did the definitions of the stakes. This is not to say that rhetorical escalation is an orderly process. Executive prose is the product of many writers; and some concepts—North Vietnamese infiltration, America's "national honor," Red China as the chief enemy— entered the rhetoric only gradually and even sporadically. But there was an upward spiral nonetheless. And once leaders had *said* that the American Experiment itself stood or fell on the Vietnam outcome, they had thereby created a national stake far beyond any earlier stakes.

Crucial throughout the process of Vietnam decision-making was a conviction among many policymakers that Vietnam posed a fundamental test of America's national will. Time and again critics were told by men reared in the tradition of those who had ruled the Philippines, defeated Japan, and at least preserved South Korea that all the United States needed was the will, and the nation would then prevail. Implicit in such a view was a curious assumption that Asians lacked will, or at least that in a contest between Asian and Anglo-Saxon wills the non-Asians must prevail. A corollary to the persistent belief in will was a fascination with power and a sense of special proprietary rights about the power America possessed as no nation or civilization ever before. Those who doubted the American role in Vietnam were said to shrink from the burdens of power, the obligations of power, the uses of power, the responsibility of power. By implication, such men were soft-headed and effete.

Finally, no discussion of the factors and forces at work on Vietnam policymakers can ignore the central fact of human ego investment. Men who have participated in a decision develop a stake in that decision. As they participate in further, related decisions, their personal stake increases. It might have been possible to dissuade a man of strong self-confidence at an early stage on the ladder of decision; but it became infinitely harder at later stages, since a change of mind there usually involved implicit or explicit repudiation of a chain of previous decisions.

The various ingredients cited in the making of Vietnam policy created a variety of results, most of them fairly obvious. Throughout the conflict, for instance, there was persistent and repeated miscalculation by virtually all actors in high echelons and low, whether dove, hawk, or something else. In addition, there was a steady yielding to pressures for a military solution and only minimal and sporadic efforts at a diplomatic and political solution—until Hanoi's Tet Offensive in early 1968 forced the Johnson administration to change course belatedly.

Throughout the conflict, there were also many missed opportunities, large and small, for American disengagement from Vietnam on increasingly unpleasant but still acceptable terms. Most notably, after November 1964, President Johnson could have used the largest electoral mandate in history to de-escalate in Vietnam, in the clear expectation that at the worst a neutralist government would come to power in Saigon and politely invite the United States out. Instead, many years, lives, and dollars later, such an alternative became elusive, infinitely more costly, and ultimately unattainable.

America's process of extrication from the Vietnamese civil war took even longer than Harold Isaacs would probably have dared to predict in early 1950 when he wrote that "the real problem is not how to implement this policy but how to extricate ourselves from it."

That process, begun with the preliminary Paris peace talks of 1968 (and Lyndon Johnson's virtual abdication), continued under a new Republican President, Richard M. Nixon, and his chief foreign affairs adviser, Henry A. Kissinger. But the process took five years, and meanwhile, American might and technology were put to use as never before in efforts to "persuade the other side." One after another—

while negotiations were opened, stalemated, or recessed—a long-available but previously rejected list of military options was used, each action to little avail except for the further devastation of Indochina. Technically neutral Cambodia was invaded (and later systematically destroyed); Laos was invaded; North Vietnam's harbors were mined and its urban areas "carpet-bombed."

What the American negotiators apparently sought was some sort of "decent interval"—at least of several years—between American withdrawal from South Vietnam ("Vietnamization" of the war it was called for a while) and Hanoi's probable reunification of the entire nation—its unchanged objective since 1945. In the minds of many Americans, however, that "decent interval" was actually forever: time for South Vietnam to become self-reliant, and a perpetuation of two separate Vietnams. Hanoi's negotiators, armies, and guerrillas sensed that hope and firmly rejected it; for Ho's Vietminh revolutionaries had been too long frustrated and too often deceived by the outside powers.

In the end, peace agreements were signed in 1973—and soon, of course, violated by both sides. But President Nixon was not only hamstrung in his response by a deep-rooted American peace movement and the congressional constraints that this movement had helped create; he was also distracted by the Watergate scandal that soon caused his resignation. As for Nixon's successor, Gerald Ford, he and Secretary Kissinger were similarly constrained and—as Americans had been so often over the years—taken totally by surprise by the worst outcome that Ford's predecessors had so much feared: the sudden and rapid collapse of South Vietnam's armed forces and government, and the fall of Saigon itself in late April 1975, with the residual American presence put to flight in disarray.

So did it finally end, a tragic, prolonged, devastating, and—most important—entirely avoidable chapter in the history of America's relations with the peoples of Asia.

(19)

The Philippine Crossroads

IN CONTRAST TO the "loss of China," the Korean War, and the Vietnam conflagration, America's postwar relations with the Philippines have seemed comparatively easy and successful. It is unlikely that they will remain so. Along with Britain, Canada, France, Mexico, China, and Japan, among others, the Philippines are often said to have a "special relationship" with the United States. As America's only major colony, the Philippines have indeed occupied a distinctive place in American foreign relations. But the heart of the relationship has always been with the ruling elite rather than with the country or the Filipino people at large.

The collaboration forged early in this century between the Americans and the Filipino elite survived, with some modification, long after the islands became independent in 1946. Along with public health measures and the English language, it has proven to be one of the major legacies of the colonial era. Even late in the 1970s, President Ferdinand E. Marcos continued to use the United States in the traditional way as a dual sanction. Although dependent upon American economic, military, and psychological support to maintain his martial-law regime, he loudly challenged the continuation of American's naval and air bases at Subic Bay and Clark Field. Since his government actually agreed with the United States that the maintenance of these bases was desirable, the main effect of Marcos's rhetoric was to manipulate nationalist sentiment, distract some of his critics, and rally public support to his increasingly unpopular regime. America's willingness to play Marcos's game—to purchase continued base rights at the cost of such rhetorical harassment—exemplifies the collaboration upon which the special relationship has been built.

This collaboration, though durable, has always been risky. Its effectiveness in perpetuating the power of the Filipino elite has postponed a reckoning with the social and economic pressures it was meant to contain. In the meantime, however, the pressures have continued to build. Beneath the facade of development, tutelage, and partnership for progress, the cement of the Philippine society—especially rural society—has been cracking.

The Americans' reliance upon indirect rule through elite Filipino collaborators gave the Philippine elite an effective veto power over social and economic policy within the islands. The results have endured. Because it suited the interests of the elite to have roads, schools, and public health measures—indeed, it suited the interests of almost *everyone*—much American energy and ingenuity went into projects of this sort, creating a proud record of achievement. But other types of reform and development—land reform, nutritional programs, taxation plans that had some potential for redistributing wealth—withered on the vine, because the elite found them either threatening or irrelevant.

This is one important reason—though not the only one—for the extreme inequities and the serious poverty and underdevelopment that characterize the Philippines to this day. Four and a half decades of ostensibly developmental, modernizing imperialism under the United States have been followed by three and a half decades of independence as America's model of decolonization. Yet in the Philippines today, the bottom 20 percent of the population still has only 3.7 percent of the wealth. Only 40 percent of the people have access to adequate drinkable water, and even fewer have electricity or waste disposal facilities. Despite a food surplus great enough to permit sizable exports of rice and fruit to other countries, 40 to 45 percent of the population is undernourished with almost one-third of children under the age of six seriously malnourished (i.e., receiving less than 75 percent of the minimum nutrient intake they need).

This is not entirely the fault of the Americans, the Filipino elite, or the collaborative political system. But it does suggest that America's success in the Philippines—its contributions to political awareness, the achievement of formal independence, and the spread of certain relatively neutral kinds of infrastructure—has not promoted social development and economic equity.

Former Senator Benigno Aquino, a shrewd student of Philippine-American relations, once lamented that Americans have taken the easy way out. "You Americans," he told the historian Theodore Friend, "you smother us with Kisses; you kill us with Hershey bars!" Hershey bar benevolence is a long way from tutelary nation building.

So the question arises: Was there an alternative to Hershey bar benevolence? Was there some way in which Americans, having forced themselves upon Filipinos, could have gotten deeper into the fabric of Philippine life and made it more progressive and more equitable? Or, recognizing that the United States was *not* going to accomplish enough to justify its occupation of the archipelago, some way in which it could have withdrawn sooner and left the Filipinos to their own devices? Was there an alternative, in other words, to the middle course actually taken?

The temptation is to say no—that these are really ahistorical questions, seeking alternatives that were not possible, given the realities and limitations of the early twentieth century. Redistributive reform took hold in the United States itself only in the 1930s, with the New Deal, and even then to a lesser degree than in many other parts of the world. How could Americans do for the Philippines something they had neither the will nor the knowledge to do at home? As for the alternative at the other end of the spectrum—simply getting out— one can argue that this was, in effect, exactly what the United States did. Leaving the Philippines as soon as a stable and responsible government of Filipinos could take charge was an idea that grew steadily upon the American public from Theodore Roosevelt's time on.

But this sort of self-congratulatory fatalism ignores perhaps the most significant sociopolitical development of the American period: the political mobilization of the peasantry (and, to a lesser degree, urban workers) outside the confines of the independence movement and the political parties that dominated it. To sense the implications of this, one has only to realize that even now more than 70 percent of the Philippine population lives in rural areas—although, of course, not all of these are peasants—and that in the American period the figure was more than 80 percent. If there is such a thing as a typical Filipino, it is the peasant who works the land, raising and harvesting the rice, corn, sugar, tobacco, coconuts, and other fruit and fiber plants, either as a share-crop tenant, a small landholder, or what is euphemistically called a wage earner, i.e., someone, often a migrant worker, who is paid either by time or by output, without having any stake or roots in the land. These are not only the most numerous people in the country but also the poorest. Agriculture, which produces less than 30 percent of the Philippine net domestic product, is the principal source of livelihood for 45 percent of Philippine families, and for 65 percent of poor families.

Although the Americans often spoke of helping these people—and to some degree actually did so through public education, public health programs, and highways—there were significant ways in which their position actually *worsened* during the American period.

The classic model of agrarian social and economic organization in the Philippines—going back to the village societies, or barangays, of early times—has been a system of mutual, reciprocal obligations, or backscratching, between patrons and clients. When it worked right, this system tended to align society vertically, linking rich and poor in a structure of mutual obligation, rather than aligning society horizontally by class. Landlords and tenants, for example, characteristically exchanged services in a way that—although profoundly unequal—benefited both. Peasants contributed their labor on the land, sometimes the animals and tools required in the work, miscellaneous services around the house and property of the landlord, and their loyalty in political and social disputes within the community. The landlord, in return, allowed the tenant to keep roughly half the crop for his own use, provided protection and patronage of many kinds for the whole family, and made available interest-free loans of food and other essentials when needed.

By modern American standards, this produced a very hard—subsistence-level—existence for the peasant and a degree of uncertainty in economic relations that appears insupportable. But from the point of view of the participants, there were many attractions. It was a *personal* relationship, flexible enough to respond to changing circumstances; and it bound the landlord as well as the peasant to local morality and customary ethics. A landlord who abused his tenants' established rights brought down the condemnation of the whole community upon his own head. He was said to be *walang hiya*, unscrupulous and shameless, one of the worst charges one Filipino can make against another.

The strengthening of the elite in the American era undermined this structure of reciprocity. Not only were the landed and professional elite of the islands secured in their political power by the dual sanction already described, but it was also they who profited most from the developmental programs instituted by the American government. As a result, they needed the support of their tenants and retainers less than ever before. Concomitantly, as they absorbed the American faith in laws and institutions, science and engineering, they became increasingly contemptuous of the established, customary ways of doing things. So, in the 1920s and the early 1930s, the second generation of Filipino landlords under American rule set out to rationalize their agricultural production. This led not only to mechanization (where possible), clarification of formerly uncertain land titles, and the introduction of a new layer of foremen and overseers between the peasants and the now often absentee landlord, but also to a wholesale assault on the tenants' customary rights. Their share of the crop was reduced to less than half; the interest-free loans of food that had tided families over the unproductive months were ended; more services were demanded and fewer benefits provided.

These pressures were not only economically ruinous but culturally shattering. Peasants interpreted the new policies as a default by landlords on legitimate obligations; and in response they began to organize for resistance and self-defense. The traditional form of peasant protest against encroachments of this sort in earlier times had been millenarian uprisings. But by the 1920s, this was giving way to a more secular orientation. In the decade and a half remaining before the outbreak of World War II, agricultural unions, eventually reaching a membership of several million, began to spread, particularly in the rice-growing region of central Luzon. In the beginning, their goals were modest. Most members would probably have settled for restoring an idealized version of the old paternalistic tenancy system: an equal division of the harvest, interest-free loans of rice and other essentials, and recognition of their right to fish and gather wood on the landlord's property and to organize in unions. In time, however, many of them linked up with the prewar socialist movement in the islands, headed by Pedro Abad Santos. Proud and nationalistic as they were, men and women like these found the official independence movement epitomized by the Nacionalista party of Quezon, Osmeña, and Manuel Roxas a cruel delusion. "Our ruling class," Abad Santos said in 1939, "has taken the place of the former [American] rulers and uses the courts to further their interests and privileges."

From that day to this, there has been an organized underside of Philippine politics, composed of people who may, either voluntarily or under some form of social or police pressure, vote for the official parties but whose interests fundamentally diverge from those represented by the elite-dominated parties. The form this takes varies from one period to another. The movements of the 1930s gave rise to the broader and more militant Hukbalahap (People's Anti-Japanese Army) during World War II, which in turn metamorphosed into the HMB (People's Liberation Army) after the war, when the target shifted from the Japanese to the landed elite and the by-then independent Republic of the Philippines that they dominated. The HMB grew out of the Hukbalahap, and the members of both groups went by the same name—Huks—because the H in HMB stood for the Tagalog word *hukbong*. But the two groups were not identical—the one was primarily anti-Japanese, the other primarily anti-landlord—and their membership, though overlapping, was not identical either.

The HMB was beaten in the early 1950s by the carrot-and-stick policies of Ramon Magsaysay, who was, first, Secretary of Defense under President Elpidio Quirino and later President in his own right until his death in an airplane crash in 1957. Magsaysay presided over a kind of minor miracle, of which the United States was one of the chief architects. In the spring and early summer of 1950, the Huks had the initiative in most of central Luzon and were making major headway penetrating other parts of the island as well. They had more willing guerrilla fighters than they could arm; and the pattern and growing boldness of their attacks so terrified the Quirino government that it began contingency plans to resist—and if necessary to flee— an assault on Manila itself. Two and a half years later, it was all over; the Huks had been reduced to a few harried bands fleeing through the mountains.

How could such a thing happen? It happened basically for three reasons. First, Magsaysay cleaned up the Philippine government—particularly the Army and the constabulary—improved its honesty and efficiency, launched major political reform programs that brought artesian wells and other desirable infrastructure to the countryside, and gave promise of a crackdown on the landlords to get them to accept less than half the harvest. Second, the Huks fell under the control of Manila-based Communists—this had been coming since 1949—whose doctrinal rigidities and whose emphasis upon American imperialism rather than upon specific injustices in the countryside were irrelevant to most peasants and eventually alienated many of them from the movement. Rightly or wrongly, most Filipino peasants thought the enemy was the landlord not the Americans: "It was hard," said Peregrino Taruc, one of the leaders of the HMB, "to make peasants see the connection between their problems and American imperialism." * Third, the United States, identifying Magsaysay as a winner, backed him more heavily than it had supported his predecessors. The United States provided one-fifth of the total Philippine defense and police budgets, half the funding for the agrarian and psychological warfare programs, improved weaponry for the Army, and some pioneer efforts at developing counterinsurgency tactics.

Since Magsaysay himself was a man of simple origins—a man from outside the usual elite sources of political leadership—peasants were inclined to believe in him. Just how much he would have accomplished if he had lived, we shall never know. There are many who argue that the image was much more substantial than the man himself. Even so, the episode suggests what might have been if Americans had more often reached beyond the spokesmen of the status quo and supported people with a broader vision.

Unfortunately, this was not the milestone that it could have been. Magsaysay's successors reverted to business as usual, and the American reformers who had advised him moved out of the fields and into air-conditioned suites in downtown Manila. Land reform became a "motherhood" issue—something everyone supported but no one really did anything about; and, as time passed, new peasant groups arose to organize the discontented.

By the late 1960s, frustration with the old politics had become so intense that students and professional people began to condemn the entire system and lend their leadership to the urban squatters and unemployed and the rural peasants. Jesuit priests, for example, began to organize the sugar workers on plantations in the Visayan Islands to the south of Luzon. And with the Huks reduced to a peripheral banditry, a new militancy emerged in the form of the New People's Army, a Maoist group that replaced the then-moribund Moscow branch of the Philippine Communist party. Urban violence grew in teeming

---

* Quoted in Benedict J. Kerkvliet, *The Huk Rebellion: A Study of Peasant Revolt in the Philippines* (Berkeley, 1977), p. 228.

Manila, though some of this may have been the work of government agents provocateurs. Finally, in September 1972, President Marcos, ambitious for a third term that he could not constitutionally have, gave the coup de grace to the whole political system by imposing a martial-law dictatorship.

By the 1980's, therefore, the United States has found itself at a crossroads in its Philippine policy. Along with the Vietnam War and the influx of American foreign investment into the Philippines during the 1960s, American support of the Marcos dictatorship has drawn down the reservoir of good will that Filipinos once felt toward the backslapping big brothers who all seemed to be named Joe. The American image today is no longer that of the schoolteachers or road builders of Taft's era, the liberators of MacArthur's time, the rural development technicians of Magsaysay's day. Now, in a way that was never true when the Americans actually ruled the islands, they are considered imperialists, interested only in the use of the bases at Subic Bay and Clark Field and the security of the American-based multinational corporations that, correctly or not, are perceived to exploit the wealth of the country. And as the United States has linked itself ever more closely to President Marcos, his enemies have, in many cases, become America's.

There is no need on this account to create a mirror image of the official mythology. Americans have not been unusually wicked, corrupt, brutal, exploitative, or even obtuse in the Philippines. But surveying the wreckage of democratic political institutions, the mass poverty and gross inequalities of Philippine life, and the growing alienation of many Filipinos from the United States, one can at least say that eight decades of collaboration have been tried and found wanting. If there is to be an American future in the Philippines, it will have to be on some other basis.

(20)

China Regained

FEW EVENTS IN THIS CENTURY can be as ironic as America's rediscovery of China even as Indochina was being "lost." For one recurrent rationale for American intervention in Vietnam was the existence after 1949 of an allegedly predatory Communist regime in Peking which hungered after conquest of the Indochina peninsula.

It was only after wider understanding slowly infused the thinking of American policymakers that China's fundamental separateness from the Vietnamese civil war became belatedly apparent. Ho Chi Minh's revolution was one thing, rooted in the Versailles conference (where Ho sought unsuccessfully to make Vietnam's case for independence), the founding of the French Communist party, and an orientation toward Moscow. Mao's revolution had a very different rooting, and took a different course—indigenous and self-sustaining in its own way, after 1927, with few obligations to Russia, Europe, or anyone else. And before and after their revolutions, despite intervals of collaboration, the Vietnamese and Chinese were much afflicted by mutual suspicions and deep-seated historic enmities.

Yet in the great blurring of vision that the Cold War produced for America's leaders in the 1950s and 1960s, all Communists looked alike. And, as even such variegated politicians as John Foster Dulles and Hubert H. Humphrey would put it, all Communists must act alike, under orders from the master planners in Peking and especially Moscow. That blurring, if mindless in terms of reality, was nonetheless both heartfelt and a great convenience in explaining America's Asian policy to the public.

Here, maps and charts long served an invaluable, if misleading, function. As civilian officials briefed congressmen or the TV public—with senior officers of the armed forces reinforcing their testimony—the use of the color red plus giant arrows made Mercator's projection reveal the horrifying story. (Also useful, of course, were columns of population figures and lists of vital raw materials.) It could be shown—as Senator Joe McCarthy had early proved—that "Communism" since 1918 had absorbed not only that immense Eurasian land mass, the U.S.S.R., but also, right after World War II, Eastern Europe. It had then absorbed all of vast China, adding a quarter of mankind to its score in the ultimate game, and now was shooting its giant red arrows into all of Southeast Asia, beginning with Vietnam.

This cartographic illusion—an offshoot of the domino theory—was often highly persuasive. All it overlooked were certain ineradicable realities, hard to show on maps: realities of history, geography, languages, religions, and most especially *competing nationalisms*. Such realities were not only hard to show, they were confusing—the minutiae of specialists, even pedants—and therefore quite dispensable.

So, thanks to such a simplistic world view in Washington—and at least rhetorical reciprocity in Communist Peking, which was both scornful and fearful of the United States—China and America began in 1949–1950 more than two decades of acute hostility and nearly all-out war. Americans fought Chinese "volunteers" in Korea and came close to provoking major Chinese intervention again in Vietnam. Meanwhile, America's protectorate of the Chinese Nationalists on Taiwan produced two confrontations over KMT-occupied clusters of small islands just off the China mainland in 1954 and 1958—the second of which nearly triggered a wider war.

Yet, with Vietnam still burning hotly, it was suddenly announced in the summer of 1971 that Secretary Kissinger had paid a secret visit to Peking and that President Nixon himself would go to China in early 1972. The lethal deadlock was about to dissolve into an astonishing new phase of amity, one not equaled since the Sino-American euphoria of the early 1940s. And most ironic of all, that amity's chief orchestrator, Mr. Nixon, had been a junior but fast-rising leader of the congressional China witch-hunters at the beginning of it all.

China policy in the 1950s was an unintended bipartisan creation: the product of beleaguered and desperate Democrats but also outraged Republicans, the latter scenting and then achieving long-denied victory

at the polls. Out of China's "loss" and the Korean War was shaped
an American posture, if not a full-fledged policy, which Eisenhower
and Secretary of State Dulles inherited in January 1953 from Truman
and Acheson. Its ingredients: first, non-recognition of Mao's Peking
regime (a Soviet creation and puppet, "a Slavic Manchukuo," as Assistant Secretary of State Dean Rusk had termed it back in 1951); second,
the exclusion of that regime from membership in the United Nations
(and thereby protection of Nationalist China's seat in the Security
Council as well as the General Assembly); third, military containment
of China through the creation of a network of bases and alliances on
the Chinese periphery (the Southeast Asia Treaty Organization
[SEATO] and bilateral treaties with Japan, South Korea, Nationalist
China); fourth, isolation of China through an embargo of all American
trade and a ban on all travel; fifth, massive worldwide efforts to persuade all other nations to follow Washington's example on each of
the previous points; and finally, a program of aid and support for America's down-but-not-out wartime ally, the Kuomintang government on
Taiwan.

This was a policy into which the Democrats had lurched uneasily
as "the dust settled" in 1949–1950, despite internal discussions of the
probable and eventual recognition of Peking. But the Korean hostilities
not only put an end to such discussions (and made them sound, to
some, treasonable); Korea also persuaded the Truman administration
to interpose the U.S. Seventh Fleet between Taiwan and the mainland,
in order (it was explained) to keep this new Asian war from spreading—
thus reinjecting American forces into the still unfinished Chinese civil
war.

Meanwhile, by 1948–1949, the victorious but bitter Chinese Communists had harassed and detained American diplomats from Manchuria southward. Hopes earlier expressed by Mao and others for postwar
cooperation with the United States had been badly soured by American
aid to the KMT during the civil war. The new China, Mao decreed,
would "lean to one side," to its Moscow partner of the 1920s.

Both sides, then, in the decade of the 1950s were constrained from
innovation—from a softening of rigidity and potentially dangerous hostility—in Sino-American relations. Indeed, the Formosa Straits Resolution of 1955 gave the White House discretionary war powers that had
a history of Latin American interventions and a sad future in Indochina.
Yet there were a few lapses, some loosenings of the deadlock. At the

Geneva Conference of 1954, Mr. Dulles may have spurned the hand of Chou En-lai; but under pressure from the UN Secretary General and others, he reluctantly agreed to permit ambassadorial-level conversations between Peking and Washington—conversations that began in 1955, and eventually became lodged in Warsaw for nearly fifteen years. (In a sense, the Eisenhower administration thereby gave de facto recognition to Peking.) For several years those meetings were a ritual exchange of polemics; and yet the two parties were finally talking.

After Geneva came the Bandung Conference of 1956, a first international celebration of the existence of independent Asian and African "unaligned" nations. There China showed a new post–Korean truce confidence on the global stage and exuded, through Chou En-lai, the "Bandung spirit" of conciliation. In that spirit, the Chinese even decreed the opening of their doors to American journalists, despite the absence of diplomatic relations. Dulles, however, guarding against the slightest breach in the stockade of containment and isolation, refused to issue passports for such travel. And a year later, when American press organizations forced him partially to relent, the Chinese were moving into a new phase of inward-turning, the "Great Leap Forward," and the invitation was suspended (except for such a trusted "friend of China" as the writer Edgar Snow).

Other than through occasional and then, later, ritualistic Chinese Communist bombardment of the Nationalist-held offshore islands—especially the Matsu and Quemoy groups—Washington-Peking relations showed no motion in any direction throughout the 1950s. And the 1960s, with the Democrats once again back in power, would look on the surface much the same. If there were differences, they were matters of nuance. In the main, Korea dominated the 1950s, Indochina the 1960s. China and America watched each other with distrust, alarm, and often-expressed hate. Yet there were other forces at work, not only within each society but especially on the part of that one power external but most deeply significant to each of them: the Soviet Union. What would evolve in 1971–1972, in the surprise of Sino-American rapprochement, was not—if one had looked closely at the forces at play in the interim—quite so totally surprising. The chief question may not be why it happened but why it had not happened sooner.

Eight years of Republican rule came to an end in January 1961 when John F. Kennedy, having narrowly defeated Vice President

Nixon, moved into the White House. He and his appointees faced the smoldering conflict in Indochina; they also inherited the China deadlock. And in the weeks before his inauguration, the President-elect was warned by General Eisenhower that any shift in China policy—any "appeasement" of Peking—would bring Ike storming out of his retirement. So John Kennedy, it seems, though flexible about China in private conversations, confided to close friends that any real changes in policy must probably await a less fragile mandate and his second administration.

Yet the Democratic party and its representatives in both the executive and legislative branches included people who, during eight years out of power, had pressed increasingly for some form of reconciliation with China—most notably men like Adlai Stevenson, the party's two-time presidential nominee and now Ambassador to the United Nations; Averell Harriman, former Ambassador to the U.S.S.R. and longtime adviser to presidents; and Chester Bowles, former Ambassador to India, and now Under Secretary of State. The new administration was divided at the outset in its approach to both communism and the developing countries. Its ranks also included men whose outlooks were often as rigid as that of John Foster Dulles—notably Secretary of State Dean Rusk, policy planner Walt Whitman Rostow, CIA Director John McCone, numerous Pentagon officials, and Vice President Lyndon B. Johnson. And in the Congress, watching carefully, were the remnants of an earlier more potent "China Lobby."

Despite such varied and contending viewpoints, the Kennedy and Johnson administrations encompassed a slow and quiet but important process of policy evolution on the searing issue of China. Between 1961 and 1969, those coming into government from the outside—specialists from universities, foundations, journalism, and "think-tanks" whose views had been spurned under Dulles—found common ground among younger Asia careerists within the bureaucracy, those untouched by the purges of the 1950s.

That common ground centered on assumptions long resisted by Dulles and his partisans: that Communist rule of the China mainland was "here to stay," in some form at least; that a stable peace in East Asia and the western Pacific region required not only recognition of that reality but also positive steps toward accommodation with the Peking regime. It was acknowledged that such steps might be rejected out of hand by Mao, at least for the time being while Taiwan remained an American protectorate; but it was argued that they should be taken nonetheless, unilaterally, in order that Peking's present leadership— perhaps changing its outlook—or that leadership's successors might sooner or later choose to reciprocate. The United States should offer, it was argued, some alternative to eternal Sino-American enmity.

The evolving internal agenda of proposed American initiatives toward China included most of the following steps as early as 1961: a lowering of polemics both in public and in the Warsaw conversations, and an effort to engage the Chinese in substantive matters; a removal of the ban on travel for American citizens who wanted to visit China; inclusion of Peking in all international disarmament conversations; the proposing of cultural and educational exchanges between China and America; a gradual removal of the barriers to trade in non-strategic goods; an end to the exclusion of Peking from United Nations membership (ideally through some formula that might still allow Taiwan a separate seat); and finally the recognition of Mongolia in order to demonstrate that the United States *could* have diplomatic relations with non-bellicose Asian Communist states (implying a similar prospect for Peking).

Such in-house planning, or at least brainstorming—which was all highly classified lest the China Lobby remnants become vicious again— was given a belated impetus by early 1962. In those weeks, State Department planners, and Mr. Rusk himself, accepted evidence, long before put forward by academic specialists and others, that a deep-seated split between Moscow and Peking had developed in the late 1950s and was not only a reality but also probably permanent, at least for the foreseeable future. The impact of that perception was profound, although its effects remained blurred by events in Southeast Asia and also China. For the first time in Washington's corridors of power, communism began to be viewed at the top as something other than monolithic. The "Sino-Soviet Bloc" was cracking open. In one nation after another rival Communist parties were beginning to contend. They were pro-Moscow or pro-Peking, leaning toward Russian aid and the Stalinist model, or toward Maoism and a Chinese model, and sometimes Chinese assistance. All too slowly, the historically enduring power of competing nationalisms—and especially Chinese versus Russian—was becoming clear, a newly understood factor in international politics both in Asia and elsewhere.

For China policy makers, the Sino-Soviet split posed fundamental questions as to the dangers and opportunities of playing one Communist adversary off against the other—also how and whether to do so. Meanwhile, a few initiatives were pushed internally, generally without success. In the summer of 1961, feelers toward American recognition of Mongolia were withdrawn, thanks to a congressional outcry; and the unnerved Kennedy administration secretly pledged to Chiang Kai-shek to block Peking's admission to the UN by an American veto if necessary. At that time, and for nearly four more years, Secretary Rusk stubbornly resisted repeated proposals from within for an easing of the China travel ban, recognition of Mongolia, or any formula that might allow Peking a UN seat. Some thought he was following President Kennedy's orders; others were convinced that his own passionate hatred of Asian Communists—stemming from the Korean War—was at the center of his formidable inflexibility.

There were some minuscule results of the evolving internal consensus. Polemics were in fact lowered; the Warsaw ambassadorial channel was used at least once to reassure Peking privately that the United States would not support the Kuomintang's grandiose aims for "reconquest" of the mainland; and in 1962 the White House left open the possibility of selling wheat to China during a time when Peking faced a particularly acute food shortage. And finally, after the assassination of President Kennedy, Far East Assistant Secretary Roger Hilsman gave, in December 1963, a long-planned speech that had been designed to create a new rhetorical base for conciliatory initiatives towards China. Although the principles of the Hilsman speech would not be implemented until 1971, under very different auspices, the document was noteworthy as the first high-level and full-scale addressing of China policy since the late Dulles years. In calling for a policy of "firmness, flexibility, and dispassion," Hilsman represented the evolving consensus and, most important, publicly acknowledged that the People's Republic of China was actually here to stay.

But meanwhile, engulfing all of Asian policy, and indeed policy elsewhere, was the Indochina war. Kennedy's death nipped in the budding whatever might have come out of his first term, much less his second. And Lyndon B. Johnson—with Rusk eventually strengthened by the President's super Cold Warrior adviser Walt Rostow—was not about to do much regarding China until the Vietnam War was won. Although the travel ban was finally dented in 1965–1966 through the bypassing of Rusk, nothing significant was accomplished.

It should be added, however, that the mood of the Congress had dramatically changed, as shown in Senator J. William Fulbright's televised China hearings of early 1966; and both Johnson and Vice President Humphrey responded to those hearings that spring and summer by using new language about Peking: "containment without isolation," "reconciliation," "the building of bridges," and the "free flow of ideas, people, and goods." There was at highest levels, it seemed, a wistful yearning for some grand gesture of amity to engulf the engulfment— some way to wrap the Vietnam calamity, at home and abroad, into a bold act of trans-Pacific statecraft.

The obstacles to action, however, were formidable and recurrent. Democratic timidity has already been cited—fear of lingering elements of the old China Lobby, even after most of its key members had passed from the scene through death, retirement, or electoral defeat. Even small efforts to rehabilitate some of the pilloried foreign service officers were quietly shelved lest they cause controversy. In these years, it must be said, the upper echelons of policymaking showed the results of McCarthyism in one vivid way: the lack of high-level China specialists—and advocates—of the stature of the well-known fraternity of Sovietologists, such men as George Kennan, Charles Bohlen, and Llewellyn Thompson. Such a lack produced a powerful related obstacle. As the Sino-Soviet split became grudgingly accepted, and as Soviet-American rapprochement began to develop after the Cuban missile crisis in the fall of 1962, Soviet specialists tended to argue strongly against China initiatives lest Washington-Moscow relations be harmed. Ironically, in this fashion, the U.S.S.R. and America's Moscow watchers gave a new lease on life, a new rationale, to the waning old China policy of containment and isolation.

Such advice found warm support in Secretary Rusk, whose adamant inflexibility on Asian Communism in general, Chinese Communists in particular, remained deeply baffling to his colleagues. When not deflecting plans for China initiatives, he would periodically (as on October 12, 1966) share with the press and the world his apocalyptic vision of "a billion Chinese on the mainland, armed with nuclear weapons" and intent upon America's destruction. As for President Johnson himself, his chief White House foreign affairs adviser, McGeorge Bundy, once put the problem succinctly. "This President," he said to a junior colleague, "will never take the steps on China policy that you and I might want him to take unless he is urged to do so

by his Secretary of State. And *this* Secretary of State will never urge
him to do so."

So China policy remained for Washington in the Johnson years
largely an adjunct to the Vietnam War. For some, simplistic and ignorant, China was still seen as the instigator and promoter of that war—
the chief puppeteer. To others, China's significance was relegated to
one ongoing question: How far could the United States go in its punish-
ment of North Vietnam without provoking massive Chinese intervention? Here the bitter lessons of the Korean War had been learned,
or at least respected, by many. So major efforts were made, usually
with success, to avoid extreme provocation and the accidental expansion of the war. Nonetheless, seven years of intermittent American
bombing of China's ally and neighbor North Vietnam was itself a continuing provocation of considerable proportions; and Peking, outraged
and apprehensive, reciprocated through verbal warnings, heated rhetoric, civil defense preparations, and—most importantly—extensive assistance to its Vietnamese co-believers.

Needless to say, the Chinese side of the Sino-American relationship
deserves strong emphasis. Even though Washington's would-be innova-
tors in the 1960s were proposing unilateral initiatives with minimal
expectation of a favorable Chinese response, it must be said that Peking's internal and external preoccupations in this decade probably
precluded much of a response, especially while the Vietnam War
burned so brightly.

A first and fundamental factor was the precipitous deterioration
of relations between Peking and Moscow. The alliance formed in 1949
could not, it seemed, survive mutual antagonisms and suspicions that
were rooted in history, geography, competing nationalisms, and conflicting personalities. It was virtually inevitable, many observers had
written in the 1930s and 1940s, that no Chinese Communist leadership
would long tolerate Russian domination. So with the death of Stalin
and a truce in Korea, Mao and the new Soviet leadership began to
part company. The valuable Soviet advisers who had been overseeing
China's race to industrialize were suddenly withdrawn by Moscow
in 1958; they took their blueprints and aid with them, and thereby
left a legacy of abiding bitterness. One Chinese response was the "Great
Leap Forward," a bootstrap attempt to perform economic miracles
through backyard steel furnaces and the like. It was a bizarre effort
that had failed badly by the early 1960s.

The Sino-Soviet rupture caused China's leadership to re-emphasize more intensively than ever the doctrine of "self-reliance" as well as a vision of Mao, not Khrushchev and his successors, as the true world-wide heir to the leadership mantle of Marx, Engels, Lenin, and Stalin. In response to what Peking saw as increasing Soviet "revisionism"— or a backsliding into capitalism and collusion with imperialists—the Chinese sought to wean away from Moscow the Communist parties and "national liberation" movements in Asia, Africa, and Latin America. Most infuriating to the Kremlin, the Chinese also courted Eastern European leaders. By the mid- and later 1960s, ideological conflict had been compounded by something much more potentially dangerous: sporadic but increasingly bitter military conflicts over disputed terrain along the 4,500-mile Sino-Soviet border, with a massing of troops on both sides.

A critical turning point in the Moscow-Peking relationship was the Soviet invasion of Czechoslovakia in the summer of 1968, and the enunciation of the Brezhnev Doctrine of intervention that accompanied it as a rationale. The message seemed clear: If today Prague, why not tomorrow Peking, or at least a pre-emptive Soviet strike against the Sinkiang (Xinjiang) bases of China's developing nuclear capability? And indeed there were persuasive rumors at the end of the 1960s that superhardliners in the Soviet military establishment were urging just such punitive action.

In retrospect, the collapse of Sino-Soviet relations seems enough to explain the turnabout in Sino-American relations that was shortly to occur. Yet there were virtually insuperable obstacles to such a turnabout on the Chinese side. Two were external, one internal. The former are self-evident: the continued American protectorate over the Chinese Nationalists on Taiwan; and, until 1968, ever-increasing American escalation of Indochina hostilities. Washington's arming of Chiang Kai-shek's KMT regime, defended (mainly symbolically) by patrols of the U.S. Seventh Fleet between a Chinese province and the mainland, was an affront to Peking's sovereignty and dignity; so were American efforts worldwide to isolate China (increasingly unsuccessful) and to keep China out of the United Nations (annually more difficult). As for America's Vietnam intervention, China continued to view the war as a threat to its own territory and vital security interests until gradually convinced, in 1968–1969, that both the outgoing Johnson administration and the incoming Nixon administration had genuinely decided to terminate, somehow, the costly Indochina military involvement and therefore no longer posed a threat to China.

The internal obstacle to Sino-American reconciliation in the 1960s was what turned out to be a quite massive Chinese self-inflicted wound: the Great Proletarian Cultural Revolution unleashed by Mao Tse-tung in 1966. This unprecedented effort by an aging Mao to re-establish his own authority and to destroy and thereby reinvigorate both party and bureaucracy—to create a continuing revolution—produced such bloody convulsions at all levels of society that it took the Army's intervention, under Mao's orders, to begin to re-establish effective governance two years later. All the pent-up tensions within the society were unleashed, old scores settled, the "Reds" taking charge and the "experts" put out to pasture, or far worse. Here was the beginning of what would come to be known after Mao's death in 1976—and the arrest of his accomplices (the "Gang of Four," including his widow)— as the "ten bad years."

The main effect of the Cultural Revolution on China's international relations, and on Sino-American relations in particular, was to create a fairly total hiatus. For many months, with China turned completely inward, with most Chinese ambassadors recalled home, and with Chou En-lai's Foreign Ministry itself under siege by the Red Guards (young Maoist partisans "making revolution" by attacking backsliders), Peking was essentially without any foreign policy at all. Not incidentally, vivid accounts of the tumult in China gave some American policymakers yet another reason to delay action on China initiatives. Once again, "now" was "not the time"; perhaps, in fact, communism in China was at last collapsing. Prior to the gradual re-establishment of a semblance of order at home, Peking's divided leadership was in no position to make or reciprocate initiatives relating to foreign powers.

And yet the slow calming of the Cultural Revolution did in fact coincide with the shock of the Czech invasion and the infamous Brezhnev Doctrine. Furthermore, in Washington, the besieged Lyndon Johnson had opted for Vietnam peace talks and had also virtually abdicated. For once, in what has been described by one observer as two decades of "oscillations" between militancy and moderation in both Chinese and American policies, the two nations were moving into a rare interval of synchronization. Since 1949, each nation had gone through phases of one or the other; but in the mid-1950s, when Chou En-lai was leading China into a time of moderate outreach based on Geneva and "the

Bandung spirit," Dulles was reinforcing a policy of militancy toward China. And in the 1960s, when small overtures were suggested under Kennedy and Johnson, Peking was talking war more stridently than ever, sensing close assault by Washington in Vietnam, assault too on its Soviet border, and then engulfed in internal upheavals. But the time had finally come in 1968–1969 for a "meshing" of the oscillations: both China and America in a stage of relative moderation and outreach, a unique opportunity to be seized by those on both sides who might have the imagination and courage.

In the spring of 1971, Americans were startled to learn that an American table-tennis team had been invited by their Communist Chinese competitors at an international tournament in Japan to visit China at once. Much more startling was President Nixon's brief announcement, in July of that year, that Secretary of State Kissinger had just completed a secret visit to Peking, and that Nixon himself would be visiting China early in 1972.

So began the era of "Ping-Pong diplomacy," one that would see its slow-motion culmination finally in formal American diplomatic recognition of the People's Republic of China—and derecognition of the Chinese Nationalists on Taiwan—under a Democratic President, Jimmy Carter, in March 1979. From table tennis to full recognition took eight years, after twenty-two years of hostility and deadlock—a puzzlement in itself, though not inexplicable.

As for the surprise caused by the Kissinger-Nixon turnabout, readers of this book should not share in it. Why did it happen? Because the time was ripe for both parties. Why had it not happened earlier? Because both sides had been deeply preoccupied with other matters, including each nation's major internal disturbances.

And what was the proximate cause of this long-delayed breakthrough? Quite simply, the existence and behavior of the Soviet Union.

For China, Russia had become a supremely dangerous neighbor and a heretical rival in the fierce struggle over Marxist orthodoxy—thus a source of real fear, given a million Soviet troops on China's borders and saber rattlers in the Kremlin well armed with nuclear weapons. Russia had been, of course, a traditional Chinese enemy since the Tsars first marched east.

For the United States, under Nixon and Kissinger, the U.S.S.R. was an uneasy sharer of nuclear power, one that Washington faced in an endless series of bargaining situations in efforts to avoid nuclear war. The question for American policymakers was how to increase their leverage vis-à-vis the U.S.S.R. And one answer—too long resisted in previous years—was to develop relations with China, thereby persuading Moscow to be more forthcoming lest America move too close to Russia's Chinese enemy—to play what would later be called "the China card." This was a move partially made in 1971–1972; and it produced— despite years of warnings by American Soviet experts—some positive results quite soon on such important Soviet-American issues as the SALT I Talks, a Berlin settlement, and trade agreements.

There were other reasons, of course, for the turnabout, all cited previously. But should there have been surprise about Nixon himself as the architect? Not for close observers of a shrewd opportunist. For during his years out of office—years that included travels in Asia as a private citizen in the mid-1960s—the former Vice President had come to the conclusion (as at least one major article he wrote would reveal) that no enduring peace in Asia could be built without the inclusion, as keystone, of the People's Republic of China. And once he was in office, in 1969, his administration's actions as well as rhetoric built upon the foundation that his predecessor had left behind. His first State of the World message, devoid of anti-Chinese polemics, hinted clearly at normalized relations with Peking; and that summer and autumn, old Korean War restrictions on trade with China were gradually modified.

Meanwhile, to support a mutual view that Chinese and Americans had more in common than divided them—with Vietnam under negotiation—various emissaries were at work to pass inquiries and messages between the two powers. Most notable among them was the long-time journalist and Mao biographer, Edgar Snow, fresh from months in China and an interview with his old friend Mao. Also involved as intermediaries were the Romanians, sharing a common interest in keeping the Russian bear preoccupied. The message became clear: Chairman Mao would welcome a high-level American visitor, even the President himself. The Chinese were satisfied that America was disengaging from Indochina. All other issues, including the status of Taiwan, remained on the agenda for further discussion.

Richard Nixon's eight-day China trip will not be forgotten by those millions who viewed it on television. As he stepped uncertainly down the *Air Force One* ramp at Peking's airport that late February day in 1972, and as he reached out to shake the senior outstretched hand—that of Premier Chou En-lai—he symbolically bridged a chasm of twenty-two years. (That was, of course, the hand that Dulles had refused to touch at Geneva in 1954.) Shortly came the ultimate blessing: Nixon's meeting with Mao himself. And that night, at a very grand banquet, Nixon and Chou exchanged toasts whose warmth—despite some reiterations of positions on matters yet to be negotiated—would have astonished the people of both nations a year or two before.

The Nixon trip ended a week later in a curious "Shanghai Communiqué," a document that would shape the new relationship for the next seven years. Its most important aspect, besides a joint pledge to move toward "normalization" of relations between the two nations, was a seriatim statement of each party's position on the one outstanding issue, the future of Taiwan. In that statement, however, the American government did not disagree with Peking's position that Taiwan was, ultimately, part of China. In effect, both parties had agreed to disagree about the resolution of the one remaining obstacle to complete normalization. Meanwhile, each government would establish a liaison office but not an embassy in the other's capital. Also meanwhile, the 1971 announcement of the Kissinger China trip had caused the increasingly fragile dike against Peking's admission to the UN to collapse entirely; and despite an American effort to keep Nationalist China from walking out of the General Assembly once displaced in the China Security Council seat, both seats were soon occupied by the People's Republic of China. To the surprise of some, the new Chinese representatives were very proper, respectable, quiet, intelligent, and even likable. After years of warnings that Peking's admission would cause the UN's destruction, this came as vindication of those within the United States government and the UN who had long argued for an end to the exclusion of the People's Republic of China.

Richard Nixon's largest, and perhaps most significant, accomplishment was the cutting of the Gordian knot of Sino-American relations. In China, he was received—and even after his resignation in disgrace rewelcomed—as a great friend of China and a great statesman. The irony of such accolades is tempered by the high probability that only a fiercely anti-Communist Republican President could have accomplished what Nixon did without major recriminations among the American electorate and their representatives. One is forced to ask whether a Hubert Humphrey, liberal Democrat, could or would have done the same, despite the magical opportunity that Peking and Washington faced in that phase of their oscillations after November 1968. Had he tried to do so, the opposition party and those further to the right would without doubt have tried to reverse his course—and perhaps returned to McCarthyite assaults. But for Nixon's right-wing opponents, there was simply nowhere to go; the President could not be accused of "softness on Communism." For the reopening of serious contact with the real China, Nixon was the right man at the right time.

The Shanghai Communiqué bypassed the issue of Taiwan and looked to "normalization," meaning full diplomatic relations, on an unstated timetable that related to a phased lowering of America's military presence in both Indochina ("Vietnamization" of the war) and Taiwan. The latter was easily done, since the American presence was neither large nor at all central to Taiwan's self-defense. Vietnam withdrawal was more complicated, given the administration's occasional re-escalation of the war in order to force Hanoi into concessions.

What heavily impeded progress toward normalization was the Watergate crisis that devoured the Nixon presidency shortly after Nixon's landslide re-election in 1972. In due course, the man who had hounded those who "lost" China and whose greatest achievement had been the rediscovery of China was himself forced to resign the presidency; and his successor, Gerald R. Ford, chose to focus his efforts on the cleansing of the office and an attempt at re-election. Once again China policy was shunted to the back burner.

By 1976, when Democrat Carter narrowly defeated Ford, American-Chinese relations were barely an issue in America. In China, however, with the old order rapidly changing, they were a major concern among contending parties. In that fateful year, Chou En-lai had died in April, then the enfeebled Mao in September; and then, within a month of Mao's death, a new group led by the twice-purged Teng Hsiao-p'ing (Deng Xiaoping) came to power and quickly put away Mao's widow and closest aides. Both the old and new leaders had counted on full "normalization"—and all that that might bring in a closer informal alliance. But Teng and his allies—heirs to the tradition of Chou En-lai—were especially eager for assistance from whatever quarter in the process of modernization and in the building of strength to fend off the Soviet threat.

Although President Carter initially seemed to give less than highest priority to normalization, his State Department and White House advisers—also his adroit Peking emissary, Leonard Woodcock—were able to negotiate an announcement of impending recognition of the People's Republic of China (and derecognition of Taiwan) in December 1978. And despite residual challenges to this move—which would, of course, cause the termination of the U.S.-Taiwan Mutual Defense Treaty of 1955—normalization was accomplished in 1979; and the treaty duly expired at the end of the year. Furthermore, in March 1980, Congress broke with the previous tradition of evenhandedness in the treatment of Moscow and Peking and voted most-favored-nation trade status to the People's Republic, thereby making China America's number-one trading partner among Communist nations.

Meanwhile, despite years of dire warnings about the abandonment of America's World War II ally, Taiwan—derecognized—found itself entirely well defended, with its trade and investment ties strengthened with the United States, Japan, and other major industrial powers. Especially on the rise—though still only covertly, through that thriving British enclave of capitalism on the South China coast, Hong Kong— was trade between Taiwan and the mainland itself. Some observers had long argued that the ultimate solution to the Taiwan problem would, in fact, be a "Hong Kong formula": in the very long run, mainland China sovereignty; but in the meantime, true autonomy for the island and mutual benefit for both sides through heavy trade and investment between two quite different political, economic, and social systems.

In the late 1970s, China's new leadership astonished the world yet again by sending out and inviting in—especially in relations with America, Japan, and Europe—hundreds and thousands of specialists at all levels of all disciplines. The purpose was to achieve the "Four Modernizations"; it was also to make up, at a somewhat frenzied pace, for the "ten lost years" of the Cultural Revolution. Suddenly welcomed back by Mao's still Communist successors were American industrialists and educators and biomedical people and technical specialists and foundations and even religious practitioners. Simultaneously, Chinese students were being sent abroad in large numbers, and with a degree of freedom that was reminiscent of the era from 1905 to 1949.

China, then, had been "regained," at least from some mythical Soviet enslavement. The poisonous Sino-American wound was finding a healing. The doing of it had taken too long. The rewards of the new relationship might be healthy for both nations. But the danger remained—as always in this relationship—that excessive hopes and illusions would be followed by dangerous despair, disillusionment, and hostility.

(21)

Superpower Japan

THE UNITED STATES since 1945 has shaped a much more consistently successful and healthy relationship with Japan, the former foe, than with the Philippines, the former colony, or China, the former ally. Yet Americans have been obliged to defer to a considerable change in that trans-Pacific relationship. The United States must in the 1980s share in various ways its economic and political supremacy with other nations, Japan among them. No longer does America enjoy absolute supremacy in the Japan-America tie.

Japan has no close ties with any foreign nation except the United States. Japan has always had much more interest in the United States than vice versa, ever since the Meiji Restoration of 1868. And even at the time of the occupation, when so many Americans were intimately involved with Japan, that nation was only one of many American concerns. For Japan, the preserving and promoting of good relations with the United States has formed the fundamental principle of that nation's foreign policy since the end of the occupation.

Japan has emerged in that time as a senior member of the international community and as a new kind of global power: without colonies, without land mass, without raw-material wealth, without military power, but with immense economic vitality. Indeed the Japanese have realized that ideal of John Adams for the young American republic: their business with the world is "commerce, not politics or war." One can say of Japan that more productivity goes on there in less space than anywhere else in the world, and the Japanese people now enjoy

293

the longest life expectancy of any national populace in the world.

Wandering through Tokyo, one can savor and partake of the richest multicultural fare of any city in the world. Only New York or London could rival it. Of restaurants, for example, one may enjoy everything from Kentucky Fried Chicken or pizza to French *haute cuisine*, with a dazzling variety of Chinese regional cooking, not to mention the entire gamut of Japanese food.

Western opera and symphonic music flourish alongside rock and soul, Japanese folk, and popular music. The theatergoer can choose among Chekhov, Brecht, O'Neill, Shaw, No or Kabuki, as well as modern Japanese drama. The avant-garde in all the creative arts enjoys an appreciative audience.

Some of these art forms live in harmony but separately; others are undergoing cultural interpenetration, a glorious mélange of East and West, experiencing fusion and enrichment through reciprocal exchanges. Film, a relatively new art whose birth coincided with Japan's emergence into the national community, is a good example of current international culture, with at least one Japanese director, Kurosawa, well-known in America. Tokyo in 1980 foreshadows the cultural ecumenism which the rest of the world may ultimately enjoy.

The Japanese have successfully capitalized upon that most important resource of all, the intellectual capability of their people. Even the narrowness of their islands has been turned to advantage: Japan's cities have easy access to the sea lanes. And the remoteness of Japan's situation has not been a liability of consequence, for the Japanese have pioneered in the building of huge ore and petroleum carriers, bringing down the cost of shipping large quantities of raw materials over great distances. Japanese steel, made of ore imported from India, with coking coal brought in from the United States, can be sold profitably in the United States. The Japanese have successfully exploited foreign techniques; they are eager collectors of information about the newest technologies. And this has bound them closely to America in the years since 1945.

But what will happen now that they have reached the frontiers and must find solutions themselves? Is Japan more than an "improvement technology"? Can the Japanese successfully develop an economy that rests upon "the knowledge industries"? What implications has this for the United States?

The Japanese agonize, suffering from what has been labeled a "vulnerability complex." This runs deep in the blood. Life on these volcanic islands, susceptible to devastating earthquakes at frequent intervals, has been alarmingly uncertain from earliest times. In the modern era, the arrival of Commodore Perry injected a new note, the menace of the outside world. The image of the predatory West has remained strong throughout Japan's modern history.

In the 1980s, the Japanese are less aware of their wealth than of their small resource base and the increasingly unfriendly and possessive attitude of much of the rest of the world toward natural resources, dramatically demonstrated by the United States after it entered the world energy market in the early 1970s. Japan is more dependent upon oil imports (virtually 100 percent) than any other industrial country. Before the world energy crisis of 1973, Japanese industry ran on the assumption of cheap oil; in that year, oil accounted for 75 percent of Japan's total energy use. As oil costs quadrupled in the later 1970s, Japan could insure supply only by being able to pay any price demanded. Hence the Japanese are energetically attempting to diversify their sources of supply. And not just of oil. For foodstuffs, for example, they are looking to Brazil, Mexico, and Australia as alternatives to the United States.

Materials are not the only problem. The Japanese now fear the competition in manufacturing that South Korea, Taiwan, Hong Kong, and Singapore are providing. These other peripheral states of the Confucian world are exhibiting the high growth characteristic of the Japanese economy, with China, of course, yet to make a significant debut as an international economy.

Japan is profoundly isolated—geographically, racially, and culturally—from other nations of like economic development and political bent, those nations which the Japanese would most like to cultivate. Americans and other foreigners do not easily master Japanese ways of behavior or penetrate Japanese society. Paradoxically, they are not encouraged by the Japanese to do so, but often they do not make the effort. The language isolates; few foreigners really learn it. Thus the foreigner is cut off from much of Japanese culture and can approach it only on Japanese terms.

Beneath a veneer of dazzling cosmopolitanism, the Japanese jealously preserve their cultural integrity. They still regard Americans and other foreigners as exotic creatures to be kept at a distance, the outside world a "zoological garden" to observe with detached curiosity.

They sally forth into this dangerous environment only to scurry back home to the embrace of a highly integrated and protective society.

The "international style" is Western; its social forum, the cocktail party, alien to the Japanese. And when at a recent summit conference one of the Westerners buttressed an argument by referring to the myth of Sisyphus, the allusion was lost upon the Japanese. Even those Japanese who speak English or another Western language fluently are handicapped by being the outsiders in any international gathering of Westerners; they do not have shared cultural roots. They are uncomfortable in the confrontational milieu of the international conference. Their style is different. The Japanese are happiest if agreements, in essence, are made in advance.

The postwar Japanese have yet to seize the initiative in international affairs; Japan simply reacts. This sense of detachment from the outside world is sometimes interpreted as arrogance by many foreigners and may well be a primary reason for Japan's failure to build closer and more satisfactory overseas relationships. Europeans and Americans both dislike Japan's competitive skills. The British have still not forgotten Japanese treatment of POW's in World War II or the humiliation of the fall of Singapore. The developing nations fear the extractive quality of Japan's current interest in them; in Southeast Asia, the Japanese are called "Yellow Yankees." Japan's lack of international humanitarianism has provoked anger from many. In terms of per capita wealth, Japan ties with the United States for bottom honors among the major democratic nations in "grant aid" (no strings attached). Japanese lack of interest in allowing entry to refugees has also stimulated foreign criticism.

Students of Japanese history have begun to ask whether the post-1945 period might be even more important than the post-1868 period for the breadth and complexity of change it brought to the Japanese. The American occupation was probably the most successful sustained military occupation to occur anywhere in modern times. Out of it the Americans got what they wanted: a pacified Japan which would not require American handouts for survival. The Japanese did not do badly either, for they were able to begin, with some American help, their successful recovery from a catastrophic war. Feelings on the part of each side about the other became remarkably good, in sharp contrast to what they had been a short time before.

The occupation trailed off without a dramatic ending, the Japanese continuing to feel dependent upon the Americans, the Americans complacently accepting the dependence. "Wall Street shivers and Tokyo catches pneumonia" summed up the American view of the economic relationship throughout the 1950s and beyond.

As for military affairs, the Mutual Security Pact of February 28, 1952, governed the association. Under the terms of this treaty, the United States retained arms, men, and bases on Japanese soil, both (as Americans saw it) to protect Japan and also to uphold American interests in East Asia. The pact ushered in a period lasting at least until the mid-1960s, a time when political and military problems were uppermost in American-Japanese relations.

The security treaty provided an American "nuclear umbrella" for the Japanese, many of whom were saying they neither needed nor wanted such shelter. Unarmed neutrality is what they demanded; meanwhile, in what Japanese historians would later call a "reverse course," the Americans were quietly pushing the Japanese to rearm, despite the "no war" clause of the new constitution.

Yet the Japanese perception of themselves in the 1950s as an over-populated nation with very limited agricultural land and scarcity of natural resources was generally shared by Americans who were not prepared to argue very strenuously against what has been called the "Yoshida Doctrine." Its three principles were that Japan should not rearm, should not get involved in any overseas conflict, and should concentrate on economic development and the creation of domestic prosperity.

The American military bases were an irritant in the relationship. They were a constant unhappy reminder of war, defeat, and occupation; they used precious agricultural land; and the Japanese saw them as threatening Japan with being drawn into American-Russian rivalries and possible conflict. On the other hand, some Japanese would admit that their nation drew economic profit from the American presence, which entailed spending by American GI's and procurement orders for material used by the American forces. War in Korea, and later in Vietnam, swelled the profits. During the early 1950s, the cash flow enabled the Japanese to balance their international payments and to lay the groundwork for their entry into the international market.

Growing tension over security matters—and growing Japanese nationalism—erupted into violence in May 1960 when the bilateral treaty was up for renewal. Hundreds of thousands took to the streets in angry protest. Despite the uproar, the government rammed the treaty through the Diet and rode out the storm. But a proposed June visit to Japan by President Eisenhower had to be cancelled. And Prime Minister Kishi was forced to resign.

Kishi's successor, Ikeda Hayato, skillfully moved away from controversy, diverting the attention of the nation toward the economy. Everyone could support Ikeda's goal to double national income in ten years. Already in 1960, Japanese economic growth—at a rate much higher than prewar and more than double that of the United States—was being described as miraculous.

That the phrase "economic miracle," first applied to postwar Germany, should be equally if not more applicable to Japan might say something about the profitability of war in the twentieth century— to the loser. First rebuilding the industrial plant, then expanding it, purchasing the best technology available on the international market, adapting and improving it, the Japanese owed little to those practices conventionally attributed to them. Their success after the war was not founded upon cheap labor, unfair foreign trade practices, or the mindless imitating of others, although this interpretation lingered in the minds of Americans and other foreigners.

The Japanese economy has primarily focused not on foreign markets and foreign tastes so much as on the home market, catering to the Japanese people and their growing and increasingly sophisticated thirst for material satisfactions. Perhaps the American presence stimulated these Japanese desires. Certainly the Japanese have relentlessly pursued the goal of economic growth, but they have done so since the early Meiji era. Into this effort, since the war, has gone all the energy and ability which previously sought expression in military muscle and empire building.

Japanese foreign trade broke out of the area coincident with the old Greater East Asia Co-Prosperity Sphere of the 1930s and became global. In the mid 1960s, the Japanese began to generate a surplus in their trade with the United States. At that time, America still boasted ten times the productive power of Japan.

By 1978, the United States was running an annual trade deficit with Japan approximating $12 billion. Including South Korea and Taiwan, the figure reached $17 billion, or more than half of the American worldwide trade imbalance. Thus, in the late 1970s, dollar deficits with East Asia were as much a problem for the United States as those generated with the oil-rich countries.

Raw materials (such as coal, lumber, cotton, soybeans) constitute more and more of Japan's imports, whereas America seeks to sell high-technology (and high-profit) goods. Textiles were the first grievance—and Japanese triumph. Then in rapid succession came radios, motorcycles, television sets, steel, and automobiles. American manufacturers were unable to compete with the quality and prices of their Japanese rivals. And the Japanese exporters seemed attuned to the needs and desires of the American public. They knew Americans wanted small cars long before Detroit did.

Japan is the single most important market for American agricultural exports. But even trade in foodstuffs has created frustration and recriminations. Americans would like to sell more beef and citrus fruits to the Japanese. Price and quality are clearly competitive, but the Japanese anxiously protect their domestic producers. In the Japanese political world, the farm vote is important; and as a result the housewife shopping in the neighborhood sees beef priced as high as forty-five dollars a pound and oranges at a dollar each.

The Japanese hope that their growing investments in the United States may ease bilateral economic tensions. Manufacturing soy sauce in Wisconsin and assembling automobiles in Ohio does provide new jobs for Americans. But international or multinational corporations add complexities and ambivalence to the America-Japan interaction.

The Ford Motor Company, for example, which sells nearly half its products (trucks, cars, automotive parts) outside the United States, would like to sell more to the Japanese, and it lobbies for import quotas on Japanese cars. At the same time, Ford owns a 25 percent interest in the Japanese auto manufacturer that exports Mazdas to the United States, and would like to form close ties, even a merger, with another—Toyota, maker of the world's all-time best-selling car.

Economic tensions deriving from conflicting goals elsewhere in the world have placed further strains upon American-Japanese ties. During the early stages of the Iranian hostage crisis in the winter of 1979–1980, Americans deeply resented Japanese trading company purchases of oil from Iran, seeing such actions as undermining American negotiating efforts. Japan conversely resented American insensitivity to Japan's lack of energy resources and to its need to salvage something from

its multibillion-dollar petrochemical investment complex lying 85 percent completed at Bandar Khomeini.

Japanese say that American businessmen don't try hard enough
to penetrate the Japanese market. Americans retort that they have
been discouraged not only by tariffs but also by more subtle barriers,
citing, among others, "buy Japanese" procurement policies, Japanese
discrimination against foreign banks, and informal "import restricting"
cartels.

American exporters of music synthesizers, anti-knock engine compounds, and bull semen chafe, believing a market is there if they were
simply allowed to get at it. And there are many other similarly frustrated American manufacturers. To them, "Japan, Inc." looms as the
image of a corporate colossus, skillfully parrying foreign attempts to
enter its own ground, aggressively combating the foreigner on his.

In the early 1970s the Japanese spoke frequently and ambivalently
of the term "economic animals" that foreigners applied to them. Other
nations, envious perhaps, have been offended by Japan's "unseemly"
success. Charles de Gaulle was widely quoted for his scornful reference
to Prime Minister Ikeda as a "transistor radio salesman." But most
Japanese find prosperity enjoyable. Who could be unhappy with a
growth in per capita income from $150 (1950) to $4,300 (1975)? As
creators of the economic wonder, business as an activity and businessmen as an elite group have won respect from the Japanese.

Yet with all the prosperity, is there a decent living for the Japanese
people? Foul air and lack of sunshine make life disagreeable for many
city dwellers living close to factories belching smoke and emitting
noisome and poisonous chemicals. Parks, greenbelts, and open spaces
are few. Japanese cities are often unattractive. But they are not scarred
by vandalism or littered with trash.

The Japanese have invested in machines rather than in economic
activity with a lower capital efficiency. There are too few roads, particularly local ones, for the number of cars. If all cars in Japan should
take to the roads simultaneously, the result would be that none could
move anywhere. The toll from traffic accidents is high. Housing is
grossly inadequate, thanks in large measure to the high cost of land.
Whereas an average Japanese salaried worker can confidently expect
to be able to buy an air conditioner and a car, and even to take a
trip to Europe, he cannot be sure of ever being able to afford his

own piece of ground for a house. Food and clothing prices may be high but the typical Japanese family has a plethora of appliances and other goods, with too little space for them, resulting in a mode of life very different from the open and uncluttered space of the classical Japanese architectural ideal. Cities have sprawled enormously as people have reached out for living space, condemning commuters to a life spent on trains. For a man working in Tokyo, two hours each day between home and office is not unusual.

School buildings are often bleak and miserably uncomfortable, especially in the damp and cold of winter. The public library is virtually unknown in Japan. If you want to read a book, you buy it. Sewage disposal systems are still rudimentary for much of Japan. This made good sense as long as night soil was always collected for fertilizer, but it no longer is. Yet the Japanese have not pushed for flush toilets and sewers; consumer goods have captured higher priority. "After all," as one Kyoto economist remarked, "we Japanese spend much more time watching television than we do in the toilet."

Recent changes in Japanese social structure have been extraordinary. Old wealth was given a hard blow both by the war and by the virulent inflation thereafter. Paper assets disintegrated, and land proved to be the most satisfactory long-term investment. With the astronomical increase in the price of land since 1945, there are no "peasants" in Japan any longer—only relatively affluent farmers.

The farmer is a person of economic privilege, often envied by his city cousin, but agriculture has become a less important part of the economy. The area of cultivated land has actually shrunk, with changes in the types of crops grown. Rice remains the most important single crop in Japan, but there is a new emphasis on fruits, vegetables, and livestock, reflecting new food tastes. Many people work their farms only part time, deriving most of their income from some other occupation.

The income spread in Japan is relatively even; thus it is not a society with a small group of people on top flaunting large fortunes, and a large majority groaning below in desperate proverty. More than 90 percent of the Japanese describe themselves as middle class. The society is remarkably egalitarian. A low—and falling—crime rate is evidence of lack of alienation in Japanese society.

Japan no longer has an aristocracy. Titles, except for the immediate members of the imperial family, were abolished by the 1947 constitution. A "meritocracy" has formed, based largely upon success in school and university. Far more Japanese than ever before attend university, and *where* one graduates carries tremendous importance in determining career opportunities. The aspiring diplomat had best go to Tokyo University, or perhaps to Hitotsubashi; otherwise his chances of entry, let alone success within that prestigious service, are—or at least were until very recently—slim. Business corporations as well as government have their preferred university sources for recruits. So mothers anxiously fret about their children and try to start them off well by getting them into the "right" nursery school.

Few societies prize education and learning as highly as the Japanese. Perhaps because of the Confucian heritage, the written word is esteemed. The Japanese are a nation of readers. Bookstores abound, the publishing industry booms. As a result, writers are among those enjoying the highest earned incomes in Japan. Television provides at least some substantial intellectual fare.

Since 1945, youth have also emerged into much greater prominence. Japanese leadership remains more geriatric than that of most nations, despite the practice of early retirement for businessmen (fifty-five), but young people give the culture much of its pulse. They are the most finely tuned to influences from abroad, chiefly American; and they set the pattern for popular culture in dress, music, and food. In politics, Japanese youth may generally be outspoken in their anti-American sentiment; culturally, the same people are avid for things American.

Japan has enjoyed remarkable political stability since 1945; it remains the world's only advanced industrialized democracy with a non-Western heritage. All the mechanisms and apparatus of Western-style democracy may be there, the American-inspired constitution of 1947 remaining untouched, but the nuances of political practice are purely and uniquely Japanese. Far more Japanese voters turn out at the polls than American ones in proportion to the population. It would be hard to forget to vote in Japan. Trucks with loudspeakers blaring the merits of a particular candidate circle city streets ceaselessly at campaign time, and every street pole is bedecked with posters. Although the same conservative party always wins a plurality nationwide (the Liberal Democrats), political life is more lively than one might suppose, because of the factionalism characteristic of Japanese politics.

Factionalism provides the Japanese with some of the qualities of a multiparty system. Although the basis of the factions is personal, loyalty to a particular leader being the cement of the system, personalities are not as significant in Japanese politics as they are in the United States. No Japanese statesman has enjoyed the personal popularity that John F. Kennedy had in the United States; he was an enormously attractive figure to many Japanese also because of his image of youth, energy, and intelligence. And the man he chose as his ambassador to Japan was also well liked by the Japanese. Harvard professor Edwin O. Reischauer brought to his post a profound understanding of the Japanese people and their culture, a willingness to listen to the whole spectrum of Japanese opinion, and a determination to broaden the information flow between Japan and America.

Regardless of the quantity of trade, the power of the military alliance, the many ties binding the two nations in friendship, each has its list of complaints to make of the other.

Americans are frustrated, even enraged, at the seemingly chronic trade imbalance between the two countries and bitter at the "free ride" the Japanese have received since 1945, enjoying the shelter of American arms and "not doing enough" in foreign aid.

The Japanese have resented the humiliating swiftness of changes in American diplomatic and foreign economic policy—opening relations with the People's Republic of China without allowing the Japanese sufficient notice to change their policy at the same time, or, to take another example, the abrupt devaluation of the dollar in the same year (1971). Moreover, they ask how *reliable* an ally is the United States, an ally which embargoes soybeans and refuses to sell Alaskan oil.

The return of Okinawa to Japanese sovereignty in 1972 removed one of the major political grievances felt by the Japanese toward the United States. Another, the Vietnam War, was ended in 1975. To the Japanese eye, that conflict was white men shooting Asians; it was hopeless adventurism, to be compared with Japan's own unhappy China experience of the 1930s.

The Japanese are deeply concerned about what they perceive as current American weaknesses: inflation, high energy consumption, low and declining rates of savings, and sagging productivity. The American domestic "mess," as the Japanese interpret it, cannot but adversely affect other nations, especially Japan, since Americans seem prone to use Japan as a scapegoat. "Stop the whale killers! Boycott Japanese goods," read the bumper stickers. No other friendly nation is singled out for such critical attention.

But the most serious problem of all in American-Japanese relations is the lack of knowledge that each nation has of the other, particularly Americans of Japan.

Wall Street and the Ivy League universities assume too large a part in the Japanese definition of how American politics works. And despite the importance of the soybean, most Japanese know little of grassroots America. Yet because America is so important to Japan, the Japanese make a great effort to learn about it. Most Japanese try to learn English (the number of English-speakers has increased dramatically since 1945); American books are widely translated into Japanese; American affairs receive wide, continuing, and penetrating attention by Japanese newspapers, magazines, and television.

American popular culture continues to be a major influence in Japanese lives, more pervasive even than Japanese goods in the lives of Americans. Vending machines, television quiz shows, billboards, and blue jeans are as ubiquitous in Japan as in America. Yet these phenomena are often thought of as simply modern rather than as American. "Oh, do the Americans drink Coca-Cola also?" a Japanese girl asked.

The United States has emerged from the extreme provincialism characteristic of large continental nations. Americans are clearly more sophisticated about the outside world than Chinese or Russians, or even Australians. And the United States understands East Asia much better than Europeans do. This is particularly true along the Pacific Coast, where most Japanese immigrants, aside from those in Hawaii, chose to settle.

Since 1945, cultural and educational relations between Japan and the United States have not been left to chance or to propaganda, as is the usual case. Probably no other bilateral relationship is so conscientiously and well served. Government grasped the initiative; other groups subsequently took it up, with John D. Rockefeller III a notable example of such private leadership. Under the Fulbright program, begun in 1946, Americans taught and studied in Japan, and ultimately Japanese came to the United States. (In 1979, the Japanese assumed half the cost of that program and it became a joint endeavor.)

President Kennedy and Prime Minister Ikeda in June 1961 established formal networks for exchange "on trade and economic affairs at the cabinet level," and two other bodies, "one to study expanded cultural and educational cooperation between the two countries and the other to seek ways to strengthen scientific cooperation."

These aims have been given substance by the Japanese with the founding of the Japan Foundation (1972), which has made major gifts to American universities; and on the American side by the forming of the Japan–United States Friendship Commission (1975), a trust fund of $36 million, drawn from Japanese government repayments for American facilities built in Okinawa and turned over to Japan. The commission has financed a rich variety of scholarly, educational, and aesthetic pursuits.

And yet . . . the gap remains enormous. To bridge it the Japanese try harder than the Americans. Most Americans seem to be content to remain largely ignorant of Japan. Too few know the language, too few study the culture, and information readily available to the American public about Japanese affairs is scanty. More Americans were exposed to the sixteenth century fictional world of James Clavell's *Shōgun* than any other book about Japan.

As Japan continues to grow and prosper, Americans, by persisting to ignore much of what Japanese have to offer to the world, impoverish themselves and their nation. Japan, after all, has been America's chief trading partner in Asia since 1890, America's only dangerous Asian rival, and is now America's chief ally and associate outside of the European community.

Epilogue: The Future
of American–East Asian Relations

IN THE 1980s, after two hundred years of American–East Asian interaction, trans-Pacific relations seemed to have entered a rare interlude of calm. Despite two hostile and volatile Koreas, despite a brutally unstable non-peace in Indochina, despite the ambiguous status of Taiwan, despite worldwide Soviet-American tensions, the interlude was indeed rare.

Never in a century had China, Japan, and the United States been into such an extended period of peace and partnership with one another. The pattern of the past had been so often lethally different: usually, but not always, America in league with China and seeking to impede Japan. There were also, of course, important times of Japanese-American collusion, usually at China's expense; but *collision* was more the norm than collusion. As for Sino-Japanese conflict, that had been tragically recurrent.

The new three-way relationship had the virtue of common sense. Despite radically different cultures, stages of development, and socio-economic systems, the three nations had needs and interests that were complementary. What they had in common was much more important than what divided them.

The foremost common bond was fear, or at least deep suspicion, of the policies of the Soviet Union. This was an ineradicable "given," something that would not change significantly in the foreseeable future.

Tsarist Russia had reached the Pacific in 1637, had negotiated with the Chinese for two centuries, annexed the Maritime Provinces, encroached upon Manchuria, fought with and lost to Japan. So Russia was no recent interloper—rather a veteran and permanent Eurasian power. As for the Tsar's successors: Soviet Russia, an early unsuccessful midwife of revolution in China, had broken with Maoist China while remaining America's very unwelcome partner in sustaining global peace through a nuclear balance of terror.

The U.S.S.R. was not only a world power; it was also specifically an Asian and Pacific power, a former ally of both the United States and the People's Republic of China, a continuing occupier of territory claimed by Japan, and now an ally of Vietnam. If Washington, Tokyo, and Peking had had no other reason to draw together, the Soviet Union's existence would have been quite enough.

But there were, of course, other attractions as well, in such fields as trade, investment, and learning. By the early 1980s, China had virtually jettisoned the heavier baggage of Maoism and had moved into yet another phase of intensive international outreach to achieve "modernization." The effort was not new in Chinese history; but the context involved more people, and greater national unity, than in any other time of Chinese outreach. And they looked both to America and Japan (as well as Europe) for trade, training, aid, and investment.

As for Japan, despite occasional setbacks, unsolved problems, and some deep-seated grounds for insecurity, that nation's unique blend of the indigenous and the Western continued to produce internal and external triumphs, if not miracles. Its partnership with the United States had never been more complexly binding or more equal. And relations with Western Europe and the reopened Chinese mainland, if more tentative, continued to grow and thrive. The politics of fear and frustration, which had once brought Japan to expansionism and ruin, seemed relegated to fringe groups. Politics, economics, and culture had joined forces to create a highly successful world enterprise.

Yet for all the rare good news of trilateral amity—China, Japan, and America—there remained some specially intractable problems and some dangerous potential flash points on the East Asian scene. Two peninsulas—Korea and Indochina—had undergone a savage history in modern times, and their future continued ominous. The Korean quest for full independence and national unity was denied success, with the nation artificially divided between totalitarian Communists in the North and anti-Communist military dictatorships in the South. And "postwar" Indochina had only achieved suspended war and occasional genocide—not peace—as the Vietnamese strove to force their rule upon the already decimated people of Cambodia, while the outside powers lined up bizarrely in support of one faction or another.

Meanwhile, other non-Communist nations of Southeast Asia were making gingerly progress toward those elusive goals of regionalism and "multilateralism" through the workings of the Association of Southeast Asian Nations (ASEAN). Washington's détente with Peking had at long last made possible normal relations between these nations— the Philippines, Malaysia, Indonesia, Thailand, Singapore—and the Chinese. Now their collective worries were focused on a closer though smaller neighbor, Communist Vietnam.

For those who knew much about the past, the present would seem somewhat unreal—even an undeserved piece of good fortune for Asians and Americans. Too much blood and treasure had been wasted in unnecessary warfare, too much ignorance and stupidity had dominated the shaping of American–East Asian relations. The respite might seem both overdue and unearned—and, for those made skeptical by past unfulfilled hopes, probably short-lived.

History is littered with the rhetoric of Americans who have foreseen, even proclaimed, a great new era in trans-Pacific relations—from diplomats William H. Seward, Anson Burlingame, and John Hay, to Presidents Theodore Roosevelt, Woodrow Wilson, and Lyndon B. Johnson, to journalists, novelists, and poets, admirals and generals, legislators and evangelists. The arrival of a "Pacific Century" has been regularly prophesied or decreed. As a euphoric Nebraska Senator put it in the 1940s, "We shall lift Shanghai up, ever up, until, God willing, it will be just like Kansas City."

And then have followed the dashing of hopes, time and again. Dashed hopes have produced their own varieties of spokesmen, interpreters, and polemicists. Revisionism is a corrective, and the correctors wait in the wings. Their easiest targets are American innocence and grandiosity.

Revisionists at various times have included writers on the Left and the Right who regarded America's entire East Asian involvement as a "great aberration" from otherwise sound traditional policy; or who saw the United States in the 1930s as plotting to goad Japan into a military first strike in a Pacific war; or who viewed the American missionary effort, wherever or in whatever form, as "cultural imperialism"; or who saw Washington's planners as using both the Hiroshima/Nagasaki bombs and other Asian policies as a means to achieve postwar

hegemony over the U.S.S.R.; or who suspected American Asia specialists in government and the universities of conspiring to achieve a Communist victory in China; or who accused the United States of instigating
the Korean War; or who were convinced that the American escalation
of the Indochina war sprang from a desire to attain control of that
region's raw materials.

One cannot dismiss all these corrective critiques. The American
record in East Asia is as complicated, in both motivations and results,
as American society itself at its many stages of development over the
past. So most correctives contain some degree of truth. But the all-
explanatory theses collapse under scrutiny.

If theses are elusive as one surveys the two-century record, recurrent themes are not.

A first theme, on both sides of the Pacific, is virtually "invincible"
ignorance. That Asians and Americans knew so little about each other
in the remote past is hardly surprising. That knowledge of each other's
histories, cultures, and languages remains so pathetically thin today is
alarming in the extreme. In this regard, Americans bear the greatest
burden of guilt, through perpetuating a system of primary and second-
ary education which largely ignores Asia except as an occasional adjunct
to some quick "world history" survey. As for the teaching of Asian
languages in the United States, that offering is rarer still; the world
is expected to speak English. Of course, Asian states reciprocate
through their own parochialisms, although linguistically they often try
harder.

A further theme is the resilient power of nationalism. Americans,
Japanese, Chinese, Koreans, Filipinos, Vietnamese, and the others all
have come out of separate crucibles that shape national identity, however that identity may grow and change, be aggressive or quiescent.
Time and again, one nationalism has misread another. The Japanese
misperceived China and America in the 1930s, much as the Americans
misunderstood first China and later Vietnam. Ideologies, such as communism and capitalism, democracy and socialism, have eventually been
bent, shaped, even transformed by the superior force of a nation's
own heritage and the superior force of nationalism. Yet Americans
especially have been slow to learn this lesson.

Then there is the theme of race or color, one that has poisoned
trans-Pacific relations too often. It showed itself in brutally discrimina-

tory American reactions to Asian immigration. But it has also shown itself in Asian approaches to one another and to outsiders—Japanese to Koreans, for example, Southeast Asians to Chinese. Racism seems a virtually universal quality, one that feeds upon ignorance and, often, nationalism.

Finally, there is the theme—recurrent in these pages—of America's sense of distinctiveness, however defined. Geography and history combined to give Americans a unique urge toward "mission and manifest destiny" in the nineteenth century, and toward tutorial benevolence in the twentieth century. When Britain and Europe dominated the world, Americans developed a parental self-image in their dealings with East Asians. The United States lacked real power but sought to "do good"—a concept implicitly enshrined in the Open Door policy. And when, after World War II, the United States achieved supreme power, the benevolent ideal became fueled by military might—and by the real or imagined existence of evil adversaries, especially communism. Throughout, the sense of America's distinctiveness persisted— and its special role in East Asia—until the trauma of Vietnam shook the nation to its foundations.

In one reading of the record, ignorance, nationalism, racism, and idealism had combined to produce nuclear-armed grandiosity. And it took the Indochina experience to begin the curing of that affliction.

In the relative East Asian quietude of the early 1980s, the past could offer Americans a number of warnings about future dangers and pitfalls in trans-Pacific relations.

For instance, Americans should beware of underestimating yet again the continuing potency of various and conflicting Asian nationalisms—Chinese and Japanese in particular. Americans should also be prepared, despite the temporary calm, for the resurfacing of deeply rooted radical and contrapuntal tendencies in Asian societies—China, Japan, and elsewhere. Another caveat: Despite good will and firmer partnership between the United States and several Asian nations, Americans should keep in mind the continuing cultural chasms that separate their country from such disparate societies as allegedly "Westernized" Japan and eagerly "modernizing" China. Most important here are the diverse authoritarian patterns that underlie societies whose traditions are not the same as those of the United States—and whose histories are far longer.

Americans should also beware of reverting to their national itch to reshape the world, especially Asia, in their own image. That way lies vexation, disillusionment, and worse. Further, there lurks the danger of mistaking the elites who rule—and who may resemble Americans—for those being ruled. All too often the United States has become wedded, or at least infatuated, with those temporarily in authority and has lost touch with those who constitute the nation.

Finally, there is the ever-present danger—especially with regard to Asia, and most especially the Chinese—that Americans will move yet again into a phase of overexpectations, grand illusions, even euphoria. Such a phase can only lead to bitter disillusionment. It has happened too often before.

In that short span of history that we call the American experience in East Asia, were Americans "imperialists"?

Yes, of course, some were—meaning that some wanted literally to carve out territorial acquisitions, and occasionally did so. And countless others strove to dominate for their own ends—cultural, economic, strategic—regions and peoples they did not literally wish to rule. Even where the reality was humble and the means bathed in the soft wash of righteous humanitarianism, the aspiration has often been imperial, in a broad sense of the word.

Yet America's westward thrust into the far Pacific and East Asia seems also to have had a missionary heart, in the secular sense of the term—indeed, time and again, more heart than head. The imperium to be established was the winning of souls or customers, the achievement of strategic security or a place in the sun, but throughout, Asian hearts and minds to match an American model. The driving force was a curious attraction to East Asian civilization and its people— an almost obsessive sentiment about their present condition and future potential.

If Americans were, as a group, imperialists, their inexhaustible fuel was sentiment.

Index

About the Authors

JAMES C. THOMSON, JR., born in 1931, spent much of his youth in China, where his parents were educational missionaries. He graduated in 1948 from Lawrenceville, spent a year travelling in China, and graduated from Yale in 1953. After two years at Clare College, Cambridge, where he received B.A. and M.A. degrees, he studied modern Chinese history at Harvard under John King Fairbank, acquiring a Ph.D. in 1961.

Mr. Thomson entered politics as an aide to Congressman Chester Bowles, and moved with Mr. Bowles who became Under Secretary of State at the beginning of the Kennedy administration. After that, he served as an East Asian specialist for Assistant Secretaries Roger Hilsman and William P. Bundy, and then for presidential advisers McGeorge Bundy and Walt W. Rostow.

An early critic of the Vietnam War, Mr. Thomson resigned from the National Security Council staff in 1966 to teach the history of U.S.–East Asian relations at Harvard. During the next seven years he was a vocal and widely printed opponent of American policies in Indochina.

In 1969 his book *While China Faced West: American Reformers in Nationalist China, 1928–37* was published by Harvard University Press. In 1972 he co-edited, with Ernest R. May, *American–East Asian Relations: A Survey* (Harvard). He shared an Emmy for co-anchoring the coverage by ABC-TV of President Nixon's first China trip.

Since 1972 Mr. Thomson has been Curator of the Nieman Foundation for Journalism at Harvard, and continues to teach U.S.–China relations. He and his wife, Diana, who is a writer and a teacher, have two grown children, three-and-a-half cats, and divide their time between Cambridge and their house on Cape Cod.

PETER W. STANLEY was born near New York City in 1940, and grew up in Syracuse, New York. His parents loved to travel and encouraged him to study other parts of the world. At Harvard (B.A., 1962, Ph.D., 1970) and at Cambridge University, where he was a Knox Fellow at Jesus College, he studied the history of American foreign relations. An undergraduate paper on the Spanish-American War had drawn him to study the Philippines, as well, and launched him toward a career teaching and writing the history of America's relations with East and Southeast Asia.

Mr. Stanley has traveled widely in Asia and lived in Manila while conducting research there. He is the author of *A Nation in the Making: The Philippines and the United States, 1899–1921* (Harvard University Press, 1974), and several scholarly articles, and has directed a major research project on Philippine-American history. In addition, he frequently writes on current topics in Asian-American relations and consults and lectures for business groups, foundations, and agencies of the United States government.

In 1979, after having taught at Harvard and the University of Illinois, Mr. Stanley became Dean of the College at Carleton College. He lives with his wife, Mary-Jane, near the College in Northfield, Minnesota.

JOHN CURTIS PERRY, born in 1930, grew up near New York City and Washington, D.C., where his first job (age 15) was as office boy at the Chinese Embassy. He attended Quaker schools. Entering Yale in 1948, he received a B.A. degree (1952) in Chinese studies and, as a Ford Foundation Fellow, earned an M.A. (1953). After Harvard (Ph.D., 1962), where he studied under Edwin O. Reischauer, a Fulbright fellowship took him to Tokyo University. Subsequently he taught for ten years at Carleton College. There he served as chairman of the History Department and as director of the Asian Studies Program, founding the Associated Kyoto Program in which students from a dozen American colleges now participate. He has traveled widely and frequently in East Asia, including a year as a visiting professor at Waseda University (1970–71), and a summer living with his family in a Zen temple south of Kyoto. Two of his five children were born in Tokyo.

Mr. Perry is an Associate of Harvard's Japan Institute and Henry Willard Denison Professor of Diplomatic History at the Fletcher School of Law and Diplomacy, Tufts University. He is the author of *Beneath the Eagle's Wings: Americans in Occupied Japan* (Dodd, Mead, 1981) and other works. He lives with his wife and children in a crumbling eighteenth-century farmhouse in Lincoln Center, Massachusetts.